Born in 1941 in Tokyo, Hayao Miyazaki is known as the 'Japanese Disney', a filmmaker as revered – and as popular – as Walt Disney or Steven Spielberg. Miyazaki, in short, is a true phenomenon in contemporary animation and in contemporary cinema, a director of animated movies that range from the lyrical, whimsical and child-like beauty of *My Neighbor Totoro* and *Ponyo On the Cliff By the Sea* to the epic sweep of *Nausicaä of the Valley of the Wind* and *Princess Mononoke.*

This book focusses on Miyazaki's 1997 masterpiece *Princess Mononoke*, which became the biggest grossing movie in Japan (unadjusted for inflation), the previous movie being *E.T. The Extraterrestrial* (1982).

MEDIA, FEMINISM, CULTURAL STUDIES

The Sacred Cinema of Andrei Tarkovsky
by Jeremy Mark Robinson

Liv Tyler
by Thomas A. Christie

The Cinema of Hayao Miyazaki
Jeremy Mark Robinson

Hayao Miyazaki: Pocket Guide
Jeremy Mark Robinson

The Poetry of Cinema
by John Madden

Stepping Forward: Essays, Lectures and Interviews
by Wolfgang Iser

Wild Zones: Pornography, Art and Feminism
by Kelly Ives

'Cosmo Woman': The World of Women's Magazines
by Oliver Whitehorne

The Cinema of Richard Linklater
by Thomas A. Christie

Walerian Borowczyk
by Jeremy Mark Robinson

Andrea Dworkin
by Jeremy Mark Robinson

Cixous, Irigaray, Kristeva: The Jouissance of French Feminism
by Kelly Ives

The Erotic Object: Sexuality in Sculpture
From Prehistory to the Present Day
by Susan Quinnell

Women in Pop Music
by Helen Challis

Detonation Britain: Nuclear War in the UK
by Jeremy Mark Robinson

Julia Kristeva: Art, Love, Melancholy, Philosophy, Semiotics
by Kelly Ives

Luce Irigaray: Lips, Kissing, and the Politics of Sexual Difference
by Kelly Ives

Helene Cixous I Love You: The Jouissance *of Writing*
by Kelly Ives

Feminism and Shakespeare
by B.D. Barnacle

FORTHCOMING BOOKS

Ghost In the Shell
Legend of the Overfiend
Fullmetal Alchemist
Tsui Hark
The Twilight Saga

PRINCESS MONONOKE

POCKET MOVIE GUIDE

JEREMY MARK ROBINSON

PRINCESS MONONOKE

POCKET MOVIE GUIDE

First published 2015.

Printed and bound in the U.S.A.
Set in Helvetica Neue Condensed, 9 on 14 point.
Designed by Radiance Graphics.

British Library Cataloguing in Publication data available for this title.

ISBN-13 9781861713711 (Pbk)
ISBN-13 9781861714947 (Pbk)
ISBN-13 9781861715180 (Pbk)

Crescent Moon Publishing
P.O. Box 1312, Maidstone, Kent
ME14 5XU, U.K.
www.crmoon.com
cresmopub@yahoo.co.uk

CONTENTS

ACKNOWLEDGEMENTS

To the authors and publishers quoted.

PICTURE CREDITS

Illustrations are © Studio Ghibli. Toho. Tokuma Shoten. Hakuhodo. Geneon. Buena Vista Home Entertainment Japan. Buena Vista Distribution. Walt Disney Pictures. Dark Horse Comics. Mash Room Co. Ltd. Kodansha. Optimum Releasing. Tokuma International.

ABBREVIATIONS

SP	Hayao Miyazaki, *Starting Point*
TP	Hayao Miyazaki, *Turning Point*
M	Helen McCarthy, *Hayao Miyazaki*
C	Dan Cavallaro, *The Anime Art of Hayao Miyazaki*
O	C. Odell & M. Le Blanc, *Studio Ghibli*
AI	T. Ledoux, *Anime Interviews*

PRINCESS
MONONOKE

GILLIAN ANDERSON
BILLY CRUDUP
CLAIRE DANES
MINNIE DRIVER
JADA PINKETT SMITH
BILLY BOB THORNTON

THE FATE OF THE WORLD RESTS
ON THE COURAGE OF ONE WARRIOR.

(Images from Princess Mononoke © Nibariki/ TNDG, 1997)

生きろ。
宮崎駿 監督作品
もののけ姫

独占
宮崎駿 最新作
「崖の上のポニョ」とは?
「崖の上のポニョ」
2008年夏 全国東宝系にて公開
©2008「崖の上のポニョ」製作委員会

WALT DISNEY HOME ENTERTAINMENT PRESENTS
A STUDIO GHIBLI FILM
NAUSICAÄ
OF THE VALLEY OF THE WIND
2-DISC SET
From Acclaimed Director Hayao Miyazaki
MIYAZAKI'S EPIC MASTERPIECE

SIGNATURE SERI
PANDA! GO PANDA

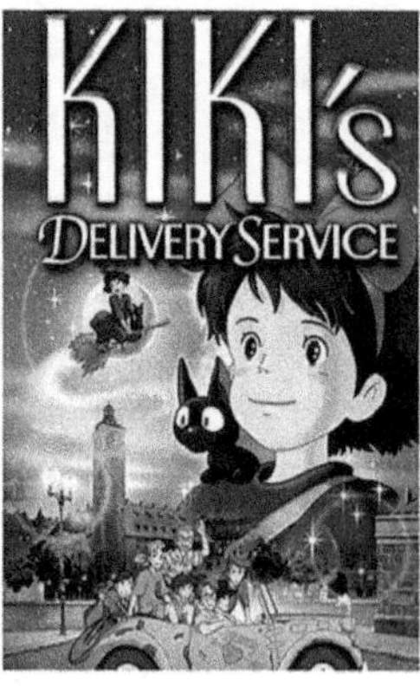
KIKI's
DELIVERY SERVICE

#1

INTRODUCTION

THE CINEMA OF HAYAO MIYAZAKI

Born on January 5, 1941 in Tokyo, Hayao Miyazaki is known as the 'Japanese Disney',[1] a filmmaker as revered – and as popular – as Walt Disney or Steven Spielberg. Miyazaki, in short, is a true phenomenon in contemporary animation and in world cinema, without equal *anywhere* in animation (as I hope to demonstrate in this book). Only Osamu Tezuka, the 'god of *manga*', is a comparable figure. The works of Miyazaki and Studio Ghibli[2] have dominated the box office in Japan for 25 years.[3] Miyazaki makes the guys at Disney, Pixar, Warners, Fox, DreamWorks, wherever, look like kids playing in a sand box (and they know it!).

For many people, particularly in the Western world, the first Hayao Miyazaki movie they would have seen would probably be *Princess Mononoke* or *Spirited Away*. Those were the two films that really brought Miyazaki to the attention of a big audience in the West. *Spirited Away* was one of Hayao

1 But Miyazaki doesn't like being compared to Walt Disney (TP, 91).
2 Like the Disney corporation, Ghibli scores high with audiences as a trustworthy brand: it had a trust rating of 43%, and 64.2% when Miyazaki's name was included (in a Toho survey). (J. Clements, 2006, 528).
3 To the point where 'most other anime features are mere marketing exercises or flashes in the pan', according to J. Clements and H. McCarthy (2006, xxi).

Miyazaki's and Studio Ghibli's biggest hits: it was the highest grossing movie in Japanese history; it won numerous awards, including the Oscar for Best Animated Feature, and the critics adored it, as they adored *Princess Mononoke* (see the reviews at the back of this book).[4] Three months after its release, *Spirited Away* had sold one ticket for every six people in Japan. *Princess Mononoke* had been a huge hit for Studio Ghibli too, with incredible box office returns in Japan: the gross was $154 million, and the rental was $92.7 million.[5]

Hayao Miyazaki may be the most talented fantasy filmmaker of his generation: not even the finest filmmakers of Hollywood could rival his films when it came to creating fantasy worlds, and fantastical characters and events.[6] Let's get real here – Miyazaki is not only 'unique', 'different', a 'genius' and a 'great artist', he is a filmmaker at a whole other level from any others in the entire history of cinema.

Once you've seen a Hayao Miyazaki animated movie, you don't forget it. We have seen all of the elements in Miyazaki's films before, it's true, so you could say that there is nothing 'original' in a Miyazaki movie – but not brought together in quite this way, and rarely achieved with such skill, such delicacy, such vision.

As inventive, imaginative cinema, Hayao Miyazaki's films are second to none: *Laputa: Castle In the Sky, Kiki's Delivery Service, Porco Rosso, Spirited Away, Princess Mononoke* and *Howl's Moving Castle.*

When you consider Hayao Miyazaki's output as a whole, you are awed by his imagination, which seems almost superhuman. There are perhaps only five or so all-round filmmakers in the whole history of cinema who genuinely possess

4 Only a few critics came out against *Princess Mononoke*. For instance, Michael Atkinson in *Mr. Showbiz*) called it 'wacky, vividly conceived but mundanely executed cartoon fantasy'. Nobody who knew anything about cinema or animation could possibly call *Princess Mononoke* 'mundanely executed'!

5 Once again, one should remember that it's box office *rentals* not box office *gross* that is the more accurate indicator of a film's financial returns. And figures should always be *adjusted for inflation*, otherwise they're even more inaccurate.

6 I agree with Mark Schilling who said that 'none of his contemporaries can equal the richness, depth and strangeness of his imagination' (2004).

the force of imagination to create entire worlds (from *scratch*, as *writers* as well as filmmakers, from *original* ideas, not adaptations). D.W. Griffith, yes, Orson Welles, yes, Akira Kurosawa, yes... and Miyazaki.

Hayao Miyazaki's cinema is marked by incredible fantasy worlds, which always remained grounded in recognizable realities; magical beings; action-packed adventures; the most astonishing portrayals of flight and flying machines in cinema; secret worlds and hidden dimensions; a passionate evocation of the wonders of the natural world, with a mystical reverence for elemental forces (embodied in animal spirits, or trees, or water, or clouds, or dragons); eccentric minor characters (with powerful, crazy, old women and crusty, old men a speciality); and young people (often girls) as the central characters. Miyazaki's films are very optimistic and life-affirming,[7] and celebrate the joy of being alive.

And, not least, Hayao Miyazaki's films are among the most technically breathtaking animated movies ever made. They are instantly recognizable as a Miyazaki or Studio Ghibli product – no one else makes movies like this.[8]

What Hayao Miyazaki's movies do is to bring you completely into a fantasy world that is instantly recognizable and familiar. It's as if these fantasy realms *have always existed* – very like J.R.R. Tolkien's Middle-earth or Ursula Le Guin's Earthsea (both influences on Miyazaki). The bathhouse in *Spirited Away* and the forests and villages of *Princess Mononoke* are so completely realized, they *must* exist, somewhere (and they do – in movies – and in the minds of millions of people). The visionary and magical elements are fused with the domestic and familial and social elements, so that it seems completely ordinary and believable that, say, flying machines soar overhead which have flapping wings like an

7 Isao Takahata described Miyazaki as someone 'who never runs from or slacks off at work, who hates defeatism and who is always optimistic' (2009, 455).
8 'He is responsible for the entire top tier of anime's undisputed masterworks and has brought the pleasures of Japanese animation to a worldwide audience as no anime director before or since has done', noted Brian Camp in *Zettai* (21).

insect (as in *Laputa: Castle In the Sky*), or that little, white creatures pop up out of trees (as in *Princess Mononoke*).[9]

In Hayao Miyazaki's fantasy cinema, the immersion in the world is total, and there's nothing to lift you out of it. There are no winks at the camera, no sending up, no intrusive movie allusions or pop culture quotes. The films of Miyazaki and his teams guide you into the filmic world with such confidence and such flair and imagination, you are happy to step inside. Partly it's because, as with the fantasy realms of Tolkien or Le Guin, Miyazaki and his teams are drawing on a long and detailed tradition of fantasy – in literature, mythology and folk tales as well as cinema. It is, in short, partly the realm of fairy tales, the classic fantasy worlds that seem to have always existed. It is that world of 'once upon a time', a place where people are put under spells, monsters roam the deep forests, and magic crystals can keep castles afloat in the sky.

Hayao Miyazaki really enjoys creating imaginary worlds – that joy in creation bounces off the screen in all of his features and TV work. It's about fashioning lies and fakery so intensely it persuades the audience that it's real, that such a world might really exist.

> It's an imaginary world [Miyazaki explained], but it should seem to actually exist as an alternate world, and the people who live there should appear to think and act in a realistic way. (SP, 307)

It's all lies[10] in animation, Hayao Miyazaki stated in 1979, it's all a fabrication of something that the animators want the audience to believe is real:

> Even if the world depicted is a lie, the trick is to make it seem as real as possible. Stated another way, the animator must fabricate a lie that seems so real viewers will

9 One of the hallmarks of *manga* and Japanese entertainment was 'twisting both time and space', Miyazaki said, in order to 'create a more fantastic, magical world' (SP, 99).
10 'Mixing fiction and nonfiction in a film to dupe the audience is the real thrill of my work' (TP, 81).

think the world depicted might possibly exist. (SP, 21)

Audiences *want* to believe, of course. They *yearn* to think that some fantasy world can really exist.[11] And they want to go there.

❦

Princess Mononoke (1997) was released in Japan on July 12, 1997 (released in North America on October 7, 1999). The other animated feature films directed by Hayao Miyazaki are (with the Japanese release date first):

- *The Castle of Cagliostro* (1979), released: December 15, 1979. U.S.A. release: Sept, 1980 and April 4, 1991.
- *Nausicaä of the Valley of the Wind* (1984), released: March 11, 1984. U.S.A. release: June, 1985.
- *Laputa: Castle In the Sky* (1986), released: August 2, 1986. U.S.A. release: July, 1987 and April 1, 1989.
- *My Neighbor Totoro* (1988), released: April 16, 1988. U.S.A. release: May 7, 1993.
- *Kiki's Delivery Service* (1989), released: July 29, 1989. U.S.A. release: May 23, 1998 (video).
- *Porco Rosso* (1992), released: July 20, 1992. U.S.A. release: October 9, 2003.
- *Spirited Away* (2001), released: July 20, 2001. U.S.A. release: September 20, 2002.
- *Howl's Moving Castle* (2004), released: November 20, 2004. U.S.A. release: June 6, 2005.
- *Ponyo On the Cliff By the Sea* (2008), released: July 19, 2008. U.S.A. release: June 28, 2009.
- *The Wind Rises* (2013), released July 20, 2013. U.S.A. release: February 21, 2014.

These are some of the most remarkable, inventive and entertaining movies in the history of cinema.

Hayao Miyazaki's original scripts have included *Laputa: Castle In the Sky, Nausicaä of the Valley of the Wind, Porco Rosso*, *My Neighbor Totoro*, *Spirited Away, The Wind Rises, Ponyo On the Cliff By the Sea* and *Princess Mononoke*. That's

11 'I personally believe fantasy is necessary' (TP, 208).

two-thirds of Miyazaki's feature movie output: the other films have been based on books or *manga* – *Kiki's Delivery Service, Howl's Moving Castle,* and of course *The Castle of Cagliostro.*

To write one hit animation movie is amazing, to write *eleven* is remarkable. To write *and* direct one spectacular animated picture is very impressive, to *write and direct eleven features*, each one a hit (and some enormous hits), is unheard-of in the world of contemporary commercial animation. Toshio Suzuki reminds us that 'hit movies don't happen by accident'. Then add to that storyboarding each movie (a big undertaking in itself). Then add to that personally overseeing drawings and cels, including drawing key animation, and you simply cannot believe one man can do it all!

And of his 11 movies as director, 5 are widely acknowledged as masterpieces – *Nausicaä, Totoro, Mononoke, Spirited* and *Wind.* I would add *Laputa, Kiki, Porco* and *Ponyo.* Some would add *Cagliostro.* Which only leaves *Howl*! (And *Howl* has plenty of admirers!).

There's no one in Hollywood or the West with a similar track record. In the West, for instance, including the Hollywood industry, such as at Disney, Pixar, Warners, DreamWorks, Fox, etc, it's typical for animated movies to have whole teams of writers and story artists. Try finding a *major* Western animation of recent times in which *one person* created: (1) the concept, (2) the story and characters, (3) the script, (4) the storyboards – yeah, and (5) directed the sucker! Nope, *you won't find a single movie*! So Hayao Miyazaki really is a one-of-a-kind filmmaker.[12]

Whatever the literary (or *manga*) source, however, all of Hayao Miyazaki's films bear a strong imprint from the director himself. It's true that animation, like all filmmaking, is a very

12 I have been guilty in this book of comparing Hayao Miyazaki and his works too often to Western and North American cinema and TV, as if everything Japanese has to be interpreted and filtered thru Western eyes, instead of on its own terms.

collaborative process,[13] and it requires a large team years of hard work to complete one of these feature animated movies. But it's also true that Miyazaki is one of the very, very few film directors working in the animation industry who can truly, properly and authentically be called an *auteur*, an artist who has a major influence on his films (and whose work sustains an *auteur* analysis, who has the way of working, the skills and the talent, the themes, the motifs, the politics and the philosophy that constitute a genuine *auteur*).[14]

But how many true *auteurs* in feature animation of recent times are there? Not *shorts*, but 90+ minute *features*. Jan Svankmajer, certainly; Walerian Borowczyk, certainly; the Quay brothers, certainly; James Selick, perhaps. And then… who?

Of all the great names of film directors in the history of animation – Géorges Méliès, Ladislaw Starewicz, Willis O'Brien, Lotte Reiniger, George Pal, Osamu Tezuka, Tex Avery, Chuck Jones, Jiri Trnka, Paul Grimault, Ralph Bakshi, Jan Svankmajer, Michel Ocelot, and Hayao Miyazaki's friend Isao Takahata – Miyazaki's remains among the greatest. (And *very* few of the great names of animation have directed, written, drawn and storyboarded as many feature-length movies as Miyazaki. And even fewer have achieved the same critical as well as commercial success).

The form of Hayao Miyazaki's animation is cel animation, also known as ink and paint animation, or 2-D animation. It is a traditional form of animated film which is based on drawings and paintings. It is all done by hand, too, with each cel drawn and then painted by hand. The process moves from conceptual sketches to storyboards, to key animation and final drawings.

There are so many vital talents in making a feature-

13 Hayao Miyazaki recognized that directors and writers could be over-emphasized in the creation of an animated work. Animation was a team effort, and no element should be over-emphasized while others were ignored (SP, 64). And sometimes there was too much attention given to the original work.

14 'If I'm going to be involved in producing a film, I want to be involved in the smallest details' (TP, 390).

length animated film, so this is not to underplay the roles of Hayao Miyazaki's producer, Toshio Suzuki, his co-producer at Studio Ghibli,[15] Isao Takahata, or animators such as Kitaro Kousaka, Katsuya Kondô, Masashi Ando, Yoichi Kotabe,[16] Kazuo Komatsubara, Tsukasa Tannai, Akihiro Yamashita, Takeshi Inaumura and Megumi Kagawa, or art director Kazuo Oga,[17] or editor Takeshi Seyama,[18] or composer Joe Hisaishi, or colour designer Michiyo Yasuda, or sound people Toru Noguchi, Shuji Inoue, Kazuhiro Hayashi, Kazuhiro Wakabayashi, and Nobue Yoshinaga. (An important aspect of Miyazaki's career, often over-looked, is how he, Takahata and Ghibli have nurtured the talents of literally 100s of artists in the *animé* industry).[19]

Studio Ghibli made *Princess Mononoke*, an animation studio best known for the fantasy films of Hayao Miyazaki, but it also produced other pictures, as well as TV shows, TV specials and commercial work.

---

15 Studio Ghibli is an animation studio best known for the fantasy films of Hayao Miyazaki, but it also produced other pictures, as well as TV shows, TV specials and commercial work. Studio Ghibli's films, particularly those of director Hayao Miyazaki, are among the most extraordinary pictures ever made, not just in animation, and are easily the equal of the best of Disney's products, including the five films of Disney's 'golden age'.
16 Kotabe's credits include *Heidi, Little Norse Prince, Little Witch Sally, Panda! Go Panda!, Nausicaä* and other Ghibli movies.
17 Kazuo Oga has provided art direction, background art and designs on most of Ghibli's works; prior to Ghibli, Oga worked on *Wicked City, Harmageddon, Urusei Yatsura* and *Dagger of Kamui.*
18 Takeshi Seyama has more formidable credits than any other film editor in Japanese animation: as well as editing most of Miyazaki's movies, they include many masterpieces and celebrated works: Studio Ghibli movies such as *Whisper of the Heart, Tales from Earthsea, From Up On Poppy Hill, Grave of the Fireflies, My Neighbors the Yamadas, Only Yesterday, Arrietty, Pom Poko* and *Ocean Waves,* the Katsuhiro Otomo movies *Akira, Steamboy, Stink Bomb, SOS! Tokyo Metro Explorers, Magnetic Rose* and *Cannon Fodder* – plus *Votoms, Conan, Adventures of Tom Sawyer, Devilman, Dirty Pair Flash, Gintama, Himawari!, Magic User's Club, Beelzebub, Lupin III, Mahoromatic, On Your Mark, Mobile Suit SD Gundam, Paprika, Paranoia Agent, Patlabor WXIII, Serial Experiments Lain, Shamanic Princess, Sherlock Hound, Sakura Wars, Golgo 13, Rurouni Kenshin, Tegami Bachi, Space Pirate Mito, Elfen Lied, Starship Troopers, Tokyo Godfathers, Ultimate Girls, Ultra Nyan, The Whale Hunt, Wizard Barristers, You and Me, Tetsujin 28* and *Little Nemo.*
19 And having Ghibli on your CV must have helped plenty of artists.

HAYAO MIYAZAKI'S BIOGRAPHY AND CAREER

Hayao Miyazaki grew up during World War Two in Japan, and was evacuated from Tokyo in 1944; he started school in 1947 aged 6, still away from the capital (the Miyazaki family moved back to Tokyo in 1950). At Gakushuin University, Miyazaki studied political science and economics. Politics has always played a significant role in Miyazaki's career. Miyazaki was active in the union at Toei Animation, for example, becoming the Chief Secretary in 1964; at Toei he was involved in a labour dispute in 1964.

The Miyazaki family business was – no surprise here – an aviation company. Hayao Miyazaki's father, Katsuji Miyazaki (1915-93), was one of the directors of the company, which constructed parts for Japanese Zero fighter planes during World War 2.[20]

The left-leaning slant of Hayao Miyazaki's politics is evident in his cinema – in the depiction of the mining community in *Laputa: Castle In the Sky,* for instance, which drew on the mining town in South Wales that Miyazaki had visited in the 1980s (at the time when Wales and other communities in Britain were struggling to hold onto the mining industry – thanks to Margaret Thatcher and her detestable right-wing regime). Socialism, of the sort that enshrines arts and crafts and making things by hand, can be discerned in Miyazaki's cinema in the collective of women that builds Porco Rosso's plane, or the painting and cake-making in *Kiki's Delivery Service.*

Hayao Miyazaki's involvement in left-wing politics would be unusual for someone who works in the animation industry in the West – you just don't find many film directors at the Walt Disney Studios, for instance, advertizing socialist ideo-

20 Hayao Miyazaki's father worked at the Miyazaki Airplane Corporation, in Kanuma City, which was owned by his uncle, Miyazaki said, making parts for war planes (not all of the parts worked, either [SP, 208]). Certainly there's an ambiguity about Miyazaki's attitude towards what his father did for a living, in manufacturing machines that were used for war. That plays against Miyazaki's fascination for wars (C, 7).

logy or membership of the Communist Party. No, no, no!

But Hayao Miyazaki became disillusioned with left-wing politics in the form of Marxism in the early 1980s. Miyazaki came to realize that 'Marxism was a mistake, that Marxist materialism was all wrong' (SP, 400). It was a common reaction among many intellectuals in the West, when they saw what was really going on in China with Maoism and in the Soviet Union with Communism, prior to the fall of the Berlin Wall.[21]

Hayao Miyazaki has an ambiguous attitude towards North America (but less to the West in general). It's a familiar position of many Japanese – after all, Amerika is the superpower which oversaw the dropping of two atomic bombs on Japan, to whom Japan lost the Pacific War, who occupied part of Japan, and who instigated the still controversial arms treaty. Miyazaki was furious about the Iraq War, and was unsure whether to accept the Oscar for *Spirited Away*. *Howl's Moving Castle* is partly a post-9/11 movie, and its depictions of war are Miyazaki's answer to the war-mongering of Amerika. (And *The Wind Rises* may've not won the 2013 Oscar because it depicted a designer who was among those responsible for aircraft used in Pearl Harbor).

Japanese movies are often about communities and families rather than individuals, and Hayao Miyazaki's cinema presents many ensembles and groups, with multiple charas 'who make different choices, take different paths in life, and thereby come to different ends', but are united by a common theme, as Gerald Mast and Bruce Kawin note of the typical Japanese film.

Hayao Miyazaki married a fellow animator, Akemi Ota, in 1965; their children are Keisuke and Goro (b. 1967), who later turned to directing. It was also around this time that Miyazaki met and grew friends with Isao Takahata; Ota and Takahata are perhaps the key collaborators of Miyazaki's career. Wives,

21 By the 1990s, Miyazaki admitted that he had 'totally forsook Marxism' (1994). Miyazaki saw his involvement with Marxism as a mistake: 'There was a time when I dabbled in the socialist movement, but I must say I was quite naive.' (2013)

husbands or lovers are often overlooked by film critics when discussing the influences on a filmmaker's life, but it's safe to assume that Akemi Ota would have had a considerable influence on Miyazaki's cinema – not least because she is an animator herself.

After he left university in 1963, Hayao Miyazaki joined the Toei Animation company, where he began working in the in-between department, on TV shows such as *Wolf Boy Ken* (1963) and *Watchdog Woof-Woof* (1963). 'I'm basically three quarters an animator' (TP, 57). Miyazaki moved into key animation at Toei, contributing to the TV series *Wind Ninja Boy Fujimaru* (1964). Miyazaki also worked on *Hustle Punch* (1965), and *Rainbow Warrior Robin* (1966).

Other credits of Hayao Miyazaki's include the feature film *The Little Norse Prince* (1968), which was directed by Isao Takahata, the TV series *Little Witch Sally* (1968), *Akko-chan's Secret* (1969), the feature film *Puss In Boots* (1969), *The Impudent Frog* (1971), *Sarutobi Etchan* (1971), and the features *The Flying Ghost Ship* (1969), *Animal Treasure Island* (1971), and *Ali Baba and the 40 Thieves* (1971).

In 1971, Hayao Miyazaki and Isao Takahata left Toei to join A-Production (a.k.a. A-Pro, now Shin'ei Doga). They went on to work for Zuiyo Company, and Nippon Animation. Miyazaki's first film as director, 1979's *The Castle of Cagliostro,* was produced by Tokyo Movie Shinsha. Miyazaki also directed some of the TV episodes of the *Lupin III* series (in 1971) with his colleague Takahata. (This show ran for 23 episodes, and Miyazaki and Takahata worked on 17 episodes as directors).

In the 1970s, Hayao Miyazaki was working in television animation, the backbone of the Japanese animation industry: *Akado Suzunosuke* (1972), *Wilderness Boy Isamu* (1973), *Samurai Giants* (1973), *Alpine Girl Heidi* (1974), *A Dog of Flanders* (1975), *Three Thousand Leagues In Search of Mother* (1976), *Rascal the Raccoon* (1977), *Future Boy Conan* (1978) and *Anne of Green Gables* (1979).

For some of these TV animated series, Isao Takahata was

directing, with Hayao Miyazaki providing concepts, scripts, layouts and key animation:[22] *Three Thousand Leagues In Search of Mother, Alpine Girl Heidi* and *Anne of Green Gables. Three Thousand Leagues In Search of Mother* was based on Edmondo de Amici's *Cuore* (1886). *Anne of Green Gables* derived from the novels of Lucy Maude Montgomery (early 1900s). *Rascal the Raccoon* (1977) was part of Nippon Animation's *World Masterpiece Theater* TV series, and adapted from Sterling North's writings about his childhood in Wisconsin. Miyazaki worked as a key animator on it (and chiefly as a scenic designer on the other shows).

Alpine Girl Heidi was an important work for both Takahata and Miyazaki, not least because it was successful with audiences and broadcasters. The success led to a feature movie being released, culled, as so often with television *animé*, from the TV episodes re-worked into a feature-length piece. *Heidi* was based on the fiction of Johanna Spyri, and included images of life in the mountains which would influence Miyazaki's later films.

Miyazaki and Takahata collaborated on some short films about the adventures of a panda and his chums, with Takahata directing from designs and a script by Miyazaki: *Panda Go Panda* (*Panda & Child,* 1973), and *The Adventures of Panda and Friends* (1972).[23]

Panda Go Panda is fun, colourful, light-hearted; the comedy is typical of Isao Takahata's work. For Hayao Miyazaki fans *Panda Go Panda* looks forward to themes, images and motifs that crop up in later outings. Such as visuals like Mimiko's hair (Dola in *Laputa: Castle In the Sky* has the same wild plaits), or Daddy Panda's wide grin and portly figure, which leads on to the giant Totoro.

22 Both Takahata and Miyazaki have discussed the issue of whether Miyazaki might've made more movies if he hadn't met Takahata or hadn't worked for Takahata. Miyazaki thought the idea was silly, and he had been quite happy being an animator: 'I had no complaint about being an animator. If I thought about my work at such a level as expressing myself in such a form, or self-display, or showing my personality, I think I could have only done a worse job'.

23 *Panda Go Panda* has been re-issued on DVD and video.

More important for future Hayao Miyazaki movies, however, are the thematic and narrative elements in *Panda Go Panda*, such as Mimi being essentially an orphan (her grandmother leaves her for a week). It's a recurring theme in Miyazaki's cinema – that young children can survive on their own – it crops up in *Laputa: Castle In the Sky,* for instance, with both Pazu and Sheeta, or Kiki in *Kiki's Delivery Service,* and right up to *Ponyo On the Cliff By the Sea,* where two five year-old children are left on their own. That is a fundamental ingredient of children's literature, though: authors have to find a way of separating the children from the parents.

In 1978 Hayao Miyazaki directed *Future Boy Conan* (a.k.a. *Conan, the Boy In the Future*) for Nippon Animation, one of his important works, and his first TV series as director (Isao Takahata and Keiji Hayakawa were co-directors, and Yasuo Otsuka was animation director). It comprised 26 episodes of 25 minutes each, with a TV movie edited from the series, entitled *Future Boy Conan: The Movie. Future Boy Conan* was based on *The Incredible Tide* (1970) by Alexander Key.[24]

In 1981 Hayao Miyazaki directed the TV series *Great Detective Holmes* (a.k.a. *Sherlock Hound the Detective*), made as a co-production with R.A.I. TV in Italy. It featured Sherlock Holmes-style capers in a dog world (a world populated only by dog characters). On *Great Detective Holmes* Miyazaki worked with Italian animators, including his friend Marco Pagott (he later named the character of Porco Rosso after Pagott).

Television animation continued into the 1980s and beyond for Hayao Miyazaki, although from *Nausicaä of the Valley of the Wind* onwards much of Miyazaki's work in animation was confined to his own movies: Miyazaki did key animation in *New Adventures of Gigantor* (1980), directed two episodes of *Lupin III* (1980), directed the first six episodes of *Great Detective Holmes* (1981),[25] and contributed key animation to the film *Space Adventure Cobra* (1982) and the TV

24 In 1999 the series was revived as *Future Boy Conan: Taiga Adventure* (directed by Keiji Hayakawa, Miyazaki's former assistant).
25 There was a short film released in cinemas.

show *Zorro* (1982).

Hayao Miyazaki formed his own company, Nibariki (Two-Horse Power) in 1984, and Studio Ghibli a little later,[26] with Isao Takahata, Toshio Suzuki and Toru Hara (former president of Topcraft). The first Ghibli studio was in Kichijoji in Tokyo, the second in Koganei.[27] In 1995 Miyazaki and Ghibli made a pop music video for the band Chage and Aska.

❦

The *manga* work of Hayao Miyazaki shouldn't be overlooked: it has provided the basis for feature films such as *Porco Rosso* and *Nausicaä of the Valley of the Wind* and has influenced movies that Miyazaki didn't direct, such as *Tales From Earthsea*.

Hayao Miyazaki's *manga* includes a history of food on airlines (*Dining In the Air*); *Puss In Boots* (1969); *People of the Desert* (1972), a war piece; *Animal Treasure Island* (1982); *To My Sister* (1983); *The Journey of Shuna* (1983); *Daydream Data Notes* (1984-92), a World War Two story about a German tank commander; *Miscellaneous Notes: The Age of Seaplanes* (1989), which led towards *Porco Rosso*; the World War 2 story *The Return of Hans* (1994); and *Tiger In the Mire* (1998). Miyazaki and Studio Ghibli have also produced '*Art of*' books for each Ghibli movie, which are useful sources of information.

26 The first Studio Ghibli film officially was *Laputa: Castle In the Sky*, but *Nausicaä of the Valley of the Wind* (1984) was really the first Studio Ghibli production (although it had been produced at Topcraft).

27 The animation under the Topcraft ægis had been produced at Asagaya in the Suhinami ward in Tokyo (SP, 443).

STUDIO GHIBLI

Studio Ghibli is an in-house animation production company: by the early 1990s and its move to its new premises in West Tokyo, it had the staff and resources to produce everything except the sound in an animated movie. It has the staff to create a movie from scratch, including the photography and computer generated work (two computer-controlled cameras were used to photograph animation). Studio Ghibli has edited its movies digitally (on an Avid system) since 1998 (in common with the commercial movie industry in general).

Of the 20 Ghibli films, Hayao Miyazaki directed 9, and has worked on 8 of the 11 he didn't direct (which only leaves three without Miyazaki credits).

The 20 Studio Ghibli feature films are (up to 2014), with Miyazaki's contribution indicated by an asterisk:

Laputa: Castle In the Sky
My Neighbor Totoro
Grave of the Fireflies
Kiki's Delivery Service
Only Yesterday *
Porco Rosso
Pon Poko *
Whisper of the Heart *
Princess Mononoke
My Neighbors the Yamadas
Spirited Away
The Cat Returns *
Howl's Moving Castle
Tales From Earthsea
Ponyo On the Cliff By the Sea
The Borrower Arrietty *
From Up On Poppy Hill *
The Wind Rises
The Tale of Princess Kaguya
When Marnie Was There

Best known for their movies, Studio Ghibli also produces work for advertizing and television (like all Hollywood studios, and most animation studios). Movies might be what the animation studios are known for, but they have to pay the bills, and commercial work is vital (for Ghibli, merchandizing also plays a key role, bringing in revenue during leaner years between the big hit movies like *Ponyo* or *Princess Mononoke*).[28] Ghibli produced some TV idents for NTV in 1992 (*Sky-Coloured Seed*), and 5 TV commercials (in 2001), plus others.

The big earner, as far as licensed characters are concerned, is Totoro, derived from *My Neighbor Totoro.* Totoro as a character and image, a mascot – like the film itself – is tailor-made for merchandizing. And it is Totoro, of course, who was chosen as the Studio Ghibli company logo (it's a drawing of Totoro against a mid-blue background. There is a Totoro store in Tokyo).[29]

Studio Ghibli is among the most successful animation houses in Japan in recent times: although it is one studio among hundreds in Japan, it absorbs a high proportion of ticket sales at the theatre or video and DVD sales, or television viewing figures (35.1% of the audience watched *Princess Mononoke* when it was broadcast on TV in Japan in 1999).[30]

Prior to *Princess Mononoke*, Hayao Miyazaki and his team at Studio Ghibli had had big hits and number one films, but *Princess Mononoke* went through the roof. It was the

28 Producer Toshio Suzuki has said that he would prefer it if a movie could make all its money back from a theatrical release, without needing video or DVD sales, let alone merchandizing (M, 207). However, in the global marketplace, sales to home entertainment formats like DVD and video can't be ignored: a Hollywood picture, for instance, will typically take less than a quarter of its total revenue from being shown in theatres. Of course, with Hayao Miyazaki's movies being such hits, they could make their money back from theatrical release alone.

29 Isao Takahata praised Hayao Miyazaki for creating such an endearing mascot in Totoro – Totoros were now found throughout Japan, Takahata said: 'Totoro lives in the hearts of all children throughout Japan, and when they see trees now, they sense Totoro hidden in them. And this is a truly wonderful and indeed rare thing' (2009, 457).

30 Mamoru Oshii commented: 'What do other animators think of Ghibli? As far as I know, they basically respect Ghibli. It's half love, and half hate. A general response would be: it's a tremendous place, but I don't want to go there. Because they control you too tightly (at Ghibli).'

highest grossing movie in Japanese history (unadjusted for inflation), until *Spirited Away.* In 1997, only *Titanic* (that one-off phenomenon that no one can fully explain – or replicate) beat it at the box office (but who watches *Titanic* now?).

In 1996, the Walt Disney corporation brokered a deal with the Japanese animation studio to distribute its films in the U.S.A. and Canada. Disney set about Americanizing the movies by dubbing them into American English, sometimes using well-known actors (like Michael Keaton and Carey Elwes in *Porco Rosso*, or Claire Danes, Gillian Anderson, Billy Crudup, and Keith David in *Mononoke Hime*). John Lasseter, later head honcho of Pixar, acknowledged the influence of Miyazaki's films. Crucially, it meant that Studio Ghibli's movies had a much wider release (in the West), and many more people got to see them.

INFLUENCES

Hayao Miyazaki has remarked that his influences are probably innumerable. At university, Miyazaki encountered some of the classic authors of children's fiction, including Eleanor Farjeon, Phillipa Pearce, Francis Hodgson Burnett (*The Secret Garden*), and Rosemary Sutcliffe (he joined the children's literature group). Ryotaro Shiba, Yoshie Hotaa, and Sasuke Nakao were also influences.

Treasure Island (1883) by Robert Louis Stevenson is a key literary influence on Hayao Miyazaki, and Jules Verne, of course, Mark Twain, Jonathan Swift, Maurice Leblanc, Robert Westall (*The Machine Gunners*), and Antoine de Saint-Exupéry. Among science fiction and fantasy authors, Miyazaki has cited Brian Aldiss (*Hothouse*), Frank Herbert (*Dune*), Isaac Asimov (*Nightfall*), J.R.R. Tolkien (*The Lord of the Rings*), Diana Wynne-Jones, and Ursula Le Guin (particularly her *Earthsea* series). He told Le Guin when he visited her in

Portland, Oregon that he kept her books by his bed, and had been re-reading her works for years.

Among filmmakers, Hayao Miyazaki has often cited the Russian film *The Snow Queen* (Lev Atamatov, 1957) as an important influence.[31] Miyazaki wrote fondly of *The Tale of the White Serpent*. Both *The Snow Queen* and *The Tale of the White Serpent* were important influences for the young Miyazaki. But he was later critical of both movies, perhaps embarrassed by loving them so much as a kid.

Among the animation influences on the young Hayao Miyazaki were toons such as Mickey Mouse and Betty Boop.[32] Much of the time animated films were scarce when Miyazaki went to the movies: he said maybe they would see one Disney *Donald Duck* or *Mickey Mouse* short during a Summer (SP, 123). Miyazaki has also mentioned animation coming out of Nihon Dogasha and Toei Animation, as well as the *manga* of Sanpei Shirato (SP, 194).

A big influence on Hayao Miyazaki's early development as an artist was the comicbook artist Osamu Tezuka (1928-89), known as the *manga no kamisama* (the 'god of *manga'* – and also the 'god of *animé'*). 'I've been powerfully influenced by Tezuka', Miyazaki admitted, 'the formative experience in my life story was Osamu Tezuka-san' (TP,153), and began to draw *manga* under Tezuka's shadow (SP, 193). Miyazaki recalled that he consciously tried to move away from being 'heavily influenced'[33] by Tezuka's comics and characters. Miyazaki has stated that: 'Tezuka's influences buried deep within me proved an extremely heavy burden'.[34]

Osamu Tezuka is of course one of the major figures in Japanese *animé*, creator/ director of *Astro Boy, Arabian*

31 Miyazaki has spoken warmly of the significance of *The Snow Queen* in the way it took up Hans Andersen's tale and reworked it, how the characters were portrayed, and how it inspired him to create better animation (TP, 184).
32 Miyazaki has cited the Fleischers as an influence. In 1980, while discussing the Fleischers in *FILM*, he noted that the endings of the Fleischers' cartoons were poor (SP, 118).
33 His mother told him not to copy other artists (TP, 153).
34 And Tezuka was in turn heavily influenced by Disney: he saw *Bambi* 80 times!

Nights, Princess Knight, Triton of the Sea, Kimba the White Lion, Bix X, Black Jack, Dororo, Jungle Emperor Leo, and *Phoenix.*[35] Tezuka was very successful very quickly: by his early twenties, he was 'the biggest selling *manga* artist in Japan'.[36]

Yasuo Otsuka (b. 1931) was a key influence on Hayao Miyazaki. Miyazaki spoke fondly of his co-worker Otsuka, and how he encouraged Miyazaki in many ways, including to see the fun in making animation, and to select material and co-workers carefully (SP, 192). And Miyazaki admitted that sometimes he pushed Otsuka hard, too: when he was directing *The Castle of Cagliostro,* Miyazaki said, Otsuka 'worked hard on *Cagliostro.* He never left his desk. It may have been because I didn't let him' (SP, 331). Otsuka had worked on the first *Lupin* TV series.

FANS OF MIYAZAKI.

In North America, Hayao Miyazaki's films have some dedicated fans, not least animators at Pixar and Disney,[37] who have often cited Miyazaki's movies as an inspiration.[38] But that hasn't translated into big sales theatrically. For instance, when *Howl's Moving Castle* was released on 202 screens in the U.S.A. in 2005, it grossed only $4.7 million (compared to $190m in Japan). As the box office figures are so high in Japan, Studio Ghibli's and Miyazaki's films can easily sustain themselves without needing overseas sales. But it's a pity,

35 As well as 21 TV series and twelve TV specials, Tezuka also produced 700 stories and around 17,000 *manga* pages (C, 30).
36 H. McCarthy, 1993, 13.
37 Films such as Disney's *Atlantis* (2001) directly took up some of Hayao Miyazaki's concepts and visuals – not least the early 20th century setting, with its world of bolts and steel and steam-powered machines. The combination in *Atlantis* of the secret world, the adventure journey to reach it, the technology employed to get there, the flying machines, the gang of characters, and the spiritual under-pinnings, all of these could be found in Miyazaki's cinema. Another one was 2004's *Steam-boy*, Katsuhiro Otomo's adventure tale entirely centred around steam and machinery.
38 A recent episode of *The Simpsons* delivered a fun spoof of the cinema of Hayao Miyazaki, with send-ups of *Totoro*'s Cat-bus, the dragon from *Spirited Away,* the witches from *Kiki*, etc.

because Miyazaki's movies would appeal to a large American audience, if they came to see them.

The influence of Japanese animation on Western movie-making is *enormous* – in terms of style, action, characters, settings, stories, and everything else. You can see it in the newer *Star Wars* trilogy, in *Avatar*,[39] the *Matrix* films, the *Lord of the Rings* movies, *A.I.*, the *Batman* pictures (and any super-hero movie).

John Lasseter spoke about Hayao Miyazaki's films:

> From a pure filmmaking standpoint, his staging, his cutting, his action scenes are some of the best ever put on film, whether animated or not... Watching one of his films is the best medicine when you have writer's block. When we at Pixar feel that we're beating our heads against the wall, we go in the screening room and put on a laser disc and watch one of his films and it's like, whoa look what he did.[40]

Other admirers of Hayao Miyazaki include Barry Cook and Tony Bancroft, Gary Trousdale and Kirk Wise, animator Glen Keane, director Hendel Butoy, director Kevin Altieri, and director Katsuhiro Otomo. Among critics: Andrew Osmond, Roger Ebert, Helen McCarthy, Dan Cavallaro and Jonathan Clements.

Aside from many of the key artists at Disney and Pixar, noted above, fans of Hayao Miyazaki's cinema include Tsui Hark (perhaps the greatest action filmmaker in the world), Guillemo del Toro and Akira Kurosawa: the *sensei* loved *My Neighbor Totoro* and *Kiki's Delivery Service*:

> It's *animé*, but I was so moved. I really loved Nekobus. You wouldn't come up with such an idea. I cried when I watched *Kiki's Delivery Service*.

---

39 Many viewers noted the influence of the floating islands in *Laputa: Castle In the Sky* on *Avatar* (2009).

40 Quoted in R. Lyman, "Darkly Mythic World Arrives From Japan", *New York Times*, Oct 21, 1999.

UNMADE FILMS.

A filmmaker such as Hayao Miyazaki is bursting with ideas, and over the course of his film career, like every major filmmaker, he will have produced many ideas and scripts and drawings and even filmed animation that never quite made it into a finished form or released product. There were some projects that Miyazaki began work on, but left, sometimes due to 'creative differences' between the project's producers and the director. Some projects Miyazaki wouldn't have been able to find funding for. Part of the reason for this is that Miyazaki is a perfectionist, workaholic kind of filmmaker, and those sorts of projects take a lot of work and a lot of time (and a lot of money) to complete.

In 2006 Hayao Miyazaki said he wanted to make a movie about Edo Castle and the 15th century period. Another unrealized project was about the survivors of the Great Kanto Earthquake of 1923 (the earthquake crops up in other *animé*, such as *Oshin, Doomed Megalapolis, Urotsukidoji* and *Smart-san*). In 2013's *The Wind Rises,* Miyazaki-sensei found a way to incorporate a Kanto Earthquake sequence. Prior to *Spirited Away* the project *Rin the Chimney Painter* had been developed but cancelled (Miyazaki wanted to set it at the time of the 1923 quake). A story based in the Meiji era (1868-1912), about transportation on the Shinkashigawa River, was another unmade screenplay. Another unrealized project was about a pig and a tank and love. Miyazaki also considered adapting the children's book *The Marvellous Village Veiled In Mist* by Sachiko Kashiwaba. A sequel to *Ponyo* was another possibility, as well as a sequel to *Porco Rosso.*

Turning Ghibli's films into theatrical musicals (for ex, *Totoro* or *Spirited Away*), must've been considered, as well as turning any of Hayao Miyazaki's movies into TV series, or filming them in live-action. (My top unmade Miyazaki movie is definitely an adaptation of the *Earthsea* books by Ursula Le Guin).

ISAO TAKAHATA

Isao Takahata (born October 29, 1935, in Ise, Japan), known to his colleagues and friends as Paku-san, is one of the most important people in Hayao Miyazaki's artistic career: they produced each other's work while the other was directing. As Miyazaki has acknowledged, they often clashed when working together, and had learnt to be very 'hands off' when they were producing the other's projects. According to the 'making of' documentary of *Only Yesterday*, while working on the movie, Miyazaki said they rarely talked – and Miyazaki was producing the film! After a screening of the finished picture, Miyazaki walked out without saying anything.

Isao Takahata is the other main director at Studio Ghibli, and has directed films such as *Ponpoko, Panda! Go Panda!, 3000 Leagues In Search of Mother, The Tale Of Princess Kaguya, My Neighbors the Yamadas, Gauche the Cellist, Only Yesterday* and *Grave of the Fireflies*. Also, Takahata had directing credits long before Miyazaki, helming TV shows such as *Apache Baseball Team, Heidi, 3000 Leagues In Search of Mother* and *Anne of Green Gables*. Takahata's first feature film as director was 1968's *The Little Norse Prince* (a.k.a. *Horusu: Prince of the Sun*). The financial failure of that movie led to Takahata and Miyazaki leaving Toei Animation.

Isao Takahata is a fabulously talented filmmaker, especially good at comedy and broad slapstick. But his films also have an emotional depth which's really striking, and some of them, such as *Only Yesterday* (*Omoide Poro Poro*, 1991), and *Grave of the Fireflies* (*Hotaru no Haka*, 1988), are deeply moving, with *Grave of the Fireflies* delivering an emotional punch that very few movies have achieved. It's on the scale of distressing emotion of *Bambi*, or the finest Ingmar Bergman dramas, or pushing-the-audiences-to-the-limits of the last minute rescues in D.W. Griffith's melodramas. Indeed, *Grave of the Fireflies* is a masterpiece of cinema, the equal of *anything else* in animation – or live-action.

TOSHIO SUZUKI.

Toshio Suzuki (born 1948), the producer of *Princess Mononoke*, joined the Studio Ghibli team after meeting Hayao Miyazaki when he was managing editor of *Animage* magazine (founded in 1978), which published Miyazaki's *manga* of *Nausicaä of the Valley of the Wind.* As one of the key players at Studio Ghibli, Suzuki is thus one of the leading figures in the Japanese animation industry, as well as being a vital influence on Miyazaki's cinema. Isao Takahata remarked that without 'Suzuki-san, there would be no Studio Ghibli today', and that Suzuki has 'steadfastly supported Hayao Miyazaki' (2009, 460).

If you want to know what a film producer does, have a look at the 2013 documentary *Kingdom of Dreams and Madness*, which shows Toshio Suzuki tirelessly working with and encouraging numerous groups of people, promoting Ghibli's products, travelling to screenings and events, meeting the press, and talking and promoting some more. A film producer, as they say, *causes* a film to happen. It's a sociable, hands-on job, where people skills are uppermost; Suzuki enjoys the process of filmmaking, more even than the movies themselves.

Other key collaborators on Hayao Miyazaki's movies, all of whom have made major contributions to his movies (there are many, many more) include: Masashi Andou, key animator, Hideaki Anno,[41] key animator (and co-founder of animation studio Gainax), Mamoru Hosoda (director of two *Digimon* movies), Tomomi Mochizuki, director, Hiroyuki Morita, key animator, Yoshifumi Kondo, key animator, Yasuji Mori,[42] animator, Yasuo Otsuka, veteran animation director, Yoshinori

41 Director Hideaki Anno (b. 1960, Yamagata Prefecture) was co-founder of Gainax Studio in 1982 (in Osaka, where he studied, with Takami Akai and Hiroyuki Yamaga); he married Moyoko Anno, a *mangaka.* Anno later directed *Nadia: Secret of Blue Water,* and *Gunbuster,* and worked on *Neon Genesis Evangelion* and *Wings of Honneamise.* An early job was animating the Giant Warrior in *Nausicaä of the Valley of the Wind.*

42 Yasuji Mori (b. 1925) worked with Miyazaki and Isao Takahata on *Heidi, Little Norse Prince, Future Boy Conan, Dog of Flanders,* and *Puss 'n' Boots.*

Kanada, animator, Yasuyoshi Tokuma, president of Tokuma Shoten, and Michiyo Yasuda, colour designer and head of the ink and paint dept at Ghibli.

#2

HAYAO MIYAZAKI'S MOVIES AND THE JAPANESE ANIMATION INDUSTRY

Japan has the biggest animation industry in the world, and Hayao Miyazaki's films and those of Studio Ghibli are very much a part of it. That Japan is one of the richest nations on Earth plays a part (at the height of the Bubble Economy in the 1980s, Japan had 16% of the global economic power, and 60% of real estate wealth). The famous TV shows, OAVs, specials, videos, and movies in *animé* include: *Akira, Digimon, Pokémon,*[43] *Dr Slump, Star Blazers, Legend of the Overfiend, Evangelion, Cowboy Bebop, Astro Boy* and *Ghost In the Shell.* According to Helen McCarthy, animation in Japan accounted for 6% of films released in late 1998, 25-30% of videos, and 3-6% of television shows made in Japan. This book isn't an exploration of Japanese *animé*, or the links between the films of Miyazaki and *animé*. There are excellent books on Japanese *animé* available, but I will note a few aspects which throw light on Miyazaki's work.[44]

The world of Japanese animation is instantly recognizable: characters with spiky hair, red hair, purple hair, long hair, hair blowing in the breeze, giant eyes, tiny mouths, snub,

43 The *Pokémon* movies have proved hugely popular in Japan, and rival Studio Ghibli's movies at the box office.

44 A good place to start, and an essential reference work, is: J. Clements & H. McCarthy's *The Animé Encyclopedia* (Stone Bridge Press, Berkeley, CA, 2015).

pointy noses, women with pneumatic bodies, guys with buff, muscle-bound bodies, superheroes, nerds (*otaku*), grimaces showing lots of teeth, elfin ears, grizzled, old guys who smoke, child-like *shojo* figures, tall, skinny villains, people who can fly, grotesque transformations, excessive violence,[45] techno-fetishism, robots, *mecha*, more robots, more *mecha*, mobile power suits, explosions, spaceships, jets, helicopters, motor-bikes, guns, guns and more guns, samurai swords, lightning storms, the ocean, the colours green and silver and red, head-bands, silly hats, comic sidekicks like dogs or cutie critters, Tokyo, futuristic cities, skyscrapers and mean streets (always with the skyscrapers!), neon signs, tentacles, monsters, demons, blood and guts, giant moons, and last but not least: the atomic bombs dropped on Japan by the United States of America.

Hayao Miyazaki's cinema certainly has numerous links to the Japanese *animé* tradition. For instance, the *shojo* figure (such as Kiki in *Kiki's Delivery Service* or Chihiro in *Spirited Away*), the ambiguous treatment of technology, Tokyo settings, Japanese mythology, war (and the two World Wars), the atom bomb, and the military machine. And the motifs that crop up in thousands of *animé* products are also found in Miyazaki's films: the giant robots, flying, rapid action scenes, explosions, gadgets, young heroes, steam-punk paraphernalia, etc.

At the same time, there are many staples of Japanese *animé* that *don't* appear in Hayao Miyazaki's cinema: high school and classroom scenes, kids riding in cars or on motorcycles, teenage parties, bust-ups between kids and parents, sword fights, and sex (Miyazaki's films steer clear of pornography or even nudity, which form a substantial proportion of Japanese *animé*).

45 Altho' Japanese popular culture is still regarded as pretty violent, Japanese society is actually more peaceful than many nations on Earth. Crime rates are low, guns are controlled, and the constitution forbids war. And in the years that *manga* sales boomed, crime rates fell (F. Schodt, 1997, 132).

THE JAPANESE *ANIMÉ* INDUSTRY

An important thing to remember about Japanese *animé* is that it is an industry that can sustain itself by producing movies and TV shows for a *domestic audience*: it doesn't need television syndication or releases overseas (but it will always take them up if available). In other words, one of the reasons that the Japanese animation industry is the biggest in the world is because there is such a large market in Japan itself for animation.

That also means that Japanese *animé* filmmakers can make their films and TV shows for a homegrown market, and don't need to pander to an international (or a North American) audience. This certainly applies to Hayao Miyazaki's movies, which producer Toshio Suzuki has remarked on a number of occasions are very much *Japanese* movies, movies that are made primarily for the *Japanese* market. So the films can reflect and explore local or national culture, and don't need to build in elements that will appeal to a global audience (no need to shift the action of their films to, say, New York or Chicago, and turn their characters into Americans).

It's an envious position to be in for a filmmaker. European filmmakers, for instance, can similarly make films only for their own national audience, but they tend to be much smaller (or cheaper) movies. A country such as France can sustain a huge production of movies per year because it has the largest film industry in Europe (that's one of the reasons why French movies travel outside France). And it means that France can make much bigger movies (it has more government investment than many other countries).[46]

Lonely Planet's travel guide to Japan makes some useful points about contemporary Japan:

---

46 And the French love Hayao Miyazaki's movies, as they love comicbooks and fantasy art. One reason that the movies of Miyazaki and Takahata were received better and were more well-known in Europe was because Europe had imported titles such as *Heidi* and *3000 Leagues*.

> First, Japan is an island nation. Second, until WWII, Japan was never conquered by an outside power, nor was it heavily influenced by Christian missionaries. Third, until the beginning of last century, the majority of Japanese lived in close-knit rural farming communities. Fourth, most of Japan is covered in steep mountains, so the few flat areas of the country are quite crowded – people literally live on top of each other. Finally, for almost all of its history, Japan has been a strictly hierarchical place, with something approximating a caste system during the Edo period. (C. Rowthorn, 2007)

As to genres, Hayao Miyazaki's cinema has included many of the chief genres of *animé*, including action-adventure and epics (*Nausicaä of the Valley of the Wind* and *Laputa: Castle In the Sky*), war stories and fantasy (*Howl's Moving Castle*), and Japanese folklore (*Spirited Away* and *Princess Mononoke*). And many of Miyazaki's movies come under the umbrella of 'children's stories'. There is plenty of comedy, though no Miyazaki movie is an out-and-out comedy. Some of Miyazaki's films combine genres: *Porco Rosso*, for example, has elements of romance, comedy, war/ politics, and plenty of action-adventure.

The genres of Japanese animation include pretty much all of those in live-action, as well as some genres particular to *animé*: comedy; romance; crime; action-adventure; horror; historical drama; science fiction (including *mecha*; cyberpunk; war; epics); fantasy (including comicbooks; supernatural tales; myths and legends; and superheroes); animal stories; martial arts; children's stories; epics; erotica; porn; and sports stories.[47]

In live-action, genres are divided into *jidai-geki* = period movies (typically in the feudal age), and *gendai-geki* = set in the contemporary era.[48] There are further categories within the two genres. Fantasy is one of the key genres of Hayao Miyazaki's cinema, as well as the youth picture.

47 Although it is regarded as popular culture, Japanese *animé* draws on high culture, including woodblock prints, *ukiyo-e*, Kabuki theatre, painting, and classical music.
48 See G. Mast, 1992b, 410.

The Japanese film industry has been one of the most prolific historically, producing over 400 movies a year. The Japanese movie business has been dominated by studio conglomerates, just like the North American system, since the 1920s (the biggies are Nikkatsu, Shochiku, Toho,[49] Toei, Shintoho and Daiei). Although the independent film sector has grown since the 1980s, the major studios continue to take up most of film production. And most Japanese film directors work for the major studios in some form or another, or for television.

In Japan, the director is king of the movie-making industry, rather than the star or producer; the director will often appear above the title, and is often used in marketing more than stars (who is the 'star' of a Miyazaki movie, used in marketing? Miyazaki, of course – and Ghibli). The director is 'the paternalistic head of his own production "family"', as Gerald Mast and Bruce Kawin explain in *A Short History of the Movies*, a social structure which echoes Japanese society (1992b, 409).

Japan is one of the major film markets in the world – for American movies, yes, but also for movies from everywhere. And when it comes to animation, there is a huge appetite for it in Japan. That helps to sustain an operation like Studio Ghibli, and a filmmaker like Hayao Miyazaki. Without that large, national market, and that enthusiastic response to animated movies and television, it would be more difficult for Miyazaki to make the kind of pictures he wants to make. For instance, if Miyazaki had to use foreign money, the economics would have an impact on the films: an investor from, say, Germany, might have certain requirements about the films being able to play in Europe and the U.S.A. A bank from, say, Australia, might have different provisos.

49 Toho, founded in the 1930s from a number of smaller companies, is best known as the studio of *Godzilla* and *kaiju* (giant monster) movies, and Akira Kurosawa. Among Toho's output were sci-fi, *jidai-geki* and *chambara*, crime, dramas, war, youth romances and comedies. Miyazaki's later movies have been distributed by Toho (thus, Toho must've made *a lot* of money out of Miyazaki).

You can see this operating in blockbuster American movies, which consciously target a range of audiences (casting actors from different countries, for instance). Those ultra-high budget American movies have to make about half their money back from international sales (since the Nineties), so the films have to be able to play in Italy or Egypt or Argentina as well as in America.

But Hayao Miyazaki's films have enjoyed a buoyant market in Japan for home-made animation: in short, the Japanese *animé* industry has enabled Miyazaki's cinema to flourish. In 2006, the best-selling *animé* titles in the U.S. of A. had 6 Studio Ghibli movies in the top 20, and 4 Miyazaki flicks in the top 11 (according to VIZ Media).

Japanese *animé* sells in the Western world via OVAs, videos and DVDs, TV shows, and related *manga* comicbooks. Animated series and movies are prepared for the Western market with English language dubs (nearly always using American actors and American-style English).

Miyazaki said that at Ghibli they regarded their movies as real 'things', not virtual (even tho' they use computers). Yes, movies might be 'information' and 'communication', Miyazaki acknowledged (in the postmodern sense), but at Ghibli films are physical 'things' (TP, 269).

Like other animators, Hayao Miyazaki thinks of his movies as movies, not cartoons: yes, it's drawings, not live-action, but for Miyazaki and his colleagues, it's filmmaking (TP, 323). The aim of Ghibli is to make 'films, not '*animé*'': they think of themselves as filmmakers not cartoonists. A lotta *animé* artists say the same thing.

Hayao Miyazaki often discussed *manga*, and how it related to Japanese culture and entertainment. *Manga* were certainly huge in Japan, and more so than in any other country (though they are on the increase in some places). North America, Miyazaki mused, doesn't have a comicbook tradition anything like *manga* culture in Japan: in Japan, a *manga* like *Shonen Jump* might sell 6 million copies a week, enormous numbers. In a 1994 speech, Miyazaki compared that 6 million with the video sales of *Beauty and the Beast* in the U.S.A.: 20 million, for a nation with twice the population of Japan. Selling 20 million in America would be like selling 10 million in Japan, Miyazaki suggested, and *Shonen Jump* sells 6 million *manga* a week!

In Japan, the audience for *manga* is pretty much everybody: the stigma in the West attached to comics and comic-books simply doesn't exist: everyone reads *manga*. The Japanese *manga* market is bigger than the *animé* market. *Manga* also requires far fewer personnel to create, and is cheaper to disseminate.

In 2000 in Japan there were 15 monthly magazines, 10 twice-weekly magazines, and 12 weeklies. Some have print runs of over a million copies. *Manga* accounted for about a quarter of all publishing sales (about 550 billion Yen). *Manga* absorbed around 40% of Japan's printed matter. The average spend on *manga* was 4,500 Yen for everybody living in Japan. According to VIZ Media, the *manga* market in Japan in 2006 was worth $4.28 billion (and $250m in the U.S.A.).

Manga and *animé* are closely aligned commercially as well as culturally.[50] Many *animé* shows are based on *manga* (and some of the big shows have their own *manga* spin-offs). *Manga* can be a cheaper means of testing out if a story will work with an audience. There are many more *manga* stories than *animé* stories. Thus, *animé* has a huge source of stories to draw on, alongside novels, plays, TV shows, video games[51] and all the other products than can be adapted.

Certainly *manga* and *animé* have been important in depicting Japanese culture overseas – and it will be for many their first encounter with Japanese culture.[52] *Manga* and

50 The crossover between *manga* and *animé* is well-known (many animations are *manga* first, and *manga* are in turn produced from movies, including Hayao Miyazaki's movies). There is also a crossover into computer games, board games, card games, pop music and online gaming.

51 Among the well-known *manga* and *animé* that were based on computer games were *Final Fantasy, Pokémon,* and *Sakura Wars.*

52 See G. Poitras, 2001, 8.

animé are popular in many Western markets, including France, Britain, Italy, Spain, Germany, and into Hong Kong, South America, and South-East Asia.[53] The U.S.A. is the primary market outside Japan. In Europe, *animé* is most popular in France (and France has a substantial animation industry). Sci-fi, cyber-punk and steam-punk are also much-loved in France, as are comicbooks and graphic novels.

CREATING ANIMATION

> Those who join in the work of animation are people who dream more than others and who wish to convey those dreams to others. After a while they realize how incredibly difficult it is to entertain others.
>
> Hayao Miyazaki (SP, 25)

Hayao Miyazaki is a hands-on animation director, a workaholic who oversees every aspect of the animation process. This is unusual: many animation directors oversee projects in detail, but not to the extent of checking every piece of key animation, for instance. Miyazaki has been known to re-draw animation if he thinks it's not good enough. Miyazaki is clearly a filmmaker who can't resist getting in there and doing the work. He is a filmmaker who really likes to make films.

That's important: the *sheer joy* of making cinema really comes across in his movies.[54] The pleasure shines through, like the elation that Hayao Miyazaki's characters experience when they fly for the first time. You really can tell when a filmmaker is having a great time making their film: you can see it in *An American In Paris*, in *Once Upon a Time In China,*

53 H. McCarthy, 1996, 7.

54 Hayao Miyazaki had to feel excited about his work in animation: 'I never want to lose the excitement I experience when I'm working' (SP, 386). Boredom is to be avoided: 'If you watch something for three minutes, you feel like you know everything about it, even what went on backstage, and then you don't feel like watching the rest' (SP, 55).

in *Vampyr*, in *Close Encounters of the Third Kind*. You can see the filmmakers letting their imaginations unfurl, and that helps to inspire the rest of the creative team to do better work. 'If I didn't enjoy entertaining people, I wouldn't be in this business' (TP, 324). As his movies demonstrate, he is one of the greatest entertainers in the history of, well, everything.

Animation is a long, hard slog – *very* labour intensive, with projects like feature films typically taking three or four years to complete. It requires a particular kind of individual, then, to maintain a high level of enthusiasm and interest, to stay focussed on the project and not be distracted into doing other things (and to maintain stamina to the end). Stanley Kubrick spoke of keeping hold of his initial inspiration for making a movie all the way through the long process of development, pre-production, shooting, post-production and distribution. You have to hang on to whatever it was that really excited you about doing the project in the first place (a production that doesn't have that initial spark of excitement and fascination can all too easily lose its momentum and energy).

I haven't visited an animation studio in Tokyo, but in every 'making of' *animé* documentary, in every photo, and in every account, every animation house is a shabby building of messy desks and work stations in which animators, ink-and-paint women, in-betweeners, *mecha* designers, character designers, CG technicians and the rest of the staff, slave away at all hours. There are no plush front office buildings, as at the Disney Studios in Burbank or Pixar in Northern California. Only the new Studio Ghibli building among Tokyo animation houses has that upmarket front office feel (but on the main floors of Ghibli, it's animators and their desks and shelves crammed into small spaces again – look at the 'making of' documentary about *Spirited Away*).

It is commonplace for animators and staff to sleep under their desks in animation houses in Tokyo. Visitors from the West to companies such as Production I.G. have been surprised by that, and by the tiny working spaces that even high-ranking animators have: just a desk and a few shelves. Cables run over the floor, DVDs, posters, toys and photocopied timing sheets are packed in everywhere, and there's not much space btn the workers and their chairs. Staff eat their *bento* boxes at their desks (taking less than an hour for lunch). They often have multiple jobs, not just one. Look at a photo of any animation house in Tokyo, and you'll see every nook is crammed with stuff. And it's not unknown for staff to have nervous breakdowns due to the heavy workload (as with director Hideaki Anno on *The End of Evangelion*, and Tomomi Mochizuki after working on Ghibli's *Ocean Waves*).

If you dream of flying to Tokyo and working at Studio Ghibli, Sunrise or Toei or one of the other 430 *animé* houses, be prepared to work very hard, and for long hours (12-14 hours a day, plus every other Saturday), to eat your lunch at your desk (and sometimes sleep there), to enjoy few perks and benefits, to do many tasks (photocopying, say, or website design), and to make barely enough to live.

Once a production starts up, it takes on a life of its own, Hayao Miyazaki explained, and his job was to find the way that the movie wants to work, to find the direction it wants to take. As Miyazaki put it – and this also happened with *Princess Mononoke*:

> The film tries to become a film. The filmmaker just becomes a slave to the film. The relationship is not one of me creating the film, but rather of the film forcing me to create it. (SP, 430)

There comes a moment during a movie's production when logic has to fly out of the window, and you have to rely on your subconscious. You have to become desperate, Hayao Miyazaki said, you have to think it's not going to work, that you can't solve the problems. At that point of desperation and hardship, the subconscious mind helps out and 'lo and behold an answer comes' (SP, 429-430).

Although you might have to draw explosions as an animator, Hayao Miyazaki said, the most important thing was to be interested in people, 'in how they live, and in how they interact with things' (SP, 125). Animators aren't just actors, Miyazaki also stated (in 1988), they have to know how to analyze, fuse and put into sequence movements 'involving gravity and momentum, elasticity, perspective, timing, and the fundamental properties of fluids' (SP, 74).

A director needs to study all sorts of things: 'Of course, the most important thing is imagination, but you have to have a constant interest in customs, history, architecture, and all sorts of things' (TP, 132). In a 1998 directing class, Miyazaki reckoned that directors need 'a "healthy ambition", a desire to express themselves or entertain others, and make money while doing so' (TP, 129). A big ego is also a common element in directors.[55]

It's no good relying on technique, Hayao Miyazaki said, because it wouldn't help to say something if you don't really have anything to say. Rather, 'technique is something people develop in order to express something' (SP, 145).

For Hayao Miyazaki, a shot must contain multiple meanings, and if it doesn't, it falls flat: 'unless three or four meanings are behind the decision on a certain shot, a film will not have a sense of urgency. It's amazing, but just by watching a video screen you can tell if it's an A-class or a B-class film' (TP, 131). The screen reveals all: 'you can't dodge the truth on the screen. Japanese films are boring because they are not infused with multiple meanings on the screen' (ibid.).

Hayao Miyazaki encourages his animators to look, look, look – at the real world, and at real people. Toshio Suzuki has spoken of Miyazaki's incredible facility for observation and recording the real world. To the point where a scene that

55 'One thing about film directors is that once you become one, you'll always be one' (TP, 327).

Miyazaki witnessed years before might crop up in a movie.[56]

> To observe and imitate is most important. He reads books, observes, etc. He often says "Don't rush for a drawing reference book – it should be inside your head".

So Hayao Miyazaki, and the key people in his creative teams – Isao Takahata, Toshio Suzuki, Yasuyoshi Tokuma, Mamoru Hosoda, Masashi Andou, Joe Hisaishi, Yasuji Mori, Yoshifumi Kondo, Michiyo Yasuda – are going to be tough, hard-working and determined individuals. Just to complete an animated feature film is achievement enough, but to make pictures that are so exquisite and visionary, is truly mind-boggling.

In 1987, Hayao Miyazaki described the typical animator as young, good-natured, and poor. They made less than 100,000 Yen a month (= $1,000. There are about 100 Yen to the US dollar). They were paid ¥400 ($4) a page for theatrical movies and ¥150 ($1.50) a page for TV animation. Miyazaki reckoned there were about 2,500 animators in Japan (SP, 135). His first wage in animation was 19,000 Yen a month in 1963, Miyazaki said, when he started at Toei Animation.

In all of his lectures and writings, Hayao Miyazaki emphasized the sheer struggle of producing animation.[57] It is an industry for workaholics,[58] to the point where Miyazaki stated: 'without workaholics, Japan's animation could never be sustained' (SP, 187). It is hard work all the way,[59] and there is no way of creating it without months of labour:

> once we start production, it's at full throttle. The schedule is always tight. I urge the staff to take no breaks, to draw, to run, while whipping myself along as well.

56 Observers said the same of the artist J.M.W. Turner: he would lean out of a carriage window and sketch something very quickly. Years later, it would become a finished painting.
57 It's worth getting the DVD release of *Spirited Away* because it has the Nippon television special about the making of the movie, and you get some idea of the sheer slog of working in animation.
58 For *Spirited Away*, 'the human investment was huge' (TP, 327).
59 For Hayao Miyazaki, work is all about passion and effort (SP, 385).

Miyazaki remarked in 1987 (SP, 138). It means checking all of the frames and key animation, if possible (SP, 183). 'Works of art are created by those who are prepared to go to the limit,' asserted Miyazaki (1991). 'I am deeply involved in checking and redrawing and touching up all the work that comes from the animators,' Miyazaki said (TP, 185).

And for Hayao Miyazaki, pursuing animation means pursuing perfection – or something as good as one can produce. 'One has to pursue it until one is satisfied' (SP, 204). When he made *Heidi, Girl of the Alps,* Miyazaki said: 'we worked at a ferocious pace. Due to lack of sleep and fatigue, we were under such stress that we didn't even catch colds' (SP, 137). And sometimes he slept on the floor in the studio: this was more common in Japanese animation in those days than one would think: it wasn't unknown for animators to stay at work all day, and sleep there too, getting up to carry on. I would imagine that today the intensive, workaholic nature of animation is still prevalent, despite unions, labour laws and all the rest (yep, and animators still sleep under their desks).

> Animated films cannot be made as easily as live-action films [Hayao Miyazaki explained]. I can't be like John Ford, who made more than 100 films, sometimes without even participating in editing his own work. Imagine me directing at this studio for two or three hours, then moving on to another studio to direct a scene like 'there, now the pig gets on the tank,' and then moving on to draw *Nausicaä* – that's just not possible. I don't do things that way, and I don't want to. Animation just doesn't work that way by nature, and if we think it can work that way then we are finished.

THE ANIMATION PROCESS.

In the Japanese animation industry, the script comes first. Storyboards and image boards are drawn when the script is completed (but sometimes before then). The storyboards are called *e-conte* (a combination of *ei*, picture, and continuity). Hayao Miyazaki likes to draw the storyboards himself.

Once the film is complete in terms of storyboards, plus indications of timing (the frames),[60] dialogue and sound effects, it goes to the key animators: they put the movie together as key animation (the animation at the beginning and the end of an action). In-between work means animating the movements between the key frames which the key animators have drawn, using time sheets. This is all mostly done with drawing on paper at desks. At the same time, the drawings are cleaned up (one single outline will be chosen, for example, from a mass of pencil lines). Throughout this and all stages of animation, drawings and artwork are being tweaked and adjusted (each stage is reviewed, and directors often oversee each process – which Miyazaki does, of course).

Once the drawings have been completed, they are transferred to cels (celluloid), and inked and painted. Finally, they are photographed (a whole complex process in itself). Photographic and special effects may be added at this stage. As expected, Hayao Miyazaki likes to check every stage in the process.[61]

It has been a regular occurrence for Hayao Miyazaki to be storyboarding a movie while it's in production, as well as producing image-boards. That's not too much of a problem in live-action, when storyboards are often cast aside anyway when the filmmakers and actors reach the set and rehearse and work out new ways of shooting a scene. In animation, it's much more problematic, because it affects the whole process. On *Laputa: Castle In the Sky,* for example, Miyazaki recalled that he was working on the storyboards throughout production:

> My daily schedule went like this: I got up in the morning, I drew storyboards, I returned to the office. At the office, I

60 In the 2013 *Kingdom* documentary, you can see Miyazaki with a stopwatch working out the timings (closing his eyes to imagine the scene).

61 However, animation doesn't always use 24 frames per second, called 'ones': it often goes to 'twos' (12 frames a second) or 'threes' (8 frames per second). Even Miyazaki's latest movies use those lower frame rates.

touched-up my staff's material. At night, I went home and did some more storyboards. After that, I slept. In Japan, I'm afraid the only one who makes animation this way is me, since no one else could take it. (1987a)

Hayao Miyazaki doesn't need a script, Isao Takahata explained, and he doesn't even bother to complete the storyboards before launching into production (2009, 458). All he needs is a clear idea of his characters[62] and the imagined world he's building. As overseen by Miyazaki, Takahata said that the production 'starts to take on the elements of an endlessly improvised performance'. And he liked to work on every process in a production at the same time, instead of waiting for one part to be complete.[63] It was as if Miyazaki 'were trying to turn the creative process into an erotic adventure', Takahata said (2009, 458).

Putting a movie into words and a script at the outset is something that Hayao Miyazaki finds difficult: he doesn't want to explain it, but to go do it. Indeed, words are only the top layer of the piece: 'the part that can be explained in words and sentences is only the surface layer of what I am thinking' (TP, 143). Yes – because if a movie could all be expressed in words, there wouldn't be any need (or desire) to make it. You could just write it down. But a movie is more than a message or a series of words (ib., 144). Akira Kurosawa said the same thing to an interviewer: if he could put the 'message' into words, he'd simply hold up a placard instead of making a movie!

One of the chief reasons for Hayao Miyazaki concentrating much more on the storyboards or continuity sketches for his own movies, rather than on producing a script, or even writing out the original story, was time: *Laputa: Castle In the*

62 Because he works with his characters for such a long time during production, Isao Takahata remarked, Miyazaki has to identify with them emotionally (2009, 456).

63 There is no set way of making a movie, Hayao Miyazaki asserted: it didn't have to develop from ideas to script to image boards to storyboards to animation. All of those events could be taking place at the same time, or in a different order (SP, 58).

Sky required 650 sketches, *Kiki's Delivery Service* 550 and *Whisper of the Heart* 450 (SP, 103). With all that work to do, there just wasn't time to write the screenplay.[64]

And Hayao Miyazaki said he couldn't work that way anyway: 'I've tried writing the story out many times before, but even if I think a story works great in text, when we render it in continuity sketches it's usually unusable' (SP, 103). Miyazaki has his own way of making movies; it wouldn't work, really, for anyone else.

It is standard procedure in Japanese animation to record the voice tracks after the animation has been completed (rather as European movies dub on the voices later, as was Federico Fellini's habit). It's the other way around in the Western animation tradition, with animators using prerecorded voice tracks for part of their inspiration (it is common for animators to employ video recordings of the actors performing the script, and also to draw on the actors' performances in other work).

Toshio Suzuki described the casting process for voices in Hayao Miyazaki's movies:

> Miyazaki does not watch TV or films, so he doesn't know many actors.[65] When we have meetings with the casting director, Miyazaki's suggestions for actors are usually dead! Especially for older characters like Old-Sophie [in *Howl's Moving Castle*]. So I usually come up with a list. We all listen to the tapes together, and Miyazaki makes the final decision. They are not always professional voice-actors.[66]

Hayao Miyazaki dislikes the Western practice, developed famously at the Walt Disney Studios, of using live-action photography as a reference or a starting-point for animation. Miyazaki hates the technique. It doesn't work, Miyazaki

64 As Ingmar Bergman noted: 'I write scripts to serve as skeletons awaiting the flesh and sinew of images' (*The New York Times,* January 22, 1978).

65 As Miyazaki admitted, 'I know who Gary Cooper is, but that's about it' (TP, 209).

66 Miyazaki has said that he does know of some of the actors that Suzuki has suggested, and he does watch TV and movies.

reckoned, and pointed to the overly expressive and unnatural movements of Disney characters such as Cinderella and Snow White, who look like they're acting in a ballet. It was no good using a young, American woman as a model in pursuing realism; even more of the symbolism of the fairy tales was lost (SP, 75).

And animation and visual effects in the West is still locked into the notion of using live-action reference material: films like *Avatar* and *The Lord of the Rings* have used motion capture technology to drive the animation of their characters (and crowed about it in their publicity).

In Japan, Hayao Miyazaki preferred his animators not to become slaves to live-action photography: if they do, 'their enjoyment of their work plummets by half' (SP, 75). Instead, Miyazaki has his animators do what artists have always done: look at real life.

MIYAZAKI'S MOVIES AND JAPAN

The films of Hayao Miyazaki and Studio Ghibli are truly a phenomenon in Japan. Every time a movie by Hayao Miyazaki is released in theatres, everyone in Japan goes to see it. Or that's what it feels like: in short, every Miyazaki movie since *Porco Rosso* has been the top film that year: *Princess Mononoke*, *Spirited Away, Howl's Moving Castle, The Wind Rises* and *Ponyo On the Cliff By the Sea.* And not just the top grossing movie, but the picture that beats all the other movies by a huge proportion. For example, in 2004, the year when big, North American movies *Harry Potter and the Prisoner of Azkaban, The Lord of the Rings: The Return of the King* and *Spider-man 2* were released in Japan, *Howl's Moving Castle* was the top film by a long way (in 2003, the biggest movie worldwide was *The Lord of the Rings 3,* and in 2004 it was *Harry Potter 3*).

From *Princess Mononoke* onwards, Hayao Miyazaki's movies have had very wide releases in Japan: 348 screens for *Princess Mononoke*, 336 screens for *Spirited Away,* and 450 screens for *Howl's Moving Castle* (compare that with the 3,000 or more screens for wide releases in the U.S.A.). *Princess Mononoke* was the most financially successful Japanese film up to that point, in Japan itself, and including all releases, not just animation. Only *The Passion of the Christ* was more successful than *Spirited Away* as a foreign language movie worldwide (and *The Passion of the Christ* is a true oddity, being an American religious movie filmed in dead languages – Latin and Aramaic).

Hayao Miyazaki has said that he is most concerned with how his movies are received in Japan: Japan is the primary market for Miyazaki's pictures (culturally as well as financially).[67] 'I'm only worried about how my film would be viewed in Japan. Frankly, I don't worry too much about how it plays elsewhere,' Miyazaki told CNN in 1999.[68]

Hayao Miyazaki was not an English speaker, and relied on other people to translate and dub his movies.[69] His chief concern was with the Japanese audience: he hoped that the translations and dubs of his pictures would be accurate. That was the main thing – to stay true to the movie as it was intended to be seen. That most especially applied to the dictum: *no cuts.*

Hayao Miyazaki didn't want to make movies for fans who only wanted one sort of movie. It was no good for film producers to categorize fans, Miyazaki remarked in 1989, and

---

67 Miyazaki, like many filmmakers, takes a dim view of critics and reviews, but values audiences: 'I never read reviews. I'm not interested. But I value a lot the reactions of the spectators'. However, a filmmaker can't just do *anything* he likes. 'I think it's impossible to do everything you want', Miyazaki claimed. 'You have to make such a movie in a different place from a movie which one or two million people pay to see and get satisfied. When I watch a movie such as Tarkovsky's *Stalker*, I feel 'this SOB is doing as he pleases!' I think he is such a talented guy.'

68 CNN, *Today*, Oct 3, 1997.

69 According to Lonely Planet's *Japan* guidebook, few Japanese can speak English as well as most Europeans, or Hong Kong Chinese, or Singaporeans, or Indians (C. Rowthorn, 2007, 50).

only make films for that kind of person.

Hayao Miyazaki warned against viewers watching his movies over and over. It was no good getting obsessed with a film, Miyazaki insisted: to a friend who said his child had watched *Princess Mononoke* over 50 times, Miyazaki sent him a letter:

> saying he was making a terrible mistake. Once a year, maybe once a lifetime, is really how often you should see any of my films.... Owning a little puppy will teach you a lot more about life than watching *Totoro* 100 times.[70]

The sentiment recalls British actor Alec Guinness, who was hounded by obsessive *Star Wars* fans. Guinness recounted meeting a boy in San Francisco who said he had seen *Star Wars* over 100 times. When Guinness asked the boy to promise never to see *Star Wars* again, he burst into tears. His mother, indignant, barked: 'what a dreadful thing to say to a child!' Guinness commented: 'I just hope the lad, now in his thirties, is not living in a fantasy world of second-hand, childish banalities'.[71]

In Hayao Miyazaki's view (which he voices often), movies should only be seen on special occasions – maybe once a year at most (TP, 163). That makes it a different experience, more potent than watching something again and again (which Miyazaki thinks can't be good for kids). Miyazaki would prefer it if children weren't allowed to watch TV until age three – then they could think for themselves (TP, 389).

Hayao Miyazaki would much prefer it if parents didn't make their kids watch movies over and over, but tried living instead. Watching *Princess Mononoke* 50 times, even if it's a 'high quality' movie, is ridiculous, Miyazaki insisted: the kids are 'losing out on something. And the adults don't realize that it's something that can't be regained' (TP, 154).

In his writings collected in *Starting Point*, Hayao Miyazaki

70 Quoted in S. Fritz, 1999.
71 A. Guinness, *A Positively Final Appearance*, Penguin, London, 1998.

repeatedly complains about the current state of animation, in movies and on TV. But he doesn't have rose-tinted glasses on: animated shows weren't better in the 'old days', either: it was just that there were far fewer of them, so each one stood out more.

As well as the sorry state of current animation, Hayao Miyazaki also thinks there is *too much* animation around today, and too many channels on TV, too much of everything. So it was impossible to judge if anything was any good anymore, because viewers were inundated with it. And it also meant that animators were more over-worked than ever before, having to satisfy television's insatiable demand for more material.

❦

In 2005, there were 430 *animé* production studios in Japan,[72] and most of them were in Tokyo. (And that's one of the reasons why so many *animé* shows are set in Tokyo, including some of Hayao Miyazaki's films). The *animé* market was worth about ¥20 billion ($200m) in 2004.

The typical 30 minute (= 23 mins) *animé* TV show costs 10 million Yen. (There are about 100 Yen to the US dollar, so 10 million Yen is about $100,000). Thus, Hayao Miyazaki's movies are very high budget movies, in Japanese *animé* terms, not only compared to TV shows, but also compared with animated feature films: the budget of *Princess Mononoke* was 19.4 million US dollars. So Miyazaki's pictures are some of the most expensive in Japanese animation history, and in Japanese film history.[73]

But $19m is still a lot cheaper than the North American equivalent (and $1 million for *Nausicaä of the Valley of the Wind* in 1984 is a bargain): the animated Disney and Pixar

72 Animation studios themselves become the centre of attention for *animé* fans, and fans will follow particular animation houses and their work. The famous ones include Production I.G., Bandai, Studio 4°C, Gainax, Madhouse, Sunrise, Pioneer, Tezuka, Gonzo, Clamp, Toei, and of course Studio Ghibli.

73 The only reason that theatrical movies are often better than TV animation was the budget, Hayao Miyazaki asserted (SP, 55), but it didn't matter to him whether he made TV movies or theatrical movies.

movies of recent times have included the following budgets: *Tarzan* $115m (or $142m or $150m, depending on sources); *Treasure Planet* $140m; *Ratatouille* $150m; and *Home On the Range* $110m.

These figures aren't really helpful, because movie budgets are notoriously difficult to check accurately: no one wants to admit how much money something *really* cost, or *exactly* how much they're earning (and Hollywood studios routinely exaggerate figures like budgets and grosses). But you know that if the budgets are one hundred million dollars or more, then *somebody somewhere* is making a lot of money. As William Goldman noted, there's a lot of money to be had in simply *making* a film, regardless of whether it's released or seen or not. And some people make a living out of producing movies, including existing on development deals and other deals, and many of those films aren't shot, and some that *are* filmed aren't released.

It's hard to believe that movies like *Home On the Range* or *Tarzan* from the Mouse House could have cost over $110 million or $115 million, but there are all sorts of economic factors to consider. The piece-work labour of Japanese *animé* is going to be cheaper than hiring staff on a permanent basis that occurs more in North American animation.[74] Living costs, unions and working conditions in Japan and America are further factors. The much longer production schedules of American animated movies must contribute to the higher costs too: Hayao Miyazaki and his teams delivered *Nausicaä of the Valley of the Wind* and *Laputa: Castle In the Sky* in less than a year, while Disney and Pixar movies can take 3 or more years. However, the large crews of hundreds of workers aren't hired for all of those years, but it's safe to say that the production teams in American (and Western) feature animation are larger than those in the Japanese animation industry, and that they are hired for longer periods. All of which drives costs

74 Miyazaki often complained about the piecework system of producing animation in Japan, which turned out work like an assembly line, instead of the hand-crafted and personal, artistic approach that Miyazaki favoured.

up (at the same time, Western animation companies farm out work to outfits in countries such as Korea, Thailand and India, just as the Japanese animation industry does).

There are a number of reasons why Hayao Miyazaki can command such high budgets for his movies: one is the simple fact that, from his first film *The Castle of Cagliostro* onwards, his movies have made money. And the later ones, such as *Porco Rosso* or *Princess Mononoke*, have been hugely successful. Miyazaki has had the top grossing movie in Japan a number of times: *Porco Rosso, Ponyo, Princess Mononoke, Spirited Away, Howl's Moving Castle* and *The Wind Rises.* That means his films can attract a lot of investment. Other reasons would include prestige: Miyazaki's movies are very high quality pictures, works of art in themselves, so that glory is reflected back on the investors (as in 'look at us, we put money into *Princess Mononoke* ').

I would imagine that hiring Hayao Miyazaki to make a film is also a bargain: you are going to get a workaholic and perfectionist who will do all he can to make his movie the best it can possibly be. Miyazaki isn't the kind of film director to shuffle on set late, mumble a couple of words, then retire to his trailer or office to loaf about for the rest of the day. As a producer himself, Miyazaki is going to stay with the movie until it's completed.

❦

Like the films of Yasujiro Ozu or Kenji Mizoguchi or Akira Kurosawa, the films of Hayao Miyazaki are very *Japanese* – they are set in Japan, draw on Japanese history and culture,[75] and are about Japanese subjects (even when they're set in[76] or about Europe).[77] But they are also – like the movies of Yasujiro

75 Miyazaki drew on Japanese history, ancient Japanese court tales, sci-fi, fairy tales, and mythology.

76 It was no wonder that Japanese movies were accepted in Europe, Miyazaki pointed out, when Japan's imported so much of European culture – 'literature, art, films, political philosophy, and ways of thinking' (TP, 323).

77 Although Hayao Miyazaki's cinema employs a huge input from European culture, history and landscapes, his films are always Japanese. Even the ones set in European places, like *Porco Rosso* or *Kiki's Delivery Service,* are very, very Japanese.

Ozu, Kenji Mizoguchi and Akira Kurosawa – films which can and do travel around the world.

Most films don't. Most movies don't get released or shown outside their country of origin. Hayao Miyazaki's movies are both very Japanese and very international. Only a few filmmakers achieve that kind of flexibility.

Hayao Miyazaki is sometimes dubbed 'the Japanese Disney'; Helen McCarthy makes another suggestion, more in tune with Miyazaki's hands-on artistry: 'the Kurosawa of Japanese animation' (2002, 10). Akira Kurosawa is of course the giant of Japanese cinema: there is a marvellous series of interviews between Miyazaki and Kurosawa, which are highly recommended (published in 1993 as *What Is a Film?*). (*My Neighbor Totoro* was one of Kurosawa's 100 favourite films; he loved the Cat-bus; Kurosawa said he wept watching *Kiki's Delivery Service;* and he also reckoned that Miyazaki's movies were more important than his own).

Other notable filmmakers in Japanese cinema, apart from the *sensei*[78] himself (Akira Kurosawa), include: Yasujiro Ozu, Kenji Mizoguchi, and Ichikawa Kon, and Japanese New Wave directors, such as Nagisa Oshima, Hiroshi Teshigahara, Masashiro Shinoda, Takeshi Kitano and Yoshishige Yoshida.

Among the classic films of Japanese cinema are: *Tokyo Story, The Flavour of Green Tea Over Rice, The Life of Oharu, Ohayu, Sansho Dayu, Kwaidan, Early Summer, Woman of the Dunes, Ugetsu Monogatari,* and *Ai No Corrida* (*In the Realm of the Senses*). And of course, *anything* by Akira Kurosawa (even one of Kurosawa's minor films is finer than many filmmakers' best efforts).

Hayao Miyazaki ranks up there with the great Japanese filmmakers, I would say. Only a few filmmakers reach those heights, but Miyazaki can rightly be placed alongside Kenji Mizoguchi, Yasujiro Ozu and Akira Kurosawa. Miyazaki does

78 Miyazaki doesn't like the word *sensei*, and persuades people not to use it. He has said: 'I am an animator. I feel like I'm the manager of an animation cinema factory. I am not an executive. I'm rather like a foreman, like the boss of a team of craftsmen. That is the spirit of how I work.'

everything that a great filmmaker can do or should do – and then he does something extra, that magical or special element that raises very good art to the status of great art.

That extra or magical or mysterious or added ingredient is a combination of (1) compassion and humanity, (2) a world vision which includes *everything*, *every* aspect of life, and (3) an ability to embrace and celebrate all forms of life (in Miyazaki's case, the natural world as well as the human realm).

Or, to put it another way: the films of Hayao Miyazaki are far, far above your regular, average movie. They are special, highly individual, very unusual, and deeply moving. To achieve that in any medium is *very* difficult. To do it with painted pieces of plastic seems particularly amazing. Once again, let's not forget that Miyazaki is not working alone, but has a huge team of collaborators, some young and new to the business, and some who have worked with him for decades.

CELS VERSUS COMPUTERS

The films of Hayao Miyazaki are traditional cel animation, but computers and computer-generated effects and devices are employed from time to time. In *Princess Mononoke*, Studio Ghibli began to use computers, but only in small amounts. For instance, computers were applied to the time-consuming process of ink and paint for about 10,000 cels (the intention was to use the computer for around 5,000 cels, but with deadlines approaching, the production resorted to more computer work). However, there were some 140,000 cels in *Princess Mononoke*, so the computer was used to ink and paint less than 10% of the cels. *Princess Mononoke* has around 1600 shots or scenes (in Japanese animation, shots are also called cuts or scenes).

Studio Ghibli's movies, though, never look computerized or digital, because by the far the bulk is conventional (hand-drawn) cel animation (and even when computers are used extensively in animation, drawing skills are still absolutely essential). However, cel animation in movies is as supremely *technological* and *industrial* as computers or digital technology. *Everything* in movies is *technological*, everything is fake, everything is a highly sophisticated cultural form created by humans for mass entertainment. So whether it's done with machines/ tools like cameras or pencils or paint-brushes or computers isn't really the point.

It *is* important, though, I think, that Hayao Miyazaki's films don't have the plasticky look of computer-generated imagery, or the 3-D look of computer animation, or the floaty appearance of computerized additions to scenes. For instance, since the mid-1990s and the success of *Toy Story*, animated movies have shifted towards what's termed 3-D (a misleading term, as all of animation is always two dimensional, when it's projected on a screen. It's more a technical term, referring to the use of 3-D models and devices inside computer programmes, and the simulation of 3-D with the use of 3-D goggles for viewing movies). But Miyazaki's works are refreshingly *not* like the 3-D animation that's seen in many animated movies from *Toy Story* onwards: all of Pixar's output, plus *Ice Age, Robots, Shrek, Chicken Little*, etc.[79]

It's significant, too, that Hayao Miyazaki's pictures don't employ digital additions to scenes which don't really mesh with traditional 2-D animation. For instance, Disney's *Treasure Planet, Atlantis, The Rescuers Down Under* and Warner Bros' *The Iron Man* have used computer-generated (3-D) elements placed into hand-drawn (but probably computer inked) 2-D animation. The digital elements often look floaty and disconnected to the rest of the scenes.

However, using computers is just another tool out of many that animation employs: a common view, still being

79 Miyazaki remarked in 2005: 'I think 2-D animation disappeared from Disney because they made so many uninteresting films. They became very conservative in the way they created them. It's too bad. I thought 2-D and 3-D could coexist happily.' However, the Mouse House brought back 2-D animation in 2007.

voiced by critics who should know better, is that:

cel animation = good, computer animation = bad.[80]

Rubbish – *all* animation is *already* highly technological. Film critics really should visit film studios from time to time, to dispel the falsehoods that they perpetuate. For instance, that some movie sets look made out of cardboard: actually, *all* movie sets are constructed from bits of wood or foam or cardboard and painted, then they're torn down as soon as shooting stops on them.

If you visited an animation house in Tokyo, London, or Hollywood (or the many out-sourced centres in, say, India or Korea), you'd find tons of technology and machines, with computers being just one among multitudes. For instance, the cameras employed to photograph the cels are very sophisticated. And they always have been: have a look at the famous multiplane camera designed by William Garity at the Walt Disney Company in Burbank in the 1930s, which required a group of technicians to operate it.

Hayao Miyazaki thought it was too late for him to convert to CGI and computers; he reckoned that hand-drawn animation would never die out: there would always be someone producing it in a garage somewhere.

MIYAZAKI AND DISNEY

So many qualities of Hayao Miyazaki's cinema would endear themselves to the makers of the Walt Disney Studios' movies. Disney's *Atlantis* (2001) seemed to be very obviously influenced by Hayao Miyazaki (sometimes dubbed 'the Japanese Disney'), and Studio Ghibli. As well as *Atlantis*, other movies in the late Victorian, steam-punk style would include *The League of Extraordinary Gentlemen* (2003), *Hell-Boy*

80 The cel vs. CGI argument merely trots out the ancient oppositions between old and new, or tradition and modernism.

(2004), *The Golden Compass* (2007),[81] and *Steam-boy* (2004), Katsuhiro Otomo's long-delayed but disappointing follow-up to his stupendous *Akira*. Pixar/ Disney's computer animated movie *Up* (Pete Docter and Bob Peterson, 2008) is among the most Miyazakian of recent Disney works.

However, Hayao Miyazaki has critiqued the pandering of Disney's movies to the lowest common denominator: there must be some kind of purity of feeling in a movie, even the popular and mainstream ones. They might invite anyone in, 'but the barriers to exit must be high and purifying' (SP, 72). For Miyazaki:

> Films must also not be produced out of idle nervousness or boredom, or be used to recognize, emphasize, or amplify true vulgarity. And in that context, I must say that I hate Disney's works. The barrier to both the entry and exit of Disney films is too low and too wide. To me, they show nothing but contempt for the audience. (SP, 72)

The Walt Disney corporation itself has been involved in many of Hayao Miyazaki's films – producing the English language versions, including *Princess Mononoke*, as well as distributing them in Western territories via its Buena Vista distribution arm[82] (the deal was made in 1996 between Disney[83] and Tokuma, the publishing company that owned Studio Ghibli). However, the Disney corporation does not handle Ghibli's merchandizing, which would seem a perfect fit at first. But Ghibli and Tokuma have held onto merchandizing

81 The fiction of Philip Pullman, including his most famous work, the *His Dark Materials* trilogy, is set in a fantasy of late Victorian to early 20th century Britain.
82 Prior to the deal with Disney, Studio Ghibli had been approached by Fox and Warners. The chief reason that Disney was selected as an overseas distribution partner for Ghibli was that it agreed to the stipulation that nothing would be cut from Ghibli's movies. Fox and Warners hadn't agreed to that, according to Toshio Suzuki.
83 Critics pointed out that Disney had been slow in releasing Ghibli's movies: only two (*Kiki* and *Mononoke*) in 6 years after the deal.

rights.[84] And they haven't allowed computer games to be produced from Ghibli movies.

JAPANESE AND ENGLISH

Another striking aspect of Hayao Miyazaki's films is the success of the English language versions. As anyone who's watched a few non-English movies will know, some dubbing can be terrible, produced with barely any care at all. The first time audiences in the West will have seen a Miyazaki movie, including *Princess Mononoke*, will probably be in a dubbed version (they are favoured by TV broadcasters, for instance: if there's a choice, a broadcaster will always go with a dubbed version). The first movie by Miyazaki I saw was *Laputa: Castle In the Sky* in the Walt Disney dubbed version; my son Jake and I watched the movie and were amazed by it.

A number of companies (such as New World Pictures, Streamline Pictures, and Manga Video) have dubbed Hayao Miyazaki's and Studio Ghibli's movies, but it is definitely the Walt Disney Studios which has made the English dubbing their own. And Disney have done it so well (many of their versions are overseen by veteran Jack Fletcher).[85] Miyazaki's films have been given the high-class treatment, with big name actors voicing the characters: Michael Keaton, Claire Danes, Jean Simmons, Christian Bale, Lauren Bacall, Jade Pinkett Smith, etc. (The principles of casting voices for animation are different from live-action, of course, but look at those names – they are still well-known actors, and also primarily

84 According to Helen McCarthy, Hayao Miyazaki is not much interested in merchandizing or having his movies distributed outside of Japan. Those issues are 'completely unimportant. To him, the movies themselves, seen full-size in the cinema, are the only things that count' (M, 211).

85 As well as John Lasseter, Rick Dempsey has been involved with many of the Disney versions of Hayao Miyazaki's movies, as producer and dialogue director, and also David Candiff as production manager, with casting by Ned Lott and voice direction by Jack Fletcher.

American).

This also happened with *Princess Mononoke*, which included Claire Danes, Gillian Anderson, Billy Crudup, Keith David, John DeMita and John DiMaggio.[86] For the Walt Disney Studios, Hayao Miyazaki's movies are prestige projects – but they also sell well (though not nearly as well as in Japan, where they are the equivalent of a *Titanic* or an *Avatar* in terms of box office).

The English language versions have altered Hayao Miyazaki's films, however, by changing some of the lines of dialogue, or adding lines (not to mention the vocal performance itself). Most Western, English-speaking audiences probably prefer the English dubbed versions (though I prefer the Japanese versions in all cases).

For instance, there are many differences between the English subtitles – which presumably translate the Japanese dialogue (though not all of it) – and the English dubbed versions. There are lines in the English subtitles which don't appear in the English dubbed version – and vice versa. Background sounds and additional lines of dialogue are also added; thus they are *not* the original sound mixes – and the sound, as many filmmakers have noted, can be 90% of what's going on in a movie. This means that Studio Ghibli's films have a slightly different impact in their Japanese subtitled and English dubbed versions (regardless of where they are screened. (Also, some companies have re-edited movies such as *The Castle of Cagliostro* to get rid of Japanese words and credits.)

86 You might recognize some of the voice cast used among the secondary charcters in the Walt Disney versions of Hayao Miyazaki's movies, as they appear in many animations, from Disney, Pixar and other studios: David Ogden Stiers, John Ratzenberger, Jack Angel, John Hostetter, Tress MacNeille, Sherry Lynn, Phil Hartman, Tony Jay, and Cloris Leachman.

ILLUSTRATIONS

Images of Hayao Miyazaki and some influences

Images of Hayao Miyazaki.
(Top right by Natasha Baucas, 2009.
Second from top left, L.A. Times).
The young Miyazaki (above right).
With his mother (above).
With Toshio Suzuki (second from top).
Isao Takahata (below right). Goro Miyzaki (below left).

Some of Hayao Miyazaki's influences:
From top left:
The Snow Queen. Antoine de Saint-Exupéry. Isao Takahata.
Akira Kurosawa. Diana Wynne-Jones. Philippa Pearce.
Rosemary Sutcliffe. Moebius. Osamu Tezuka. J.R.R. Tolkien.
Ursula Le Guin. Taiji Yubushita & Kazuhiko Okabe. Lewis Carroll.
Betty Boop. Walt Disney. Frank Herbert. Chuck Jones.
Yasujiro Ozu. Robert Louis Stevenson. Jules Verne. Charlie Chaplin.

Some of the films and filmmakers influenced by Hayao Miyazaki. Clockwise from top left: Toy Story. Atlantis. Avatar. The Lord of the Rings. Batman. The Princess and the Frog. Star Wars.

Some animé products released 1980s-2000s. Only a few have a theatrical release (either in Japan or elswhere).

Miyazaki drawing the Nausicaä manga (above).
The Nausicaä storyboards (below).

Miyazaki working on the storyboards
for The Wind Rises

Miyazaki working out timings for animation using a stopwatch.
This is how large parts of Ghibli's movies are made:
sitting at a desk with a pencil and a piece of paper.

Studio Ghibli during the production of Princess Mononoke.

Miyazaki working the animation staff at Studio Ghibli.
At the time of Kiki in 1989 (above), and during
The Wind Rises in 2013 (below).

#3

ASPECTS OF HAYAO MIYAZAKI'S CINEMA

MOVIES FOR EVERYONE

A significant element in Hayao Miyazaki's cinema is that it doesn't talk down to its audience. It takes its fantastical scenarios seriously – but also allows for humour and silliness. His films are not patronizing, but also not lecturing or hectoring. Pedagogical, yes, but not over-zealous, or hitting the audience over the head with moralizing.

Hayao Miyazaki's movies, like all great fantasy movies, are not (just) for children, but for people of all ages. In fact, like fairy tales, their primary audience is not children at all, but adults. Children don't write fairy tales, don't publish books, and don't make fantasy films. Adults do. And fairy tales always were for adults, until the 19th century, when they became part of the commodification of childhood.[1]

But originally, and for always, fairy tales have been written *by adults, for adults.* Similarly with fantasy movies. That's not to say that the films of Hayao Miyazaki and his teams are not enjoyed by children, and do not contain elements that address children directly. And of course Miyazaki's films often feature children or young people as their heroes.

Childhood is 'the best time of one's life' for Miyazaki (TP,

1 See any of the excellent books by Jack Zipes in the bibliography on this topic.

163). 'Our basic awareness must be that childhood doesn't exist for the sake of the humdrum lives of adults' (TP, 168). For Miyazaki, childhood is special, and should be a time of anti-consumerism and anti-capitalism, where children are not exploited, and are not regarded as future workers for society.

Working for children meant *beginnings*: for children, something is new for the first time: the first time you took a train journey by yourself. Miyazaki explained:

> The single difference between films for children and films for adults is that in films for children, there is always the option to start again, to create a new beginning. In films for adults, there are no ways to change things. What happened, happened.

Hayao Miyazaki did not make movies wholly for children, but his desire to entertain children was certainly vital: 'I try to create what I wanted to see when I was a child, or what I believe my own children want to see' (SP, 50). However, he also acknowledged that producing movies for children can be even more challenging than producing movies for adults, because 'they deal with origins and fundamentals' (SP, 91).

> When I hear talk of children's futures, I just get upset, because the future of a child is to become a boring adult.[2] Children have only the moment. In that moment, an individual child is gradually passing through the state of childhood... but there are children in existence all the time.[3]

Being a parent was certainly a spur to Hayao Miyazaki wanting to make pictures for children. Why? Because, he said in a 1995 interview, when you have a child of three, you want to show it something good. And when you see there is nothing good enough out there, you have to make a movie yourself (SP, 432).

2 'Present-day children have not done anything wrong, so why have they been handed such a dreary world?' (TP, 123).
3 Quoted in A. Osmond, 2008, 20.

Detractors would probably trot out the same criticisms of Hayao Miyazaki's cinema as they do of Walt Disney's films, or children's book authors: they would see only that Miyazaki's movies are very colourful and stylized and so can't be 'serious' or 'important'. They would say that Miyazaki's films are intended for children, and so can't be as serious or as valuable as films by, say, Ingmar Bergman or Wong Kar-wai. They would say that Miyazaki's pictures are 'lightweight' or light-hearted, as if the only kind of serious movies have to be heavily melancholy or dramatic or tragic. And finally they would complain that Miyazaki's pictures are fantasies, and fantasy doesn't have the cultural kudos of Shakespearean or Sophoclean tragedy.

All junk, of course.

A recurring theme in Hayao Miyazaki's writings is the ambition to make something for children that's meaningful and special, that has more value than the run-of-the-mill animation on television (SP, 187). 'I want to create works that children can enjoy, or that they can spend some quality time with', Miyazaki asserted (SP, 55).

All adults were children once, and that is partly what Hayao Miyazaki's movies trade on: not childishness so much as a return to a child-like view of the world – which includes wonder and awe as well as fear and anxiety. In this respect, Miyazaki's cinema shares much with Disney's cinema, or many of the great filmmakers who have taken children or young people as their protagonists.

Most of the Walt Disney Studios' films since the revival of the Disney Studios in 1984 by Michael Eisner, Frank Wells and Jeffrey Katzenberg have been what I call 'dual track' or multi-layered movies. That is, pictures which simultaneously target different segments of the audience: action and knockabout comedy for the kids, and knowing, self-conscious quips and in-jokes for the adults. Actually, Uncle Walt knew all about that, about how to talk to parents and their offspring at the same time.

But the films of Hayao Miyazaki and his teams are not like that. They don't split up the audience, and they don't wink at the audience (or at the adult members of the audience). Miyazaki's movies are not self-conscious or 'postmodern' or cleverly allusive of other movies. Oh, they draw on other films often, but they don't do superficial *hommages* or spoofs of other movies. They don't deliver those in-jokes and clever satires of other films, which are so much a part of the Hollywood family movie.

Contemporary animated films are stuffed with those allusions and pop culture references: *Finding Nemo, Chicken Little, Cars, Ice Age,* and, most notoriously, the *Shrek* series.[4] But *Laputa: Castle In the Sky, Porco Rosso* and *Princess Mononoke* don't contain those silly references to the rolling boulder in *Raiders of the Lost Art,* or Norman Bates in *Psycho*, or the shark in *Jaws*, or numerous quotations from pop music. Hayao Miyazaki and his teams are too busy telling the story in their films to stop for jokes about *E.T.* or martial arts movies. They don't want to take you out of the story with bitter snipes at Disney or DreamWorks or Fox or Warners, or turning the film halfway through into a dumb, TV game show. They are not, in short, theme park movies, consumer movies, commodified movies, or pop culture movies.

While contemporary Hollywood cinema endlessly cannibalizes itself (remakes on top of sequels on top of remakes – when was the last time you saw a *new* American movie based on an *original idea* released in a first-run *theatre*, not on DVD or TV?), Hayao Miyazaki's cinema just gets on with making the films and telling a cracking tale. Miyazaki's pictures are boundless when it comes to ideas and inventions.

But the movies of Hayao Miyazaki and his teams are also

4 DreamWorks' *Shrek* (2001) replayed fairy tale clichés in a knowing, ironic, postmodern and comic fashion. There were many digs at Disney films and the Disney corporation in *Shrek.* It seemed a bit odd, even obsessive, that Jeffrey Katzenberg (via DreamWorks SKG) should still be attacking Disney, his former employers. By the time *Shrek* came out, it was seven years since Katzenberg had departed the Mouse House. Some critics exalt the *Shrek* movies, but you can't even place them beside the films of Hayao Miyazaki.

not deadly serious – they are not po-faced and do not take themselves too seriously, like the films of Andrei Tarkovsky or Carl-Theodor Dreyer. There's just too much warmth and tenderness and *life* in a Miyazaki movie for it to be solemn for too long.

FLIGHT

Flight — the sky — transcendence.

Few filmmakers have been so preoccupied with flying as Hayao Miyazaki (Steven Spielberg is definitely one).[5] One wonders if Miyazaki would really liked to have been a pilot[6] – in World War One, and into the 1920s (just like Porco Rosso). Spielberg remarked:

> I am absolutely fascinated and terrified by flying. It is a big deal in my movies. All my movies have airplanes in them. You name the movie – they all fly. To me, flying is synonymous with freedom and unlimited imagination but, interestingly enough, I'm afraid to fly.[7]

One of the reasons that Hayao Miyazaki is able to include so many flying sequences in his movies is surely cost: a flying scene can't be much more costly to produce than other action scenes in animation. But if you had to do those scenes in live-action, they would be much more expensive.

'Alles will schweben',[8] said the German poet Rainer

---

5 Moments of flight in Steven Spielberg's work include the helicopters and flying UFOs in *Close Encounters of the Third Kind*; the airship and planes in the *Indiana Jones* series; the planes in *1941*; the magical bike flight in *E.T.*; the fairy tale Peter Pan flying in *Hook*; the flights and pilots in *Always*; the futuristic flying vehicles in *A.I.* and *Minority Report*; the airliners at the airport in *The Terminal*; more jets in *Catch Me If You Can*; and the last image of *Jurassic Park* is of flight; *The Lost World* also ends on flight. And Spielberg's WW2 film set in China, where the Japanese are the villains, 1987's *Empire of the Sun,* contains many flying scenes.
6 Miyazaki has remarked that he enjoys flying (particularly thru skies with interesting clouds), but has no ambitions to become a pilot (AI, 29).
7 Interview with A.M. Bahiana, *Cinema Papers*, Mch, 1992
8 *Sonnets to Orpheus,* tr. J.B. Leishman, Hogarth Press, London, 1946, II, 14. 5.

Maria Rilke in his *Sonnets of Orpheus.* All things want to fly. The image of flight is the symbol of transcendence, as the *Pancavimca Brahmana* says: 'he who understands has wings'.[9] Mircea Eliade, the historian of religions, wrote in *A History of Religious Ideas*:

> we must always take into consideration the primary experience of the sacrality of the sky and of celestial and atmospheric phenomena. This is one of the few experiences that spontaneously reveal transcendence and majesty. In addition, the ecstatic ascents of shamans, the symbolism of flight, the imaginary experience of altitude as a deliverance from weight, contribute to consecrating the celestial space as supremely the source and dwelling place of superhuman beings: gods, spirits, civilizing heroes. (1979, 27)

Mircea Eliade reckoned that the sky was the first symbol of transcendence, and remains the primary emblem of the sacred, of spirituality, flight, ascension and revelation. The sky is heaven, where the gods live.

> I believe, personally, that it is through consideration of the sky's immensity that man is led to a revelation of transcendence, of the sacred.[10]

And it's not only flying in machines and aeroplanes in Hayao Miyazaki's cinema, although there are 100s of those – many characters fly by themselves, whether it's Totoro, Ponyo, Howl, Sheeta and Pazu (using the crystal) in *Laputa: Castle In the Sky,* or Kiki on her broomstick, or Yubaba as a bird, the River God and Haku as a dragon in *Spirited Away.*

9 *Pancavimca Brahmana,* in M. Eliade, 1985, 4.
10 M. Eliade, 1984, 162.

HAYAO MIYAZAKI AND FEMINISM

Not a few commentators have noted that Hayao Miyazaki is a feminist. At Studio Ghibli, Miyazaki has been concerned about the working conditions for women (the jobs in animation production have traditionally been partly arranged along gender lines: at the Disney Studios in the Classical Hollywood era, for instance, all of the key animators were male, while the inking department, which comprises dull, repetitive work, were largely female). (Japan is still a rather patriarchal society: women earn 66% of what men earn (compared to 76% in the U.S.A., and 83% in Britain), and only 9% of seats in the government (in the Diet)).

Studio Ghibli has nurtured women in animation jobs: Eiko Tanaka, for instance, now a big name in Japanese *animé,* founded Studio 4°C (she had been a producer on *Totoro* and *Kiki*); Atsuko Tanaka (a key animator at Ghibli), animated the short film *Mon-Mon the Water Spider* for the Ghibli Museum; and Makiko Futaki has been an animator on most of Ghibli's output.

Certainly a pro-women stance comes out in Hayao Miyazaki's films, including *Princess Mononoke*, in the roles that he and his writers assign to women (his mother is the source of inspiration for many aspects of his female characters, according to Dan Cavallaro [29]). Second wave feminists and third wave feminists could likely criticize the films of Miyazaki and his teams on numerous counts in their portrayal of women. But it's certainly significant that so many of Miyazaki's protagonists are female. You can search through the work of many of Miyazaki's contemporaries and struggle to find movies with a female lead. But *Nausicaä of the Valley of the Wind, My Neighbor Totoro, Kiki's Delivery Service, Howl's Moving Castle* and *Spirited Away* have female characters as the chief protagonist.[11] And it's not only Miyazaki's films, but

11 In *Laputa: Castle In the Sky,* both Pazu and Sheeta are the heroes, in *Ponyo On the Cliff By the Sea* it's Ponyo and Sosuke, and in *Princess Mononoke* it's Ashitaka and San.

those of Studio Ghibli: *Whisper of the Heart, The Cat Returns* and *Only Yesterday* have women in the main roles, while *Grave of the Fireflies* is about a boy and a girl.

The people who put together Marco\s plane in *Porco Rosso* are all women (a plane factory's traditionally a male preserve, as is the foundry where the women work in Irontown in *Princess Mononoke*), and the workers in the bath-house in *Spirited Away* are women (there are men there too – but they are giant frogs, which's somehow apt).

For instance, only two of Steven Spielberg's pictures have women as the main character: *The Color Purple* and *The Sugarland Express*; none of George Lucas's films; one of Tim Burton's films (*Alice in Wonderland*); and only two of Francis Coppola's movies (*Peggy Sue Got Married* and *The Rain People*, though his entry in *New York Stories* would also count). Some Western filmmakers, of course, have specialized in creating stories with women in the lead: Woody Allen, Ingmar Bergman, Josef von Sternberg, George Cukor, and Pedro Almodóvar.

It should be noted, though, that the most famous animation studio in film history, the Disney Studios, has put women at the forefront of many of their movies: *Snow White and thc Seven Dwarfs, Cinderella, Alice In Wonderland, Sleeping Beauty, Lady and the Tramp* and *Mary Poppins* during Uncle Walt's lifetime, and in later movies such as *Mulan, The Little Mermaid, Beauty and the Beast, Pocahontas, The Princess and the Frog,* etc.

Having a female character in the lead role doesn't make much difference, though, if everything else in the film is patriarchal and masculinist. So the notions of feminism, and female agency, and women's empowerment, and how women are portrayed and perceived, is problematic. It's not enough to point out that a picture has some key female characters; it's much more complicated than that.

It's important, for instance, that women are not often depicted in a very negative light in Hayao Miyazaki's cinema, as they are in so many North American movies. The images of women in Miyazaki's tend to be positive and life-affirming. Some of the women in Miyazaki's movies are very strong characters: you wouldn't mess with San in *Princess Mononoke* or Dola in *Laputa: Castle In the Sky* or Yubaba in *Spirited Away.* And the young heroines of Miyazaki's movies are also tough, practical and assertive characters: Kiki, Nausicaä, Fio, Chihiro (and sometimes they might not start out wholly confident and independent, like Chihiro, but they usually end up like that).[12]

Why so many female characters? One reason Hayao Miyazaki offered was that when girls do something, it's kinda automatically more interesting than when boys do something:

> If a boy is walking with long strides I think nothing of it, but if a girl is walking boldly, I think she looks so full of vitality. That's because I'm a man: women might think a boy striding along looks cool. (SP, 428)

Because Hayao Miyazaki is a man: yes, it *is* that simple sometimes. Miyazaki would rather look at girls than boys, and would rather have girls as the main character than boys. Asked about his preference for female characters, Miyazaki replied that it was a complicated issue, but reduced his explanation to this: 'it's because I love women very much'.

A criticism of the depiction of female characters in Hayao Miyazaki's cinema might be that he and his writers have simply transferred male/ masculine attributes to a female character (as Hollywood movies do – consider Hollywood action movies, such as *Alien, G.I. Jane, Catwoman, Lara Croft, Underworld, Kill Bill*, etc).

I don't think that Hayao Miyazaki's films do that, though; I don't think of Miyazaki's female characters as simply female versions of male characters. In fact, it's more that in some cases, Miyazaki's cinema doesn't make that much of gender

12 *Spirited Away* charts the journey of a young girl from insecurity, anxiety and dependence to self-confidence and independence.

differences. His characters don't angst about being female or male – they are too busy getting on with being themselves. There are few examples of characters voicing views such as 'girls shouldn't do that', or 'women don't do that'.

Hayao Miyazaki has commented a number of times on wanting to provide positive role models for young, Japanese women (and *Spirited Away* was made partly to do that). It was partly a movie produced for young women, who weren't being catered for, Miyazaki thought, in movies. Certainly *shojo* characters[13] such as Nausicaä and Kiki and Fio (in *Porco Rosso*) are positive role models – they are hard-working (a vital Miyazaki characteristic), independent (also important), idealistic, optimistic, helpful, confident, warm-hearted, and (crucially) compassionate. They are characters who believe in themselves and what they are doing.

It's true they can be too idealistic (and naïve) at times, and have to adjust their hopes and dreams to fit reality; they can be irritatingly enthusiastic, and have to temper their enthusiasm; they can be headstrong, and stubborn.

But they are seldom negligent of other people's feelings; they are deferential (and remember their manners when others remind them); they are trusting, and loyal. And, unlike too many young characters in Western animation, they are never bratty.[14] Ghibli and Miyazaki have also avoided overly cute depictions of young women, which are everywhere in Japanese animation: they do have the large eyes[15] and tiny

---

13 The *shojo* character is a young girl, somewhere between a child and an adult. The *shojo* is marked by a fondness for popular culture, for cute consumer goods (*Kawaii*), a wistful nostalgia, and an innocent eroticism (S. Napier, 118). Many of Hayao Miyazaki's characters are *shojo*, of course, although some critics have seen Miyazaki's young women as 'youths wearing *shojo* masks'. Cuteness is certainly a key element in Miyazaki's young female characters. It's no surprise that many of Miyazaki's *shojo* characters are linked to flight, because flying represents escape *par excellence.*

14 Hayao Miyazaki has also avoided portraying *shojo* characters as sexually objectified (called *loli*) and 'play toys for Lolita complex guys' (SP).

15 Why does Miya-san persist in using the big eyes of *animé*? One reason is that he finds them beautiful, and another reason is economics: to be commercial for a Japanese audience, Ghibli needs to stick to the styles of popular culture (TP, 91).

mouths of *animé* women, but they are not babes or dolls.[16] Large breasts are common in Japanese *animé*, but in Miyazaki's films they are reserved for older matriarchal figures, like Dola in *Laputa* or *Yubaba* in *Spirited Away.*

Hayao Miyazaki recognized that *shojo manga* (comicbooks depicting young women)[17] were really psychological: the real story took place in the text and the blank spaces of the page, not in the visuals. Thus, in turning a *shojo* comicbook into an animated movie the real question was: 'how much of a person's psychological state can really be represented with visuals' (SP, 101).

Hayao Miyazaki's female characters are at their worst when they are self-absorbed, like Kiki when she's lost confidence in her witchy ability. When they are passive, like Clarisse in *The Castle of Cagliostro,* they conform more to stereotypes of princesses in towers who need to be rescued by dashing princes (Lupin III).

Hayao Miyazaki's women are at their best when they are brave, and kind-hearted, and compassionate, and confident in their decisions. When they trust themselves, and when they gain the trust of others. They can be just as heroic as guys, and often more heroic (Nausicaä, Kiki) – because they are the heroines, the chief characters, and no one else is going to do it if they don't. Often they have to act alone, without help or back-up, and sometimes without really knowing what they are doing.

16 A. Osmond, 1998.

17 In 1995, there were 45 magazines aimed at girls (*shojo*), compared with 23 *manga* magazines (*shonen*) aimed at boys.

CHARACTERS: THE LOOK

In terms of compositions and figures, the films of Hayao Miyazaki feature recurring types. The children, for instance, are wonderfully energetic, laughing characters, with large eyes and enormous mouths that stretch across their whole faces when they laugh. They are squat, round body types, that bounce around a scene like basket balls.

The heroes and heroines tend to be rather intense, with the clean, pure lines of classical beauty, and the familiar features of Japanese *animé*: wide eyes (always with a couple of eye lights), tiny, button noses, small, neat mouths, and fabulous, spiky, wild hair (that usually wafts in the breeze, and not only in flying or magical scenes). They are usually highly agile and dynamic, sometimes clumsy, and usually possess slender bodies like dancers.

The older men in Hayao Miyazaki's cinema run from tall, skinny, neurotic types to gruff, burly, muscular figures. Short, portly figures recur (like Marco in *Porco Rosso* or the old engineer in *Laputa: Castle In the Sky* or Jigo in *Princess Mononoke*). Some are dynamic adventurers, like Lord Yupa in *Nausicaä of the Valley of the Wind,* and some are dynamic but comic, like the Mamma Aiuto boss in *Porco Rosso.* Miyazaki loves moustaches and beards (in films such as *Nausicaä of the Valley of the Wind,* there's no mouth at all for some of the male characters, just a giant, bushy shape).

Another character type that Hayao Miyazaki has made his own is the powerful, older woman, usually rather large, sometimes with a vast bosom, very big hair, and typically an enchantress. The costumes are usually skirts and dresses, with hair in traditional styles, such as buns: the crone in *Nausicaä of the Valley of the Wind,* the Witch of the Waste in *Howl's Moving Castle,* and the one that tops them all, the totally incredible, once-seen-never-forgotten Yubaba in

Spirited Away.[18]

Few Hayao Miyazaki heroes or heroines wear jeans and Tee shirts, crop-tops or bikinis,[19] baseball caps, tattoos or piercings. Sometimes overalls or dungarees, sometimes army uniforms, and sometimes, like Pazu in *Laputa: Castle In the Sky,* a shirt and breeches. The young women tend to wear dresses or skirts (Kiki hates her dark witch's dress).[20] The costumes are dictated very much by the periods which Miyazaki and his teams like to explore, of course: the late 19th century and early 20th century, or, occasionally, more mythical eras, as in *Nausicaä of the Valley of the Wind* or *Princess Mononoke*.

As well as using women in the lead roles, Hayao Miyazaki also likes to pair up characters, so that the hero is essentially split into two. Often, they are male and female, and are usually regarded as a couple (sometimes they actively resent being seen as a couple, like Porco with Fio in *Porco Rosso*, and sometimes they are not quite a romantic couple, like San and Ashitaka in *Princess Mononoke*). And sometimes Miyazaki likes to subvert expectations, and reverse gender roles. For instance, he makes the leader of the pirates in *Laputa: Castle In the Sky* a powerful woman, Dola. And in *Mononoke*, the tough boss of the industrial, Irontown community is not a man, but a beautiful woman, Eboshi.[21] And in *Kiki* it's the girl who rescues the boy.

---

18 Yubaba is the finest example in all cinema of the crazy, powerful matriarchs in Lewis Carroll's *Alice* books, the Duchess, the Red and the Queen of Hearts.

19 Ariel the mermaid in Disney's 1989 flick sports one of the more preposterous costumes for a fairy tale character.

20 There's an erotic component to this – Hayao Miyazaki has commented that he likes skirts and dresses. And like other Japanese *animé*, the skirts and dresses tend to blow in the wind all the time.

21 A recurring motif in Miyazaki's cinema are the pairings between older women and younger women: Kushana and Nausicaä in *Nausicaä of the Valley of the Wind,* Clarisse and Fujiko in *The Castle of Cagliostro,* Dola and Sheeta in *Laputa: Castle In the Sky,* and Gina and Fio in *Porco Rosso.* Even Chihiro and Yubaba work together in *Spirited Away.*

CHARACTERS: TYPES.

One of the strongest elements in Hayao Miyazaki's cinema, and one of the chief reasons for its enduring popularity, is surely Miyazaki's ability to create convincing and likeable heroes and heroines. These are young people (sometimes older people) that are resourceful, hard-working, brave, dignified, and creative, but also sometimes vulnerable, sometimes moody, sometimes doubting themselves and their abilities. They are not superheroes, however, though they do occasionally have some superhero traits – such as the ability to fly.

They are not petty, not greedy, not envious, not small-minded; they are generous, and kind, and helpful, and loyal. All of these positive qualities might make them insufferable and arrogant, but no, the characters in Hayao Miyazaki's films are very appealing. These are genuine people; sometimes they can be very serious, but they are also ready to laugh and fool around (but I don't think San or Ashitaka laugh once in *Princess Mononoke*). At the level of characterization, the movies of Miyazaki are as convincing and persuasive as any of the great filmmakers – Charlie Chaplin, D.W. Griffith, Ingmar Bergman, Akira Kurosawa, whoever.

Most of the characters in Hayao Miyazaki's movies are white – either Japanese or European, with one or two Americans. If they're European, they tend to be French or Italian (not so many Brits or Scandinavians, for instance). 'White' meaning 'Caucasian' – but that is a visual convention of Japanese *animé*: to Japanese audiences, they would look Japanese; to Westerners they look 'white'.

DAILY RITUALS.

Another significant ingredient in the films of Hayao Miyazaki is their domesticity and everydayness: every single one of the interiors in these magical movies is a believable, lived-in space: there are pots of coffee or kettles and saucepans on the stove; there are onions or tomatoes on the table; there are bowls of milk on the floor for cats and vases of flowers on the table; there are clothes hanging up inside and outside; and there are pictures on the walls. These are places where real people live – the walls and floors are not spotlessly clean, the doors are scuffed at the bottom and around the handles, and the brickwork has cracks in it.

There is an emphasis on daily rituals, like eating, cleaning, cooking, and washing. And scenes of characters going to bed or getting up out of bed. The scenes may only be little slips of colour on a plastic animated cel, but you really can believe that Kiki is lying on her back in that big, dusty room above the baker's store in *Kiki's Delivery Service.*

STYLE

In terms of style, the animated movies of Hayao Miyazaki run from conventional cinema to sudden explosions into fantastical or heightened modes of narration. Miyazaki's use of the camera is largely traditional – classical camera moves such as slow pans to reveal an environment, or slow tilts, or slow zooms, often across verticals and horizontals.[22] Like all the best filmmakers, Miyazaki does not wave the camera around pointlessly or use self-conscious or tricky effects.[23] However, when dramatically necessary, he will employ crash zooms, or whip pans, or rapid tracking shots, or flash cuts, or extreme close-ups. In short, Miyazaki uses the camera for a dramatic reason every time. He will not cut to a God's-eye-view, for

22 Hayao Miyazaki's animation simulates live-action cinema, as if the spaces were being filmed with a real camera, as does Japanese animation (and most Western animation) in general: that is, it includes camera movements like pans and tilts (favourite Miyazakian shots), tracking shots, zooms, dynamic backgrounds, selective focus, wide angles, and so on. Western animation (including computer animation added to live-action movies) also simulates photographic elements such as lens flare.

23 I'm glad that Miyazaki hasn't got into speed ramping or self-conscious editing techniques (as some fans would like to see). There's so much going on in a Miyazaki movie, you don't need that look-at-me fussiness.

instance, when having the camera at eye-level will do just as well, or better.

One of the striking aspects of Hayao Miyazaki's cinema is how often he uses movement in space, along the right angle to the screen. Traditionally, this's trickier to achieve convincingly in animation (the flattened movement from right to left or left to right is more common. Think of the 1960s Hanna and Barbera cartoons, where characters run past recycled backgrounds).

In films such as *Princess Mononoke* or *Laputa: Castle In the Sky,* characters race towards the camera, or away from the camera, creating a dynamic sense of movement and composition. There's never a feeling that Hayao Miyazaki and his teams are limited in any way by the animation process. Characters move from and into all corners of the frame.[24]

In some pictures, such as *Spirited Away* and *Howl's Moving Castle,* there is an interior space where the production teams decide they are going to go all-out, to throw in every idea, every colour, every prop, every and any thing they can think of. In *Howl's Moving Castle,* this occurs in Howl's bedroom (and also the castle itself), while in *Spirited Away* it's Yubaba's apartment (and in *Arrietty,* it's the heroine's bedroom). On the visual level, the interiors are reminiscent of the highly ornate and decorative art of Symbolist painters Gustave Moreau or Odilon Redon, or the British Pre-Raphælite artists (such as Edward Burne-Jones or John Everett Millais or James Tissot).[25]

One of the most impressive aspects of Hayao Miyazaki's cinema is invisible: the editing and pacing. Not a frame is wasted, and none of his films seem too long or slow or padded-out. One of the beauties of animation for the viewer is that because it's so expensive and so labour-intensive, anim-

24 Characters walking towards the camera is one of the most difficult things to do in animation, Miyazaki said (SP, 320) – and Miyazaki's cinema is full of such scenes.

25 For Chris Lanier, *Spirited Away* is 'one of the most visually baroque films ever made. Its look and density are so unique', recalling ancient Buddhist frescoes or Byzantine art.

ated movies are rarely too long. Miyazaki's pictures are as exquisitely-paced as any in the history of cinema. That is a vital element of their success. Compare, for instance, with so many Hollywood films of the same period – 1980s-2000s – and you'll find movies that drag on and on, that have every dramatic highpoint s-t-r-e-t-c-h-e-d o-u-t mercilessly l---o---n---g, each plot point will be hammered home bluntly, and the films out-stay their welcome by twenty, thirty or forty minutes.

Instead of including meanderings and atmospheric incidents, the best Japanese films focus on the main theme ruthlessly, as Bruce Kawin and Gerald Mast explain in *A Short History of the Movies*:

> the great Japanese films seem to rivet every incident of the plot, every character, every visual image, and every line of dialogue to the film's central thematic question or dominant mood. (1992b, 410)

Hayao Miyazaki's movies have wonderful, enormous and spectacular endings, and that's a key reason for their success. There are quite a few major filmmakers, for instance, who had real trouble with endings (Orson Welles, Stanley Kubrick, Steven Spielberg, and Francis Coppola, for instance). But in Miyazaki's movies, the ending is fully worked out on the narrative and thematic and emotional levels: that is, Miyazaki's movies don't only deliver fantastic action and thrills and stunning set-pieces and gags and stunts, they also completely convince emotionally and thematically.

Instead of happy endings, Hayao Miyazaki said it was enough for him to have the hero deal with a single issue for the moment. It might be easier to make a movie where everyone is happy because the villain has been defeated, but Miyazaki just couldn't do that (SP).[26] 'A film should show some

26 For Miyazaki, movies like *Pearl Harbor* and *Saving Private Ryan* were 'films like video games' (with *Ryan* as 'one of the worst films of this sort. The aerial forces do their bombing, and then it ends').

problem being overcome, even if it's a small one', Miyazaki remarked in 1995 (SP, 423). Just creating evil villains in order to destroy them at the end of a story to produce a catharsis makes animation 'a despicable profession' for Miyazaki (TP, 178).

> In American films, as long as it's an enemy, you can kill as many people as you want, and that's true of *Lord of the Rings* too. You can kill indiscriminately without worrying about whether they are civilians or military. As long as it can be called collateral damage. (TP, 287)

Discussing *Future Boy Conan* in 1983, Hayao Miyazaki said that he liked it when stories ended with the characters cleansed or liberated: they become, in effect, *more* child-like or innocent at the end, rather than the conventional narrative development from innocence and naïvety to maturity and knowledge. Instead of gaining something, like wisdom, or values, or morality, or a message, things drop away. So, for Miyazaki liberation is one way to go: 'I feel that viewers should feel liberated after watching cartoon films, and that the characters should also ultimately be liberated' (SP, 304).

THEMES

Among the themes that Hayao Miyazaki's cinema takes in are ecology, war, politics, depression, loyalty, the loss of innocence, consumerism, and creativity (C, 1). You can add animism, good vs. evil, nature, age and youth, flight, feminism, the future, technology, and machines to that list.

Animism is the most ancient form of religion or spiritual feeling, and predates all religions. E.B. Tylor famously defined animism as 'the belief in spiritual beings'. Animism is found throughout Hayao Miyazaki's cinema, and he has referred to it in his writings. A film such as *Princess Mononoke* or *My*

Neighbor Totoro is a pæan to animistic sensibilities. And animism of course is a foundation of Shintoism,[27] Japan's main religion. In Miyazaki's movies, there are offerings to spirits (*kami*),[28] sacred gates (*torii*), and Shinto shrines (*jinja*).[29]

Nature and ecology is such an all-pervasive theme in Hayao Miyazaki's cinema, and all of his films and his narratives relate to the natural world and protecting the natural world in some form or another.[30] And some movies, such as *Nausicaä of the Valley of the Wind* and *Mononoke Hime,* make ecological politics central to the narrative (*Mononoke* is the sequel to *Nausicaä* in its ecological theme). For Miyazaki, ecological issues could not be ignored from around 1960: that was the time when it was no longer possible to ignore the wider world (SP, 107).[31]

Society isn't automatically progressive, always developing to greater and greater things. Although the utopian desire is all-powerful, and humans cannot live without it, Hayao Miyazaki reckoned there will be a time when, for example, there is no electricity: there will be power lines, but no electricity (SP, 421). Miyazaki often talks about the future, how technological societies will find resources and fuel running

27 As the *Lonely Planet* guide to Japan explains: 'In Shinto there is a pantheon of gods (*kami*) who are believed to dwell in the natural world. Consisting of thousands of deities, this pantheon includes both local spirits and global gods and goddesses. Shinto gods are often enshrined in religious structures known as *jinga, jingu*, or *gu* (usually translated into English as shrine') (C. Rowthorn, 2007, 54).

28 As well as *kami* or spirits, Hayao Miyazaki's movies – and Isao Takahata's – feature Buddhist icons, such as *jizo* statues (C. Odell, 28).

29 Although *Nausicaä of the Valley of the Wind* contains images of a messiah, there are few overt references to Christianity in Hayao Miyazaki's cinema. Miyazaki said he was shocked when he first saw the images of Christ in Western art: 'I couldn't believe what repulsive images the artists had used to represent God. I was simply aghast; there was no way I could have regarded them as beautiful' (SP, 121). Miyazaki is not the only artist of recent times to react that way.

30 Japanese want to be one with nature in old age, Hayao Miyazaki wondered, but Europeans want to confront nature and stare at it (SP, 146).

31 In *Tales From Earthsea* by Ursula Le Guin, the young wizard Otter remarks: 'I look at the world, at the forests and the mountain here, the sky, and it's all right, as it should be. But we aren't. People aren't. We're wrong. We do wrong. No animal does wrong. How could they? But we can, and we do. And we never stop.' (45).

out, with over-population a major issue.

There is no absolute good or evil in Hayao Miyazaki's cinema. This is a fundamental moral perspective. Miyazaki is critical of stories and movies which end up happily – as if everyone is now going to live happily ever after because the villain is dead. No. Miyazaki much prefers ambiguity in all of his characters – including the good guys. (Characters are often more complex in *animé* than in comparable products in the Western world. It's not unknown, as Gilles Poitras pointed out, for main characters to die, to fail, or to lose the girl/ boy [2001, 55]).

Hayao Miyazaki noted that Ursula Le Guin suggested that dark was more powerful than light in her *Earthsea* books (SP, 359), but not 'dark' in terms of 'evil'. One of the reasons that the bad guys in Miyazaki's cinema are ambiguous and not wholly evil is emotional: that is, it's due to Miyazaki's tendency to empathize with his characters emotionally, so he can't see them as all bad.

> I tend to proceed on an emotional basis. I can't do the work unless I have an emotional investment in it. I tend to pour myself into the characters. And when I do so, I start to empathize with the characters, to feel sorry for them. (SP, 299)

This *emotional basis* for Hayao Miyazaki's cinema is one of the reasons why his stories proceed at times illogically, but emotionally true. His narratives do not have strictly good or evil personalities, and they often take routes which seem odd or unusual. It is an intuitive approach to storytelling which is Miyazaki's own, and one of the things that makes his cinema so extraordinary – and so different from everyone else's. 'I'm not making a film; instead, it feels like the film is making me', is one of Miyazaki's mantras (SP, 110).

Hence the villains in Hayao Miyazaki's cinema are not your usual villains:

> I'm really not good at depicting the bad guys, frankly. They always wind up to be people who are at the core basically good. (SP, 303)

Only bad people, Hayao Miyazaki asserted, such as Mao Zedong, try to change history dramatically (SP, 298). If you turn a villain into an ugly, bad guy, it's too easy to get rid of them, Miyazaki said in 1994: but if you make them more sympathetic, it becomes more complicated, a richer mix (SP, 413).

The idea of portraying good and evil in movies as simple polarities is anathema to Hayao Miyazaki:

> I know it's considered mainstream but I think it's rotten. This idea – that whenever something evil happens someone particular can be blamed and punished for it – is hopeless.[32]

Hayao Miyazaki has often said that he likes to make films he would like to see himself: 'I just want to make films I want to see' (SP, 306). Animated movies might help people feel more liberated, Miyazaki wondered, more refreshed, more relaxed: they might be able to suggest ways of liberating oneself from fears and anxieties.

Underlying the fantasy and spectacle of Hayao Miyazaki's cinema is plenty of unease and ambiguity – and sometimes Miyazaki consciously foregrounds that moral ambivalence and ideological uneasiness.[33] For instance, by making his villains not out-and-out baddies, like Eboshi, the boss of Irontown in *Princess Mononoke*, or making his heroes not wholly good guys, like Howl in *Howl's Moving Castle.*

In a conventional narrative, for example, such as a Western (Brothers Grimm) fairy tale, Yubaba in *Spirited Away* would be evil, and would be punished. But she is a much more ambiguous figure: thus, there is no villain in *Spirited*

32 Hayao Miyazaki, quoted in C. Winstanley, 61.
33 'I have inherited my old man's anarchistic feelings and his lack of concern about embracing contradictions' (SP, 209).

Away, and no evil force to be defeated. It just doesn't work like that in Miyazaki's moral universe.

Hayao Miyazaki's cinema is also not Gnostic or Manichæan: it does not believe that the world itself is tainted or corrupted or evil (there are more filmmakers who promulgate Gnostic philosophies than one would think, even if they are not aware of it).

But it is important to stay aware of the potentially damaging politics of fantasy. For Miyazaki, ignoring the ethnic or racial aspects of fantasy novels is dangerous. The enemies in *The Lord of the Rings* are clearly meant to be Asians and Africans, Miyazaki insisted: 'I think the people who don't understand that, who go around saying how much they like "fantasy works", are really idiots' (TP, 288).

The scene in *Raiders of the Lost Ark,* where Indy shoots the Arab with the sword, was another example of the racism of fantasy: 'it makes me incredibly ashamed to think that there are Japanese who get a thrill out of that. They're the ones being blasted in scenes like that' (TP, 288).

Time is a recurring concern of Hayao Miyazaki's cinema: the importance of the past, of ancestors, of earlier generations, and of the future. Read any interview by Miyazaki and he often discusses the past and the future. What the past was *really like* is a concern, and what the future is *really going to be like* is another.

The emphasis on time, on the past and the future, comes out in Hayao Miyazaki's movies in the depiction of ruins and abandoned spaces, another Miyazakian speciality, from *The Castle of Cagliostro* onwards, emphasizing a sense of history and the past. *Nausicaä of the Valley of the Wind* and *Laputa: Castle In the Sky,* for example, with their abandoned relics of earlier civilizations, offer a poignant commentary on what the past meant to the people at the time (excessive mechanization and industry), and just how much of that civilization and community has lasted.

The message is crystal clear: you might think that

advanced capitalism and technological sophistication is wonderful and life-enhancing and is here to stay, but this current phase of civilization is just as transitory and ephemeral as the clouds or the wind. What is the final image of Miyazaki's final film? – a windy, cloudy, grassy plain (when humanity's gone, nature will take over).

Flight is of course a major, major theme, as outlined above.

Feminism and pro-women ethics and morality is a recurring theme, to the point where Hayao Miyazaki stands far ahead of almost every other comparable filmmaker (including in Japan). You have to look to arthouse filmmakers such as Walerian Borowczyk, Ingmar Bergman or Pedro Almodóvar to find a (male) director so keen on placing women at the centre of their stories.

Growing up and finding one's place in the world is a theme found in pretty much every Hayao Miyazaki movie: it is given a particularly Japanese flavour, but also of course it's a universal theme (D. Cavallaro, 8). The related themes of the strong bonds of socialization and the institutionalization of the individual are set against the importance of finding one's individuality and independence. It's about being both a complex individual and being a part of a complicated society.

Social responsibility, loyalty, hard work, respect, generosity, companionship, kindness and solidarity are explored at both the individual and the social level in Hayao Miyazaki's cinema, in a manner so deep and detailed – separating Miyazaki's cinema from nearly all animation, and certainly from the Disney and American type of animation.

In short, the level of *maturity* in the outlook of Hayao Miyazaki's cinema is very rare not only in animation, but in any kind of commercial cinema. We are moving far beyond good vs. evil and good guys versus bad guys, way beyond the Western world's simplistic moral duality which still pervades all of popular culture – *and* high culture.

Hayao Miyazaki wondered if animators were dealing with

something 'left undone in our childhood', as if they hadn't quite fully grown up, 'we must all be pursuing what we couldn't do during our childhood' (TP, 154-5). And Osamu Tezuka was acutely self-conscious, Miyazaki said, as he himself was: Tezuka was dealing with 'a gap between his inner self and the world', which Miyazaki also struggled with (ibid).

Youth and old age, the differences of age and of generations, is both a theme and a common motif in Hayao Miyazaki's cinema, and in Japanese animation (and not just because his movies are about children, and children and parents). Miyazaki likes to put characters of different ages together – often they are women: Chihiro and Yubaba in *Spirited Away*, for example, or Sheeta and Dola in *Laputa: Castle In the Sky,* or Kiki and Osono in *Kiki's Delivery Service.* And often communities rely on young people to do what they cannot do anymore: for instance, the Eboshi people in *Princess Mononoke* need Ashitaka to discover what is happening in the rest of the country.

Though utopian and often optimistic, Hayao Miyazaki's art is also carefully realistic and pragmatic. Not pessimistic, not defeatist, but certainly practical. His movies end with the recognition that there is plenty more work to be done. However, Miyazaki has also described himself as a pessimist, but said that he wouldn't force his own life-philosophy onto the audience of his movies, in particular children.[34]

It's important, Hayao Miyazaki said in 1979, to have characters that are fully fleshed out, who are 'life-affirming and have clear hopes and goals', and then make sure that the story 'develops as efficiently and simply as possible' (SP, 34). And Miyazaki stuck to this proviso: the *life-affirming* or positive aspects of his characters is vital, I think, to his

34 At the time of *Spirited Away*, Miyazaki remarked: 'In fact, I am a pessimist. But when I'm making a film, I don't want to transfer my pessimism onto children. I keep it at bay. I don't believe that adults should impose their vision of the world on children, children are very much capable of forming their own visions. There's no need to force your own visions onto them.'

cinema. Miyazaki doesn't want to give out 'messages', or lecture his audience (there are other places to do that than in an animated movie or TV show, he said), but he does want to send out positive, life-affirming views when it comes to his lead characters and their hopes and dreams.

Hayao Miyazaki would never, and has never, created an anti-hero as his main character, or featured characters who are nihilistic or even pessimistic. Miyazaki's characters might be subject to bouts of depression (like Kiki), or might be 'cursed' by the gods (like Ashitaka in *Mononoke*), or under a spell (like Sophie in *Howl* and Marco in *Rosso*), but they are not pessimists or nihilists. However, they might be anarchistic, and rebellious[35] – but usually that's part of their bid for independence and individuality, or their recognition that doing things in the accepted manner isn't going to get the best results.

A decent motive: in a 1988 lecture, Hayao Miyazaki decried the motives of characters in current animation: there are two: work and sex (SP, 84). Robots fight because they are robots, police pursue criminals because they are police, and so on. Nothing but the work ethic. Or it was sex. For Miyazaki, there had to be better motives than that.

Technology is a key theme in Hayao Miyazaki's cinema, in particular how human societies relate to technology, and how technology is being used to exploit the Earth's resources. There is also a fetishistic exaltation of technology in Miyazaki's movies,[36] which sometimes runs counter to the deeply critical treatment of technology.[37]

'Fan service' in Japanese animation means delivering to audiences something fetishized and glamourized: *mecha*

35 Miyazaki is opposed to self-righteous groups, to authorities who 'parade their righteousness': 'th
others through huge military power, economic power, political power or public opinion' (AI, 29).

36 Only filmmakers such as George Lucas rivalled Hayao Miyazaki in creating myriad forms of technology. Miyazaki's films were deeply in love with machines and technology, especially vehicles such as planes.

37 Hayao Miyazaki liked people who looked after machines, he said, who didn't trade in their cars every year for a new one. 'I prefer people who detect a kind of animistic power in the marvel of machines' (SP, 420).

(robots and machines),[38] for example, lovingly depicted, or something sexy – glimpses of underwear or parts of the body. Needles to say Hayao Miyazaki's movies contain 'fan service' – though almost always of the *mecha*, fetishistic kind.

War is one of Hayao Miyazaki's fascinations, and it crops up in many of his films, from *Nausicaä of the Valley of the Wind* to *Howl's Moving Castle.* 'I'm fascinated by wars and I read a lot about them' (SP, 399). And it fascinates his colleague, Isao Takahata too: Miyazaki produced the movie *Grave of the Fireflies*, which was directed by Paku-san.

War corrupts people, it corrupts their sense of ideals and justice: *pace* the war in the Balkans of the early Nineties, Hayao Miyazaki said (in 1994): 'the thing about war is that even though people may have a sense of what is just in the beginning, once you start a war that sense of justice inevitably becomes corrupted' (SP, 399).

One thing is very striking about the cinema of Hayao Miyazaki: altho' he publicly denounces the military machine, at least half of his movies depict military forces in action and in some detail. There is a technofetishism, an adoration of *mecha* (which you find throughout *manga* and *animé*), which is at odds with the political attacks on the military-industrial complex. Yes, you could say that Miyazaki & co. evoke the military solely in order to show them in a negative light (as rampant capitalists in *Laputa*, for instance, or brutal perpetrators of pointless warfare in *Howl*), but it's also a case of artists wanting to have things both ways (as they always want to!).

38 One could discuss at length the significance of cyborgs and robots and hybrid lifeforms in Hayao Miyazaki's cinema, in the light of the theories of Donna Haraway or Slavoj Zizek – you know the theories: the 'return of the repressed', the undead, zombies, ghosts in the machine, animated machines, dolls, puppets, computers with souls, etc etc etc... but I'll leave that up to other writers. (See, for instance, D. Haraway's "A Manifesto For Cyborgs", and *Primate Visions* (Routledge, London, 1989), and *Simians, Cyborgs, and Women* (Routledge, London, 1991).)

MORE ASPECTS OF MIYAZAKI'S CINEMA

LOVE STORIES.

There are love stories in Hayao Miyazaki's cinema, but they tend to either be youthful and idealistic romances between teenagers, or detached, wistful relationships among older characters which are not consummated. There are many tender and affectionate scenes in Miyazaki's cinema, but only a few kisses (hugs being more common).[39] And no sex scenes. Instead, flying scenes or some other experience stands in for sexual desire, which's common in movies (dancing being the most obvious synecdoche for lovemaking in Hollywood cinema – think of Ginger and Fred, or Leslie and Gene). As flying is so central to Miyazaki's art, it's understandable that flying scenes should stand in for sexual expression (the flying scene with Chihiro and Haku in *Spirited Away* is exactly that, a love scene: they fly with their heads together, holding hands, and Chihiro weeps).

The typical love story in Hayao Miyazaki's cinema is between two young people; they might be ten years old (as in *Spirited Away*), or thirteen (as in *Kiki's Delivery Service*), or around that age (in *Laputa: Castle In the Sky*). And when Miyazaki did portray a 'grown-up' sexual relationship – between Gina and Marco in *Porco Rosso* – it was similarly virtuous and restrained. The emotion was certainly there, but the expressions of it were demure.

It hardly needs to be said that the love stories in Hayao Miyazaki's movies are always heterosexual. And though the families he depicts might sometimes be broken, they are usually the classic configuration of mom, dad and two kids.

THE OCEAN AND WATER.

Pretty much every Hayao Miyazaki movie features the ocean, and sometimes it's such a prominent element: the sea

39 Although porn and *hentai* takes up a large part of Japanese animation, much of *animé* is chaste and restrained. For instance, the first onscreen kiss in all Japanese cinema occurred as late as 1946 (G. Mast, 1992b).

in *Porco Rosso*, for instance, with its numerous islands, including Rosso's idyllic island retreat.[40] Or the coastal town in *Kiki's Delivery Service.* Halfway thru *Spirited Away,* the bathhouse becomes surrounded by the ocean.

And just think of the numerous towns that are set beside the sea: in *Kiki's Delivery Service*, in *Porco Rosso*, in *Howl's Moving Castle,* in *Ponyo On the Cliff By the Sea*, and in *Laputa: Castle In the Sky* (the military island).

And even those movies which don't contain the ocean – such as *My Neighbor Totoro* or *Princess Mononoke* – feature rivers or lakes or forests so big and juicy with life they are equivalents of the ocean. (*Mononoke Hime* has a large lake, the beautiful pool at the heart of the forest, and a river in flood).

And one of Hayao Miyazaki's specialities is the sunken land or town, which appeared in his first film, *The Castle of Cagliostro,* the Roman ruins underneath the lake. The underwater areas of the flying land of Laputa. The submerged forest in *Nausicaä of the Valley of the Wind.* The flooded railroad line in *Spirited Away.* And the deluged Japan in *Ponyo On the Cliff By the Sea.*

In short, water is everywhere in Hayao Miyazaki's cinema, for all of the obvious reasons: it adds life and beauty to scenes, it is perfect for animation in a variety of styles, it is central to human life, and it has any symbolism you want to attach to it.

And when it comes to animating water, one of the tough challenges of animation (you could portray the history of animation techniques by studying how animators depict water), Studio Ghibli is extraordinarily accomplished.

ANIMALS.

It's impossible to miss the importance of animals in Hayao Miyazaki's cinema: a staple of animation since its

40 And even when *Porco Rosso* moves inland, to Milan in Italy, there's a major sequence involving the chase and escape via a river.

earliest incarnations, animals in Miyazaki's art perform a variety of functions. The cuddly, cute sidekick is a recurring animal, just as it is in the Walt Disney canon. Miyazaki is as happy to sentimentalize animals as much as Disney or Fox or Warners or any other contemporary animation studio.

Particular specialities are cats and dogs (the dog in *Howl's Moving Castle,* and the cat Jiji in *Kiki's Delivery Service,* for instance). *Sherlock Hound* was an entire TV *animé* series of anthropomorphic dogs. Miyazaki and his animators have clearly studied cats and dogs very closely (only Mamoru Oshii among Japanese animation directors rivals Miyazaki for dog-loving). Some Miyazaki and Studio Ghibli products have animals at their heart: *Ponyo On the Cliff By the Sea, Ponpoko* and *The Cat Returns.*

And there are also animals as nature spirits, fierce, independent, unmanageable, wild – dragons, Totoros, forest spirits. Animals as pets and friends: the red elk that Ashitaka rides in *Princess Mononoke.* Hayao Miyazaki's films also invent plenty of animals – the giant bugs in *Nausicaä of the Valley of the Wind,* the Forest God in *Princess Mononoke,* and of course the Totoros.

FOOD.

As all great storytellers for children know, food plays a huge part in a child's life, and Hayao Miyazaki knows this very well. There are many scenes involving food and meals in Miyazaki's cinema:

❦ there's a humorous scene in *Ponyo On the Cliff By the Sea* where Ponyo and Sosuke eat dinner and drink honeyed tea, and the details are exquisitely realized – of children waiting patiently at a table, of being desperate to eat, of making a mess, and Ponyo's little look of disappointment when her pack of noodles comes out broken in her dish, while Sosuke's remains neatly whole.

❦ in *Laputa: Castle In the Sky,* Pazu has breakfast on the go when Sheeta wakes up, and when he returns home, disheartened, halfway through the movie, he finds Dola and her boys happily eating their way through the place. Dola's gang are over the moon when Sheeta joins them – it means good food.

❦ the breakfast scene in *Howl's Moving Castle*, in which Sophie cheers Markl up no end by providing a cooked breakfast.

❦ Kiki delivers food on her broomstick in *Kiki's Delivery Service.*

❦ in *Porco Rosso*, the pig takes a meal in Gina's hotel.

❦ in *Spirited Away*, food takes on negative connotations – the monster spirit No Face wolfs down everything, and Chihiro's parents are turned into pigs when they break a fairy tale taboo, and eat without getting permission. Food is linked to inner emotions, too: Haku gives Chihiro something to eat which'll stop her literally fading away, as she cowers in fear in the early scenes. Later, Chihiro weeps as she eats.

HUMOUR.

It's reassuring for me that the films of Hayao Miyazaki and his teams aren't crude; they don't resort to fart jokes and toilet humour (like the farting warthog in *The Lion King* or the farting pirate in *Treasure Planet*). Nothing wrong with fart or piss or shit or whatever jokes, but they would certainly detract from the impact of Miyazaki's movies. Personally, I don't reckon that kind of childish goofing off in a fantasy movie helps any. Not that Miyazaki's films don't contain some grosser moments.

CIGARETTES.

Like the films of Jean-Luc Godard, and the *film noirs* of the 1940s in La-La Land, the films of Hayao Miyazaki are very much what I call cancer films – movies which feature a lot of smoking. These days smoking in movies means a bad guy, and smoking's been banned everywhere on Earth (except for casinos in Nevada).

But the pictures of Hayao Miyazaki – and Jean-Luc Godard, François Truffaut, Howard Hawks, John Ford, etc – are movies where many characters happily smoke. In *Porco Rosso* and *The Wind Rises*, for instance, the lead characters light up with a regularity only matched by the young rebels in Godard's 1960s flicks. Yubaba in *Spirited Away* breathes out billows of smoke, as does the Witch of the Waste in *Howl's Moving Castle* (in the latter case, the smoke is part of the sorceress Suliman's bad magic).[41] And *The Wind Rises* was criticized for showing so many smoking scenes.

STYLE AND TECHNICAL ASPECTS

ACTION.

There's no doubt that a key feature of Hayao Miyazaki's cinema is fantastic action sequences. Like the filmmakers of *Akira* or *Naruto* or *Bleach* or the *Legend of the Overfiend* movies or *Ghost In the Shell* or other classic exponents of Japanese *animé*, Miyazaki and his teams are geniuses when it comes to staging chases, or battles between flying machines, or gun fights in enclosed spaces. It's not a question of being 'free' in animation to draw anything, or being able to do things you can't do in live-action, it's a question of imagination (and staging, and timing, and research, etc).

An action scene in a Hayao Miyazaki picture is not your usual action scene. Take the chase at the beginning of 1986's *Laputa: Castle In the Sky:* for a start, it takes place on a railroad track built from wood hundreds of feet above the ground in an incredibly deep valley surrounded by mountains. And it's a dual chase, with Muska the arch villain and his army train and soldiers on one side, and Dola the formidable pirate and her pirate gang in their car on the other. In the middle are

41 Maybe there's a biographical aspect to this – one can't help noticing that both Miyazaki and his producer, Toshio Suzuki, smoke, as do others on the production teams.

our teenage heroes, Pazu and Sheeta, and an old-timer engineer in a slow freight train. It's a summary of every (silent) movie train chase – such as Buster Keaton or the Marx Brothers (from *The General* or *Go West*). One can imagine Walt Disney loving this chase (Disney was famously a railroad enthusiast).

After some incredible stunts, explosions, near-misses and the like, our heroes escape by falling into space (it's another literal cliffhanger moment). The question – how are they going to get out of this one? – is answered by the film's McGuffin, the magic crystal that Sheeta wears around her neck. Sheeta and Pazu float gently down an enormous mine shaft, and the picture moves into a quieter moment, setting the scene for the meeting with the wise, old man character, the old miner.

All of this is meticulously worked out, and plays like gangbusters. Although it's tempting, action set-pieces in a Miyazaki movie don't stretch belief, in the way that Hollywood movies, not only from the last 20 years or so, so often do. Simply on the level of action-adventure, the movies of Hayao Miyazaki are spectacular, and have no superiors.

COLOUR.

One of the vital collaborators in Hayao Miyazaki's cinema is undoubtedly Michiyo Yasuda (b. 1943), the colour designer. As Miyazaki's movies are among the most exquisite in the history of cinema in terms of colour, Yasuda's contribution is immense. As well as organizing the hundreds of colours used in every Miyazaki film, Yasuda and her team have also helped to create a unique look for Miyazaki's pictures.[42] Simply, there are no other movies which look quite like these. Even amongst the 1,000s of *animé* OVAs, TV shows, cartoons, pop promos, commercials and movies produced by the Japanese

42 One of the favourite devices of Hayao Miyazaki's films is to alter between light and dark, particularly within the same scene. Miyazaki's movies love to show lights being switched on or off, for example. Colour-wise, this means adding greys and blacks to colours, to take out the warmth and saturation.

animation industry, the films of Hayao Miyazaki are instantly recognizable.

LAYOUTS.

As to compositions and layouts, the films directed by Hayao Miyazaki are sumptuous to look at, with classical compositions being favoured (using the Golden Section, or the horizon along the lower third, for instance). The action generally takes place within the safe area for television and video. Sometimes, however, Miyazaki and his teams will turn in a deliberately off-kilter composition, for dramatic effect. When Nausicaä explores the underworld forest in *Nausicaä of the Valley of the Wind,* for example, she is framed very low in one shot, to emphasize the majesty of the enormous trees above her.

No expense is spared on the backgrounds and layouts of Hayao Miyazaki's movies, with a level of detail that rivals and often bests Disney's 'golden age' films. It seems that every Miyazaki movie is at the level of the finest of Disney movies from the 1937-1942 period: *Snow White and the Seven Dwarfs, Bambi* and *Pinocchio.*

MOVEMENT.

The movement of the characters in Hayao Miyazaki's movies is deliberately naturalistic, and far away from the exaggerated motion of the Walt Disney canon. Miyazaki has commented that Disney's characters tend to move like ballet dancers or actors in a musical[43] – just too heightened, with lavish arm gestures, for example, and exaggerated squash-and-stretch movements.[44] Disney's characters move as if they're performing to the upper circle in a vaudeville show, while Miyazaki's characters are far, far more subtle, and naturalistic (as if they know the camera is right there, and

43 Indeed, the filmmakers of Disney's *Beauty and the Beast* studied ballet dancers for the depiction of Belle.

44 Hayao Miyazaki also acknowledged that much of Japanese animation 'suffered from over-expressionism' (SP, 79).

tone down their performances).

Hayao Miyazaki's people are recognizably based on real people, even though they are stylistically drawn. In Disney's films, the figures seem to be made of dough or balloons or some squashy, bouncy material (and that's not only in the 'golden era' movies like *Fantasia* or *Dumbo*, but in the more recent movies like *Treasure Planet* or *Home On the Range*).[45]

Difference in scale is one of Hayao Miyazaki's recurring motifs, and it is a key element in Japanese *animé*: so in Miyazaki's cinema there are giant robots, giant babies, and giant men. The macho guys in *Laputa: Castle In the Sky,* for instance, are much larger than real people, sporting huge, barrel chests (in the fight in the street in Slug Valley, where the men pop their shirts open like Popeye or Superman). Yubaba and her son in *Spirited Away* have enormous heads, while the baby and Yubaba's bird are transformed into very small creatures.

And Hayao Miyazaki and his animators use differences in scale all the time for dramatic purposes: in some scenes, they will make their heroes appear small, to emphasize their vulnerability, say, or their fear, or their diminished dramatic influence. In particular, Miyazaki and his teams like to place something very large next to something very small: so the *ohmu* are enormous insects, and Nausicaä next to them is tiny; Tombo, hanging off the giant airship at the end of *Kiki's Delivery Service*, is a minuscule dot. In *Nausicaä of the Valley of the Wind,* Asbel flies a small fighter, but he's able to bring down most of the Tolmekian fleet.

Yes, in Hayao Miyazaki's cinema, one person *can* make a difference: his films are stories of individuals who shift the balance of power in their worlds: Nausicaä most spectacularly, perhaps, but also Sheeta and Pazu in *Laputa: Castle In the Sky,* Sophie in *Howl's Moving Castle,* Marco in *Porco Rosso*, and on a more modest scale, Kiki in *Kiki's Delivery Service.* And in *Spirited Away,* Chihiro saves her parents,

45 *Home On the Range* cost $110 million to make: what a truly dull film.

brings about shifts in the power relations in the bathhouse, helps to free Haku, and even teaches grand, old dame Yubaba a lesson in humility. And in *Princess Mononoke,* Ashitaka certainly makes a difference, often acting on his own.

THE SETTINGS.

The settings of Hayao Miyazaki's films have included: Monte Carlo and a fictional European country (Cagliostro) in *The Castle of Cagliostro;* a fantasy land in *Nausicaä of the Valley of the Wind* (which draws on Europe and North African deserts); another fantasy realm in *Laputa: Castle In the Sky* (which also looks to Europe, with Slug Valley being inspired by South Wales, the Rhondda Valley); a fictionalized Europe is again the setting for *Howl's Moving Castle, Porco Rosso* and *Kiki's Delivery Service;* but Japan is the setting for *My Neighbor Totoro, Ponyo On the Cliff By the Sea, Spirited Away, The Wind Rises* and *Princess Mononoke.*

It's ironic, perhaps, that many of Hayao Miyazaki's movies have been set in Europe, and have dealt with European history and culture, but three of Miyazaki's biggest successes, *Spirited Away, Ponyo On the Cliff By the Sea* and *Princess Mononoke*, have been very Japanese (i.e., set in Japan, and drawing on Japanese mythology and culture). However, wherever they are set, Miyazaki's movies are very definitely *Japanese.*

They are movies made in Japan, by predominantly Japanese crews, for the Japanese film market, and financially backed by Japanese companies. But the European (specifically *Western* European) *milieu* and tropes give Hayao Miyazaki's pictures a curious and fascinating cultural hybridity. And it works – Miyazaki's films never feel as if the European or Japanese elements aren't meshed at the deepest level.

And notice, too, that Hayao Miyazaki's movies are not set in North America, or about North America, or draw on North American culture, and have only used one or two North

American characters. Sorry, Amerika – Miyazaki-san just isn't interested: 'I just don't seem to like American culture', Miyazaki admitted (TP, 247). 'I don't feel very beholden to America'.

EDITING.

One of the reasons that the films of Hayao Miyazaki are so successful is invisible: their editing, pacing and structure. Watching a Miyazaki movie, you know you are in the hands of a master, and a master storyteller. Simply put, Miyazaki and his teams (Takeshi Seyama and Katsu Hisamura are his editors) know when to place action, when to slow a film down, when to insert back-story or motivations, and when to reveal elements of the plot (it's significant that Miyazaki has an editor credit on many of his movies).

It's not something you can learn from a book, this feeling for pace and timing and structure, and each picture is different, with different demands and possibilities. And there are no formulas (there are screenwriting manuals that claim to have the mechanics of scriptwriting down, but it ain't that easy).

But without this magical feeling for how time flows within a 80 or 90 minute movie, films soon become wearying and boring. A bad or disappointing movie is often one which hasn't been edited smoothly or successfully (of course, studios and producers meddle with filmmakers' work all too often – but usually to the extent of taking out or altering individual scenes, but they don't take apart an entire movie, so most of the editing remains largely intact).

But all of Hayao Miyazaki's pictures swim by with such grace and ease. This filmmaker does not waste a second of precious screen time. His films don't feel rushed, or disjointed, or awkward, or jagged around the edges.

The pacing of Hayao Miyazaki's movies was something that John Lasseter at Pixar found inspiring, and applied it to films such as *Toy Story* and *A Bug's Life*: 'Miyazaki-san is a master of pacing', how he lets certain scenes breathe, and doesn't rush them: 'there are certain moments in a film you cannot rush through. It's important to allow the audience to reflect on what's happening on the screen' (SP, 13).

Hayao Miyazaki derided Eisensteinian montage, where shots coalesce with other shots, combining to create a greater meaning. No, Miyazaki insisted, it's a 'totally worthless theory': rather, 'each shot should express the film in its entirety. I myself still hope to make a film like that' (TP, 131).

SOUND.

The sound of the wind is a recurring motif in Hayao Miyazaki's cinema, as it is in the cinema of Federico Fellini and Pier Paolo Pasolini.[46] In Miyazaki's films, the sound of the wind has both a practical or 'realistic' function or mean-ing, but also a spiritual or magical one. It is the sound of the flying scenes, of course, and it's the sound of the wind in the grass or crops, or the sound of a character's clothes in the breeze. But it is also the sound of something magical happen-ing. As it is in traditional symbolism: the wind is the breath of the eternal, of the divine, of God... it is the Creative Word, the Word made flesh, etc.

And the sound of the wind is linked to all of those manifestations of the natural world in Hayao Miyazaki's cinema – thunder, and storms, and clouds, and rivers, and oceans, and trees, and mountains.

MUSIC.

The music for most of Hayao Miyazaki's films is by Joe Hisaishi (b. 1950), and it contributes so much – especially to the emotional core of the movies: *Nausicaä of the Valley of the Wind, Kiki's Delivery Service, Laputa: Castle In the Sky, Porco Rosso* and *Spirited Away*. The collaboration of Miyazaki and

46 The films of Fellini and Pasolini seem to use the same wind sound effect in numerous pictures – maybe there was only one wind sound effect in the library at Cinecittà.

Hisaishi is not to be underestimated;[47] it may not be as well-known in film circles as the partnership of, say, Alfred Hitchcock and Bernard Herrmann, or Tim Burton and Danny Elfman, but it's certainly a vital part of the success of Miyazaki's cinema.[48]

As well as Hayao Miyazaki's films, Joe Hisaishi has also scored many other Japanese movies, including *Ario, Sonatine, The Water Traveler, Kids Return* and *Venus Wars.* In addition to film music, Hisaishi has composed electronic music, minimal music, piano music, pop music, and orchestral music.[49] Hisaishi has given concerts of Ghibli's scores, including to 14,000 at Tokyo's Budokan.

47 It was Isao Takahata was brought Joe Hisaishi onto *Nausicaä of the Valley of the Wind* – music is one of Takahata's special skills.
48 And one should not forget that Isao Takahata has often undertaken the production of the music in Hayao Miyazaki's films, liaising with Joe Hisaishi.
49 Andrew Osmond has identified the emphasis on innocence as being particularly important to Joe Hisaishi's music, and also 'its sense of the magical, the holy' (2000).

ILLUSTRATIONS

Images from *Princess Mononoke,* and of Miyazaki's other movies. Plus some influences and correspondences.

Hayao Miyazaki and Studio Ghibli update Akira Kurosawa in a movie so incredible you can't believe anyone could produce it.

(Images from Princess Mononoke © Nibariki/ TNDG, 1997)

THE FATE OF THE WORLD RESTS ON THE COURAGE OF ONE WARRIOR
PRINCESS MONONOKE
GILLIAN ANDERSON
BILLY CRUDUP
CLAIRE DANES
MINNIE DRIVER
BILLY BOB THORNTON
JADA PINKETT SMITH

STUDIO GHIBLI DVD COLLECTION

もののけ姫

Ein Film von Hayao Miyazaki

PRINZESSIN MONONOKE

Hayao Miyazaki's Western; but no horse for the hero; instead, a red elk.

Irontown: the depiction of industrialization is more ambiguous in Princess Mononoke than in previous movies from Studio Ghibli.

The heart of the forest in Princess Mononoke,
an evocation of a place of peace, rest, unity and spirituality
almost unknown in recent cinema.

The world of the ancient gods, Miyazaki-style.

Ever tried to kill a god? It's more difficult than you think, especially when the god is life itself.

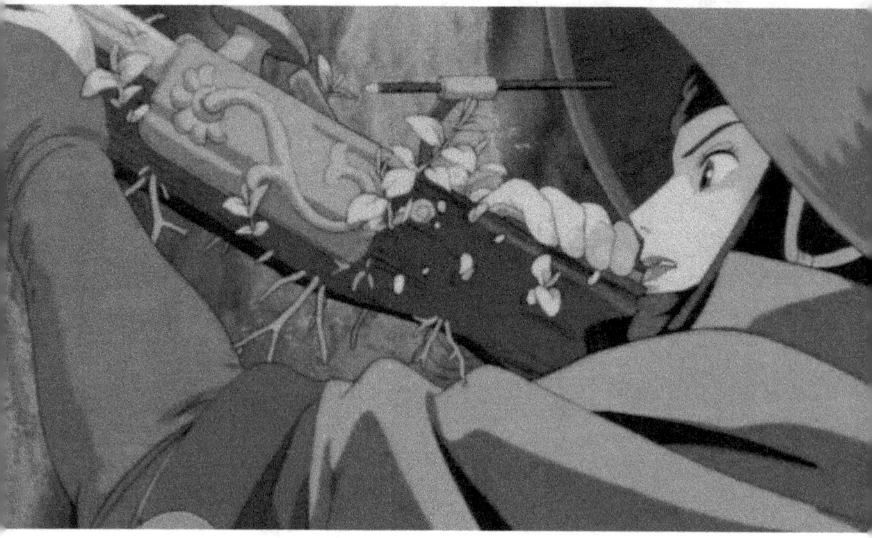

Classical and mythological motifs which work every time:
light, the sun, the sky, clouds, trees, and nature.

The ending of Princess Mononoke:
the friendly farewell of the two main characters.
Below: the kodama, forest spirits

Artwork for Princess Mononoke

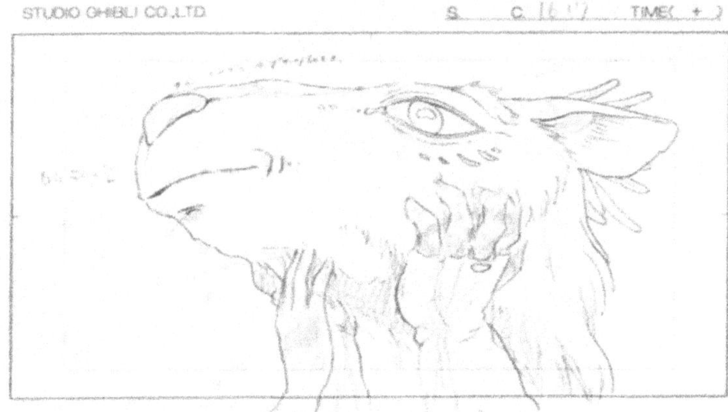

Stills from Akira Kurosawa's reworkings of John Ford Westerns

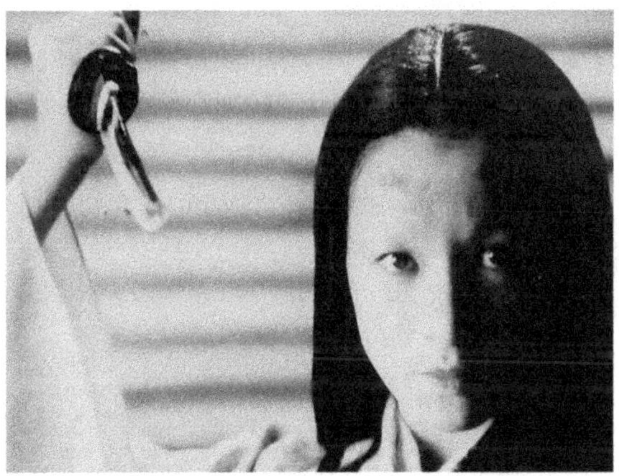

Images from Akira Kurosawa's films

Images fom Japan's Edo period
(this page and over)

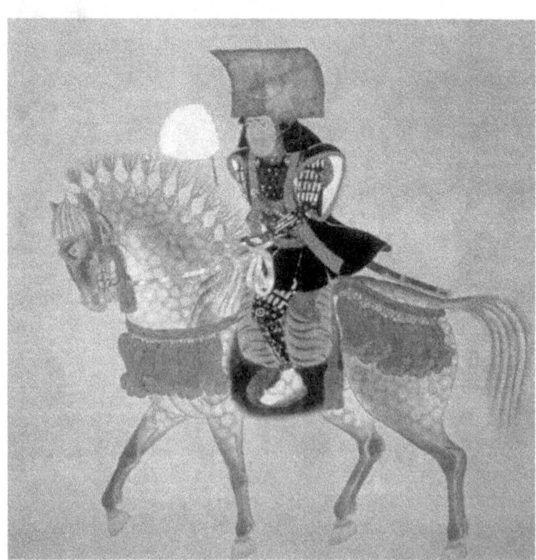

江戸近郊八景之内
玉川秋月

Japanese pottery from
the Jomon period

(© TMS-Kyokuichi Corporation/ Monkey Punch/ Manga Entertainment 1979)

(© Nibarki/ Tokuma Shoten/ Hakuhodo, 1984)

(© Nibariki/ Tokuma Shoten, 1986)

(© Nibariki/ Tokuma Shoten, 1988)

(© Eiko Kandono/ Nibariki/ Tokuma Shoten, 1989)

(© Nibariki/ TNNG, 1992)

(© Nibariki/ TNDGDDTM, 2001)

(© Toho/ Walt Disney Pictures/ Wild Bunch, 2004)

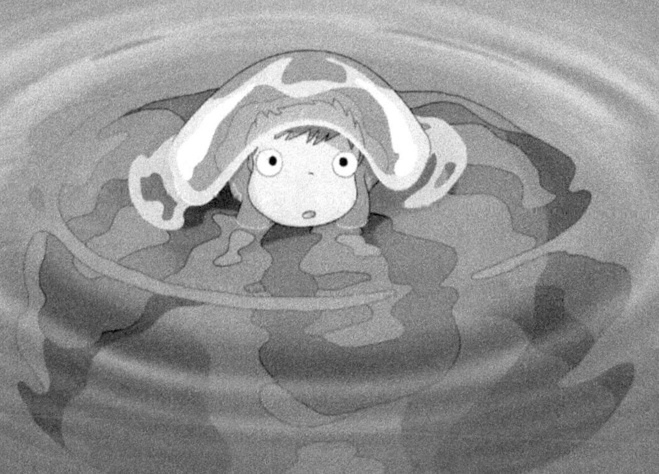

(© Toho/ Walt Disney Pictures, 2008)

(© Toho/ Studio Ghibli, 2013)

#4

PRINCESS MONONOKE

> I will depict hatred, but only to show that there is something more valuable.
>
> I will depict a curse to show the joy of liberation from it.
>
> I will depict the boy's understanding of the girl and the process by which the girl opens her heart to the boy.
>
> Hayao Miyazaki, 1995 (SP, 274)

A WORK OF GENIUS.

Princess Mononoke is a work of genius. It is a masterpiece. It is one of the most staggeringly incredible films you will ever see. By any standards you want to apply, the level of imagination and artistry and detail and insight and energy in this movie is simply astounding.

As well as being a visionary piece, with the highest quality animation achievable,[1] with fascinating characters, stupendous action, brilliant set-pieces, and with some deeply poetic episodes, *Princess Mononoke* is also a thematically rich movie. There are many levels to this wonderful picture; it is multi-layered, and can withstand countless explorations.

Moebius, Hayao Miyazaki's friend, remarked:

1 Some of the scenes – such as the market, the samurai attack in the rice fields, and Irontown – are filled with figures moving all over the screen (those shots that demand a huge amount of labour from the animators).

when I saw *Princess Mononoke*, and even more *Spirited Away*, I was struck by the fact that I couldn't imagine a producer, any producer in the world, accepting the script.

Or put it another way: only one person in the world could've conceived, written and directed *Princess Mononoke*.

PRODUCTION

Princess Mononoke (*Mononoke Hime,* 1997, Tokuma Shoten/ Nippon Television Network/ Dentsu/ Studio Ghibli) was written and directed by Hayao Miyazaki, produced by Toshio Susuki, Seichiro Ujiie, Yutaka Narita and Yasuyoshi Tokuma, with music by Joe Hisaishi, cinematography by Atsushi Okui, sound by Kazuhiro Wakabayashi and Muchihiro Ito, computer graphics by Yoshinori Sugano, Yashiyuki Momose, Mitsunori Katama and Masafumi Inoue, the animation directors were Masashi Ando, Yoshifumi Kondo, Katsuya Kondo and Kitaro Kosaka,[2] the art directors were Nizo Yamamoto, Naoya Tanaka, Yoji Takeshige, Satoshi Kuroda and Kazuo Oga, editing was by Miyazaki and Takeshi Seyama, the ADs were Koji Aritomi, Masakatsu Ishizone and Hiroyuki Ito, and colour design was by Michiyo Yasuda. Most of the principals in the crew had worked with Miyazaki and Suzuki before. Pre-production for *Princess Mononoke* began in August, 1994.[3]

The filming schedule at Studio Ghibli for *Mononoke Hime* ran from August, 1994 to June, 1997. Hayao Miyazaki began writing *Princess Mononoke* in August, 1994, completing the first treatment in April, 1995. Production kicked in with the creation of the storyboards from May, 1995 onwards (which were drawn, as usual, by the *sensei*). In July, 1995 the

2 Kitaro Kosaka has credits on *Angel's Egg, Akira, Metropolis, Grave of the Fireflies, Nasu, Pon Poko,* and Miyazaki's movies.

3 The origins of *Princess Mononoke* went back to at least 1980, when Hayao Miyazaki began drawing image boards for elements that would be used in the movie.

animation schedule began, and was finished in June, 1997.

Toshio Suzuki recalled that the financial backers of *Princess Mononoke* were against making the movie because: (1) the budget was too big, (2) there was a similar Hollywood movie coming out the same year (*Jurassic Park 2*), and (3) it was a historical drama (which were thought to perform poorly at the box office).

The budget for *Princess Mononoke* was US $19.4 million,[4] and the box office rental was $92.7 million (the domestic gross was $154 million), with approximately 13.53 million admissions in Japan (between July and November, around 12 million people had seen the film in theatres – about 10% of the population).[5] The film was released on July 12, 1997. *Princess Mononoke* was also the first Hayao Miyazaki movie to be shown in a wider release in theatres in the U.S.A. (on October 7, 1999), as part of the 1996 agreement between Tokuma and the Walt Disney corporation.[6]

Princess Mononoke had become the biggest grossing movie in Japan (unadjusted for inflation), the previous movie being *E.T. The Extraterrestrial* (1982).[7] *Titanic* (1997)[8] knocked off *Princess Mononoke* from the top spot,[9] but *Spirited Away* trounced *Titanic* in Japan (quite right, too!).

On video, *Princess Mononoke* fared amazingly well, sell-

---

4 The biggest undertaking by Studio Ghibli up until then. Miyazaki said it was 2.35 billion Yen (TP, 76). Miyazaki noted that the team at Ghibli was ready for this movie: they were at their peak, and if they didn't make it now, they wouldn't make it at all (TP, 44).

Toshio Suzuki in 2014: 'People say I've never had to bow my head and beg, but that's not true. I've had to beg so many times to get projects made.' He adds that *Princess Mononoke* was 'a fluke. We thought we were definitely doomed this time.'

5 And Japan at the time had 1/10th of the cinema screens of the U.S.A.

6 Although *Princess Mononoke* is regarded as a Studio Ghibli production, other companies were involved, including: Telecom Animation Film, Studio Killy, Trace Studio M, IM Studio, Toei Animation, and Takahashi Production/ T2 Studio.

7 *Princess Mononoke* broke *E.T.*'s record in a quarter of the time that *E.T.* had taken to make its record.

8 Sometimes I like to believe that *Titanic* never existed – a movie that audiences went nuts over and had so much about it *not* to like.

9 As well as *Titanic*, the big American movies of 1997 were *Jurassic Park 2* (*The Lost World*), *Men In Black, Tomorrow Never Dies, Air Force One* and *As Good As It Gets.*

ing two million cassettes in 3 weeks, and four million by the end of 1998.[10] In January, 1999, *Princess Mononoke* premiered on television in Japan and gained a 35.1% share of the audience.

144,043 cels[11] were produced (using 550 colours). Hayao Miyazaki personally checked around 80,000 of those cels, including re-drawing or adjusting many of them (that is an astounding amount of work – in addition to writing, storyboarding and directing).[12]

Personally checking over half of the cels took its toll on Miyazaki: he explained, after the film was released, that it was an exhausting process:

> A pictorial animator has to make pictures move. Even if I have others do it, I end up having to fix a majority of it anyway. This is the most exhausting aspect of my day-to-day work. Physically, I just can't go on. I suffer from everything from poor eyesight to shoulder tension and hip and thigh pain.[13]

Voice-wise, Yoji Matsuda (b. October 19, 1967)[14] played Prince Ashitaka, Yuriko Ishida[15] (b. October 3, 1969) was Princess Mononoke, Yuko Tanaka was Eboshi-gozen, Kaoru Kobayashi was Jokio-bo, Tsunehiko Kamijô was Gonza, Sumi Shimamoto[16] was Toki, Tetsu Watanabe was Yamainu, Mitsuru Satô was Tatari-gama, Hisaya Morishige was Okkoto, Akira Nagoya was Usi-kai, Akihiro Miwa was Moro, Mitsuko Mori was Hiisama, and Nishimura Masahiko was Kouroku. (Both Matsuda and Ishida have done very little *animé*. For two such crucial roles, in a very important production, many

---

10 According to *Screen Digest* (Nov, 1998), only children's animated films usually sell above 200,000 copies.

11 One and a half times the usual amount for a feature film (TP, 50).

12 About 80,000 of the cels were key animation.

13 Hayao Miyazaki in *Asia Pulse*, May, 1997.

14 Yoji Matsuda was Asbel in *Nausicaä.*

15 Yuriko Ishida also appeared in *Pon Poko* and *From Up On Poppy Hill.*

16 Sumi Shimamoto was a Miyazaki regular, appearing as Clarisse in *The Castle of Cagliostro,* the mother in *Totoro,* and the lead in *Nausicaä of the Valley of the Wind.*

producers would select veteran voice actors. But Miyazaki often casts voices that aren't heard everywhere in *animé*).

English language voices were provided by Gillian Anderson, Billy Crudup, Claire Danes, Keith David, John DeMita and John DiMaggio (Jack Fletcher oversaw the English dub, and Neil Gaiman[17] wrote the English language script).[18] The American version was released by Disney in 1999.

Joe Hisaishi provided music before animation was completed for *Princess Mononoke*, so the production team had music they could draw inspiration from. Usually, Hisaishi would create the music after the film was finished (as with most Western movies). The collaboration between Hisaishi and Miyazaki and his team was much closer on *Princess Mononoke*. As Miyazaki noted in poetry written to help composer Hisaishi:

> The people revered the gods of the forest and listened to the breath of the forest
> They lived as they made songs of the forest's voice (TP, 20)

There are percussive cues using drums for the Kurosawan battle scenes in the last third of *Princess Mononoke* • a haunting, soft piano cue for the rebirth of the landscape in the final moments (one of Hisaishi's beloved musical modes, which he employs a good deal) • mysterious, bubbling woodwind sounds for the appearance of the *kodama* • and a beautiful, melancholy cue using sustained strings in the scenes involving the Forest Spirit in its stag form.

Princess Mononoke was the first Hayao Miyazaki production to employ computers and CGI on a big scale. They were used on *Princess Mononoke* to colour the cels – about 10,000 out of 144,000 cels. Around 10 minutes of *Princess*

---

17 Actually, it was translated by Steve Alpert or Ian McWilliam, according to Jonathan Clements, with Gaiman acting in an editorial role; Gaiman got the job because he was recommended by Quentin Tarantino (2009, 239).

18 *Princess Mononoke* was marketed as a prestige project, and using name actors was a key element in selling Japanese *animé* to a U.S. audience.

Mononoke employed digital ink and paint work, and 15 minutes overall employed CGI (C, 127). Computer composition to combine elements of animation was deployed, as well as particle animation, morphing, 3-D rendering, and texture mapping.

The computer dept at Studio Ghibli for this show included computer graphics director Yoshinori Sugano, animators Yashiyuki Momose, Mitsunori Katama and Masafumi Inoue, and digital paint artist Horoaki Ishii, among others. The computer work was done in-house at Studio Ghibli, using 21 computers, two servers, and systems such as Silicon Graphics and Avid.

THE CURSE

Hayao Miyazaki had apparently had the idea for *Princess Mononoke* a long time – back in the Seventies he had wanted to do a movie about a princess who lives in a forest with a beast. The *mononoke*[19] was an animal spirit that the young woman was forced to marry. The echoes of *Beauty and the Beast* were obvious (the fairy tale, most famously in the version by Charles Perrault, is the basis for many stories, and many movies. Miyazaki reprised it in *Howl* and *Ponyo*).

To the initial *Beauty and the Beast*-type narrative Hayao Miyazaki added many layers, such as the political struggle for power in mediæval Japan, the industry/ human versus nature/ environment conflict, and a love story. (The most difficult part of *Mononoke* was the story, Miyazaki confessed [TP, 80]).

Hayao Miyazaki also wanted to have a character with a curse: 'for the longest time I wanted to make her the heroine of a movie,' Miyazaki recalled.[20] The princess would have had

19 'Mononoke' can be translated as a spirit, as animism.
20 In H. McCarthy, 2002, 183.

a birthmark;[21] over time, the curse shifted to a young prince (Ashitaka's curse, the *tatari,* has the look of a birthmark, of course; also, for a moment, both San and Ashitaka have the cursemark on them, when they hold up the Forest God's head during the finale).

As well as having a symbolic or philosophical aspect, the curse or mark Ashitaka bears is also a real wound that hurts, particularly at crisis moments, like the village massacre, or the first sight of the Forest Spirit. For Hayao Miyazaki, Ashitaka's curse could be linked to contemporary diseases such as AIDS.[22]

> Ashitaka was cursed for a very absurd reason [Miyazaki explained in 1997]. Sure, Ashitaka did something he should not have done – killing Tatari Gami. But there was enough reason to do so from the humans' viewpoint. Nevertheless, he received a deadly curse. I think that is similar to the lives of people today. I think this is a very absurd thing that is part of life itself.

The leper Osa in Irontown, who's so fragile he's completely bandaged, voices some key Miyazakian beliefs: that suffering is everywhere, but somehow you still find reasons to live. Osa also says 'the world is cursed'; but this Gnostic view is not that of Miyazaki.

Hayao Miyazaki described Ashitaka as someone who has no home anymore, has no place to live, is not particularly welcome anywhere, cannot go back to his village, who fights alone and usually without thanks, who has to live with a curse and with conflicts. A man with no country, no home. An outsider, a *ronin,* a warrior who doesn't want to fight. It is no easy path, and there are no easy answers.

> Ashitaka is the kind of person who is willing to live with the thorn. So, I think that Ashitaka is a person of the 21st century, who decided to live with the thorn, San. He does

21 The purple colour is both sort of 'realistic' and also a colour often used in *animé* for things strange – it's taken up in the finale.
22 Hayao Miyazaki in H. McCarthy, 2002, 192.

not say 'well, I can't do anything about it'.

Ashitaka is part-god himself. Or at least, some of the crazed god's powers have infected Ashitaka. Unfortunately, they are the kind of powers that anyone could do without, unless they happened to be a warrior intent on slaughtering people. The powers give Ashitaka added strength during combat, enabling him to decapitate soldiers with one arrow from afar. Ashitaka, though, is much more of a peacemaker than a war-monger, and he has to keep those powers firmly in check (the *intent* is critical here – the god's powers enable him to subdue both Eboshi and San, two ferocious women, and to open Irontown's gate, but when the intent is violent – as with firing an arrow – the results match the intent).

Notice too that the Forest Spirit does not cure Ashitaka of his god-curse: when the Forest God heals Ashitaka of the gunshot wound, which kills a normal person, it does not also heal the curse of the boar god on Ashitaka's arm. Ashitaka checks both wounds when he wakes by the lake in the forest glen (amazement at one, disappointment at the other). There's no doubt that the Forest Spirit could heal Ashitaka's wound if it wanted to – it is the master of life and death, as San explains. It's left the curse in place maybe because it's something that Ashitaka has to deal with and heal himself.

Several times in the movie, Ashitaka is topless, with a tunic tied around his chest. Is it 'fan service'? Is Ashitaka a Hollywood action hero, who sometimes strip down? Or is it to allow us to see the extent of the god's curse? (as well as the moment at the very end, when the mark has receded).

The slogan for *Princess Mononoke* was simply 'Live'. It is a phrase or concept that is dear to Miyazaki: repeatedly he insists that humans must live, they must walk on. If life is suffering, still you must live. It was the message of the final scene in his last film, *The Wind Rises*: 'you must live'.

THE WOLF PRINCESS

Princess Mononoke evokes all sorts of mythological and legendary narratives. One of the strongest is the wolf girl, the feral child, the human who grows up amongst wild animals[23] in a forest or jungle. It's *The Jungle Book* or *Tarzan*. In the 1997 film, San was left behind by her parents as a child, and is brought up by Moro and her children, the wolves (Moro is 'the wolf goddess is a survivor from the old world' [TP, 22]). She is also part of the prehistoric era, a human who might be found 10,000 years ago in Japan; wolves were worshipped by the Ainu until their extinction in 1905. (That *Princess Mononoke* was either about San or Ashitaka was reflected in Miyazaki's two titles[24] for the movie in his 1995 memo for the project: *Princess Mononoke* and *Ashitaka Sekki* (*Ashitaka Story*) (SP, 272).)[25]

Wolves are powerful symbols, which cinema has regularly employed. *Princess Mononoke* is one of those less frequent outings which evokes the maternal, nurturing side of wolves, as well as the more usual predatory, aggressive, hunting aspects. And the elements of wildness, of otherness, of mystery. These are no ordinary wolves, though, and their mighty forms place them very much in the realm of spirits or gods.[26] They are the wolves of fairy tales and fantasy fiction.

23 *Mononoke* is filled with animals – the whole retinue of Miyazakian beasts are here.

24 Note that the English title is half-English and half-Japanese: *Princess Mononoke*.

25 Her name is San, which also means three (she can be regarded as the 3rd child of the wolf-god Moro [P. Drazen, 2003]). The name 'mononoke', which means 'evil spirits', is given to her by the people of Irontown. As a princess, San is in the fairy tale mold: a princess without a king or queen as parents, a princess in spirit and attitude, a princess without the usual kind of realm to rule over – she has the ancient forest.

26 In *Mononoke*, and in *Spirited Away*, Miyazaki and co. attempted to portray something abstract and unknowable – gods. Miyazaki said he wasn't quite sure how to depict the gods and the spirits.

The gods in the forest exist apart from humans, with no relation to humans: they are not petty gods who guide souls to heaven after death: the forest 'is the central core, the navel, of the world, and we want to return in time to that pure place' (TP, 36).

Together with the wolf girl, Mononoke, the wolves constitute a family or community of their own, obeying their own laws, and roaming where they will. Moro is an enormous wolf, all white, while the brothers are smaller and blue-white. The image of San riding Moro or one of the brother wolves, with her hair streaming back, wearing her mask and white fur cloak and clutching a spear, is unforgettable,[27] one of the icons of Hayao Miyazaki's cinema.

The first proper view of Princess Mononoke,[28] when she turns to the camera (which takes Ashitaka's point-of-view, across the river),[29] is extraordinary. She stands proud and glares at Ashitaka, with blood smearing her mouth (she is sucking out poison from a gun fired by Eboshi). This's no ordinary heroine: that defiant look, her unusual costume, the blood around her mouth, and the giant form of the white wolf behind her, all spell otherness and wildness. And San remains true to that first image: she stays with her wolf family after the events in the narrative, including her encounter with her equal, Prince Ashitaka.

Princess Mononoke is one of the toughest of all Hayao Miyazaki's female characters – certainly the toughest of his younger, female characters. She is a rough and tumble woman, tomboyish, untamable, fierce in combat, incredibly brave and boundlessly energetic and athletic.

The Princess is a very appealing character: she has little or no fear: she hurtles down on the caravan of cattle and supplies led by Eboshi and her men, with only a dagger for a weapon (but it does help that she rides a mighty wolf). Later, she makes an assault on Irontown completely alone, taking on soldiers on the battlements and roofs, fighting with Gonza, and finally duelling with Ashitaka and then Eboshi herself (before Ashitaka steps in). San's hatred of humans never lets

---

27 Later, San wears a headband and red war paint on her face.

28 We don't see her in lengthy close-up during the nighttime attack on the caravan of oxen.

29 Ashitaka stands up, takes off his scarf, and gives his name – the polite, Japanese way of introductions.

up, and she is eager to kill Eboshi right up to the end (even when Ashitaka intervenes (yet again), you feel that San would still like to be rid of Eboshi).

For Hayao Miyazaki, part of San's journey was to show 'the kind of development that makes them a good person in their heart', to grow as a character to the point where she can feel affection for one human, if not the rest of humanity (this journey was reflected somewhat in Chihiro in Miyazaki's next film, where the ten year-old girl moves from selfishness to compassion for Haku, another prince).

The look of Mononoke Hime is expressive of an earlier historic period: she has short, roughly-cut hair, a necklace of white teeth (probably wolf teeth), white, shell earrings (which tinkle), and a white tunic over a knee-length, dark blue dress (roughly made, it looks as if San's created her own clothes). Most impressive is her warrior costume: a spirit mask that evokes a wolf, a white fur cloak (presumably wolf fur), with a white fur headdress at the top (which has wolf ears). Plus a very sharp dagger, and a spear.[30]

Where does Princess Mononoke live? In a spectacular, granite boulder wolf lair, high up in the hills, overlooking a narrow, river valley below. This is where San takes Ashitaka to recuperate (following the raid on Irontown and the healing in the forest glen). Some of the tenderest scenes in *Princess Mononoke* occur here, when Ashitaka wakes and watches San sleeping next to him, covered in a wolf fur. It's apt that Ashitaka wakes at night, into the quiet world of the forest, where Moro the wolf-god stands guard in the moonlight. The conversation between Moro and Ashitaka is unusual but important (and it's a lengthy scene). It develops the themes of the film, and also offers some back-story into San's past (Moro says she was abandoned by her parents when they fled, so was brought up as a wolf. It would be interesting to see flashbacks of San's childhood). Ashitaka states simply his

30 One of the enjoyable aspects of *Mononoke* was the design of the clothing: Miyazaki drew on reference, of course, but also made up many of the costumes.

guiding moral: can't humans and animals get along? Moro is doubtful: humans have one advantage: technology.

I have a lot of sympathy with Princess Mononoke's point-of-view: for her, humanity is cruel and stupid and is destroying her home, the forest, and trying to eliminate the gods, her friends. Though human, San has good reason for despising humanity.

San is right: humans are without doubt the most violent, the most idiotic, the most aggressive, and the most dangerous species on the planet (they are also the most neurotic, the most damaged, and the most messed up).

And there are far too many of them, and they are consuming everything in the world.

That's part of the ecological message in Hayao Miyazaki's cinema,[31] but the scientific facts bear it out. The true size of the human population, if it were in correct proportion to other mammals and natural resources, should be about the size of a London suburb. 50,000, or 100,000 or maybe 300,000. But not 10 million in one city, and not 6,000,000,000 spread across the planet. 'We need to realize fully that human beings are a tragic presence in the world' (TP, 84). Miyazaki admitted that as the *Princess Mononoke* project developed, he found humans less and less appealing: 'I wanted to punish human beings. Part of me is disgusted with hordes of people' (TP, 58).

This is the world we live in, Hayao Miyazaki wanted to say in *Princess Mononoke,* and that 'we share this despair', whether we are adults or children. It's not the world that's cursed, but the human world.

> It's not like we can coexist with nature as long as we live humbly, and we destroy it because we become greedy [Miyazaki explained]. When we recognize that even living humbly destroys nature, we don't know what to do. And I think that unless we put ourselves in the place where we

31 'I've come to the point where I just can't make a movie without addressing the problem of humanity as part of an eco-system,' Hayao Miyazaki said in 1997 (*Asia Pulse*, May, 1997).

don't know what to do and start from there, we cannot think about environmental issues or issues concerning nature.

The problem of ecology and the environment is a complex one, Hayao Miyazaki wanted to stress in *Princess Mononoke*: he talked about the historical aspects of Japan's forests, how in the Edo period forests were planted, but not for beauty or ecology, but to finance feudal domains (called *Hans*).[32] That is, it wasn't as simple as saying that bad people have ruined the planet: hard-working people have been doing it too.

LOVE

For Helen McCarthy, *Princess Mononoke* is also about love and loss:

> Miyazaki is making a film about love, the extent to which love involves loss of many kinds, and how that loss can be borne. San and Ashitaka, the human embodiments of love and loss, come to an agreement that is ideal for neither but respects both. (2002, 200)

Princess Mononoke once again depicts a love relationship in which the lovers remain apart, as in *Porco Rosso*. Once again, it is self-imposed. Because *Princess Mononoke* is a love story: in amongst all the action, the giant gods, the warring factions, there are two people who grow to love each other. But this is a more 'grown-up' version of the idealized love relationships depicted in *Laputa: Castle In the Sky* or *Spirited Away* or *Kiki's Delivery Service*. For a start, San and Ashitaka are a little older – maybe 16 or 17 or more. While

32 Miyazaki noted in 1997 that 'for the power balance between humans and animals, that was decidedly changed when humans started using gun powder. Really, though, the biggest reason why mountain animals decreased so much is agriculture'.

Chihiro in *Spirited Away* is meant to be 10 years-old, and Haku a little older, and Kiki is thirteen, and Tombo about the same age, and the heroes of *Laputa: Castle In the Sky* might be twelve or so, both San and Ashitaka are at an age when they could get together and make love, get married, have children,[33] etc. But no, there isn't even a kiss.

Yet this love story is convincing and tender – and especially moving from Mononoke's point-of-view, how she eventually realizes how much Ashitaka means to her, and how he accepts her as she is, and isn't trying to change her into something she isn't. It's true that the love story is subordinated to the action-adventure plot – *Princess Mononoke* is definitely not first and foremost a love story (however, it is highly romantic: the romanticization glows out of every frame). But the romance is an important element in the piece, because it is part of San's re-humanization, if you like, part of her journey of coming back to humanity.

And only someone noble and heroic and kind-hearted and brave is going to be her equal, and Ashitaka is certainly that. Ashitaka is a more suitable mate for San than Asbel is for Nausicaä in *Nausicaä*. And that San and Ashitaka decide to stay apart for the time being is a more satisfying resolution of the narrative than the Hollywood happy ending of togetherness, partly because it is true to their characters, and partly because it doesn't rule out them being together in the future (Ashitaka says he will come to the forest to visit San, for instance).

There's an intimate moment in the 1997 film between San and Ashitaka – some of my favourite scenes in this movie are those between San and Ashitaka when they are alone together. He lies on his back on the grass in the sacred glen, with Yakul nearby, and San has brought him some healing plants to eat (a subtle touch has San appearing with the light foot of a forest spirit – she steps swiftly on a little clump of

33 Indeed, as feminists remind us, in primitive societies young women of San's age would already have borne several children.

grass – *manga* and *animé* often include images of feet, emphasizing movement, and the contact with the Earth).

We sense that the princess of the spirits is intrigued by this human that was shot by his own people (as she puts it – though we know that the people of Irontown aren't Ashitaka's people), and who carried her away from Tatarba (for San, all humans are lumped together, and they're all evil). She sends her wolf brothers away and decides to deal with him herself. The Forest God has brought Ashitaka back to life, but he is still very weak. And he can't chew his food, so San chews it for him. Here is the kiss – well, it's a good reason for what is really a kiss (if you want a love scene between San and Ashitaka, this is it, right here – but it's typical of Hayao Miyazaki that it ain't a conventional love scene! – although it is intimate. It's also classic Miyazaki that it's the *woman* who initiates the intimacy, not the man).

Instead of chewing the leaves and placing them in Ashitaka's mouth, which would probably do the job just as well, San leans down and passes the chewed leaf into his mouth (like an animal mother might do with its offspring). Notice how the camera stays back to keep them in a two shot, from behind (so there's an ambiguity about whether Ashitaka is conscious when San is pressing the food into his mouth.) The subtle touch of having Ashitaka starting to weep and, significantly, San's bewildered reaction, says more about her increasing interest in this brave youth (a warrior who weeps... San is also startled because she is a girl who has never shed tears. She is too busy surviving to bother with tears).

ASHITAKA

Although the film's title is *Mononoke Hime,* the chief protagonist is really Prince Ashitaka: the 1997 film begins and ends with him, the narrative spends more time with Ashitaka than anyone else, and much of the plot is seen from his perspective (the titles suggested for the film were *The Legend of Ashitaka* and *Princess Mononoke*). But this is a movie with so many memorable characters competing for attention – not least the Forest Spirit (Shishigami), or Toki, or Lady Eboshi, or Jigo, or Moro.

Princess Mononoke the wolf princess is the other main character, but she appears after Ashitaka has been well-established (some twenty minutes into the first act; and initially we see the princess thru Ashitaka's eyes). Mononoke is one of Hayao Miyazaki's young women, tough, independent, fearless, energetic, athletic, practical and skilled.

Ashitaka is another Miyazakian type: a young hero – brave but thoughtful, energetic and athletic but also tender and compassionate. Miyazaki and his team of animators give the hero a number of unusual attributes to differentiate him from other movie heroes. He rides a red elk (from the *Nausicaä manga*) which sports two enormous horns, for instance, rather than the regular horse. He has an unusual, red hood and mask,[34] and a *mino*, a rainwear cloak made from woven, dried straw.

Note how Ashitaka appears to be an orphan – he has a sister, Kaya, who idolizes him, and who says goodbye to him as he leaves, giving him her precious dagger (however, Hayao Miyazaki remarked that Kaya calls Ashitaka brother meaning someone older in her clan).[35] Apart from that, Ashitaka has few or no relatives, and his allegiance is to the village; when the

34 A little like Lord Yuba in *Nausicaä of the Valley of the Wind.*
35 Kaya is also a brave girl: when the rampaging boar-god Nago is hurtling towards the village, she draws her sword when one of her friends stumbles, and turns to face it.

village elders reluctantly tell him he must leave,[36] he follows their request. But there is no mom or dad in Ashitaka's life. Hii-sama is clearly a surrogate mother, or at least a mother or grand-mother figure, and the man who's keeping look-out in the wooden tower at the edge of the forest is a kind of father figure (note how Ashitaka protects him when they fall from the look-out tower when the boar-god crashes into it).

Narratively, the quests in *Princess Mononoke* pile up for the hero: he begins the film as the young prince of the community, but is soon marked and cursed by the *boar* god Nago (the Tatarigami or cursed god),[37] and has to leave the village. At that point, his narrative goal is to make good his curse: if this were a simple fairy tale, that would be one of the primary goals. But as Ashitaka travels to the West,[38] the goals and quests alter: he becomes involved in an attack on a community, encounters the wolf princess San, meets Eboshi and the denizens of yet another community, Tatarba, and so on.

It's the classic storytelling device of opening out the world of the hero as he undergoes a journey.[39] Along the way the goals (and motives) develop, so that by the end of the film

---

36 That Ashitaka was forced out of his village was an important point – but Miyazaki found that young viewers didn't really understand that, and thought he was leaving to go on an adventure (TP, 113).

37 The boar-god can be regarded as a 'death god' (*shinigami*), who also crop up in *animé* such as *Naruto, Legend of the Overfiend, Yu Yu Hakusho, Descendants of Darkness, Death Note* and *Bleach.* The 'visualisation of 'hatred' as an organic shape-shifting entity of worms covering the form of the boar is a landmark in imaginative realisation,' noted Philip Brophy (2005, 189). A computer was tried in animating the writhing worms in the boar god scene, but it didn't work. And the first time it was animated, it was too tame – Miyazaki was after an image to express incredible rage, the 'vehement fury' that he sometimes experiences, when he becomes 'so vicious': 'when I get enraged, I have the sensation that black worms are crawling out of my body' (TP, 52, 186).

38 The setting for *Princess Mononoke* was meant to be somewhere like Chugoku in the West of Japan (TP, 99).

39 In the next village, there's a market scene, where Ashitaka meets Jigo; these sorts of films always have a bustling market scene; they're typically an opportunity for the hero to meet new characters, some who might help her/ him, as well as to obtain information. They also allow the filmmakers to show off some of the movie's production values. They're called 'watering hole' scenes in screen-writing manuals (famous examples would include the cantina scene in *Star Wars*, and any saloon scene in a Western).

Ashitaka (and Princess Mononoke) are both changed. (Thus, from a storytelling perspective, Ashitaka being an outcast from his village serves to push the hero on his way in the first act: yes, it is a curse that must be healed, but it is a way for the filmmakers of getting the hero in motion).

And the ending too of *Princess Mononoke* isn't the classic, Hollywood ending: there isn't a kiss and a hug and a wedding for Ashitaka and Mononoke: instead, the wolf girl, who can't forgive what humans have done to the forest, returns to her homeland, and Ashitaka says he will go to Tatarba to help them rebuild it. (However, these two heroes are shown in a scene on their own, and they do promise to see each other again).[40]

'Part of me does dislike human beings', Miyazaki confessed, but it would've hurt the film to endorse that negativity. So the iron-makers weren't portrayed as villains – because people acting from good intentions still exploit nature, as Miyazaki repeatedly insists (TP, 104-5).

Similarly, the two people who are daubed villains and by rights should perish, if this were a regular (Westernized) movie, Eboshi and Jigo, don't die.[41] *Princess Mononoke* is not as clear-cut as that, and won't follow the conventions of action-adventure movies. It's true that Eboshi is maimed (the wolf Moro bites off her arm), but neither Mononoke and Moro don't get to kill her,[42] as they are desperate to do, and Jigo survives intact (even though in some respects he's been the worst villain in the piece, using Eboshi to kill the Shishigami, and playing off the warring factions of the people of Tatarba, Lord Asano and the Emperor's forces against each other. Jigo is the familiar adventurer-mercenary and treasure-hunter: he's in it just for the reward. His goals are the lowest and

40 'I expect San will repeatedly break Ashitaka's heart after this' (TP, 83).

41 Jigo is like everybody, Miyazaki said: 'I had no intention of killing off Jigo. If we disown this kind of person, we would have to disown almost all human beings' (TP, 34).

42 The first time we see Moro occurs during the attack by the wolves on Eboshi and her men: the wolf-god hurtles straight for Eboshi; she is repelled by rifle's shots, and is engulfed in flames. Her final act is also to hurl herself at Eboshi.

basest – pure capitalism).

Ashitaka is a peacemaker, an intermediary between warring communities; he tries a peaceful solution *first*, before reacting with aggression. His is the familiar liberal message of 'can't we all just get along?' Why can't the animals and gods of the forest and humans get on with each other? It's a familiar question, and the answer is simple: they can't. Or they won't. Anyway, they don't.

It's important that, although Ashitaka is an outstanding warrior, he isn't depicted attacking too often – he defends, or he reacts, or he helps, but he doesn't attack. He tries words first, and negotiation. Early on, he kills some of the samurai (who are scorned as thugs by other characters), but only after warning them off, and only reluctantly (and feels remorse afterwards). It's also the curse which's enhancing his actions[43] – maybe he was only trying to wound or scare off the samurai, or to defend the villagers. (And Hayao Miyazaki did not want Ashitaka to be a samurai: 'I wanted to have a boy, not a samurai boy, in the movie'. Hence he rides Yakul, not a horse, and doesn't wear a samurai costume).

It's often Ashitaka who's standing physically in between the characters, trying to get them to negotiate or at least talk. San does the same – between Lord Okkoto and Moro, for instance, towards the end of the film. And when San is white with anger at the apocalyptic climax, and wants to kill Eboshi, just after Ashitaka's saved her and carried her through the lake, Ashitaka again steps between them.[44]

There's less humour among the main characters in *Princess Mononoke* than in other Hayao Miyazaki movies. Ashitaka and San (and Eboshi) smile or joke or laugh far, far less than, say, Tombo in *Kiki's Delivery Service* or Pazu in *Laputa: Castle In the Sky* (they don't laugh once in *Mononoke*,

43 The writhing, glowing movement of the curse around Ashitaka's arm when it's activated in moments of crisis, such as the scene where Ashitaka rescues San in Irontown, recalls the way that *ki* or life energy is portrayed in *animé* and *manga*. *Ki* appears as flames, as Gilles Poitras noted, 'a larger-than-life image of a person's "battle aura," or as someone sensing a person's "battle spirit"' (1999, 67).

44 He says he promised Toki and the girls he'd bring Eboshi back to Irontown.

and smile rarely). Instead, the humour is diverted to the secondary characters, such as the husband-and-wife bickering of Toki and Kohroku, or the wry quips of Jigo.

I guess for some viewers Ashitaka is a little solemn and serious. I don't think so; but he does take his quest of reaching the far West seriously. Hayao Miyazaki commented that Ashitaka

> is not a cheerful, carefree boy. He is a melancholy guy who has a destiny. I feel that I am that way myself, but until now, I haven't made a film about this kind of character.

The *sadness* of Ashitaka is so central to his character. It is a fundamental melancholy in his personality, not in his circumstances (or as a result of his curse). The introspection is one aspect that differentiates Ashitaka from heroes in Western, Hollywood movies.

One of the clues to Ashitaka's character occurs in the opening sequence: not just the battle with the crazed god Nago, which reveals Ashitaka in his heroic, action mode: we see he is a fearsome warrior (although he does try to negotiate with Nago first). But just as significant is the aftermath: the scene in the hut with the wise woman and the village elders is the key scene: here the witch woman gives Ashitaka his task (to discover the solution to his curse in the West), the familiar exposition of a million movies (and to learn to see unclouded by hate,[45] an important moral precept).

But notice Ashitaka's reaction; he sits quietly and listens. He does not argue with the wise woman, nor with the elders. He accepts what she says. And when he is given his task, he cuts off his topknot,[46] places it on the altar, rises, bows and walks out. He is calm and polite: this prince is definitely not a

45 Ashitaka repeats this to Eboshi; she laughs, then she decides to show him other sides to Irontown.

46 Cutting off the topknot in this village means that Ashitaka is a non-person, Miyazaki explained, and he is forced out by his community (it is a Chinese-style topknot).

spoilt brat, and not a selfish guy either: he is going to do what's best for the community.

The way that Ashitaka acts in that whole scene says a huge amount about his character. (This is great storytelling).[47]

Towards the end of the 1997 movie, Ashitaka has become more like one of the gods – or at least, the god-curse has now infected more of his body (one of the reasons that Ashitaka takes off his jacket, to keep San warm, is to reveal that the skin-stain has spread to his chest. And he's also one of those male heroes who strips down like in North American action flicks). And the design of the Forest Spirit in his decapitated state also evokes Ashitaka's skin curse: the swirling colours of purple and black link with those on Ashitaka's arm. Certainly, the movie is clear that both Ashitaka and San are not your average sort of person, and are closer to divinity in some respects than humans.

Another intriguing aspect of Ashitaka's characterization is his ability to sense what's happening to San at key moments. Yes, it is a dramatic device, developed sometimes to get information across, or to leap over gaps in the narrative. But it never seems contrived here (the scene where Ashitaka senses that one of the wolves is buried under a pile of dead boars, for instance, some way off, would be just silly in some other movies).

It also pays off to introduce the audience to the flash-backs to scenes which Ashitaka did not witness. And it pays off at the end, when the wolf mother Moro asks if Ashitaka wants to save the girl he loves.

47 The filmmaking might be something out of the classic Japanese movies of Yasujiro Ozu or Kenji Mizoguchi: the camera is stationary, at waist height, in medium shots – the way that actors have been filmed millions of times in Japanese movies (often sitting on cushions on the floor around a low table).

OTHER CHARACTERS

Jigo is an ambiguous character: a monk in red and white garb, squat, rotund, gnarled, with a large wart on his face, he is also one of the Emperor's men. He has a bunch of motives: one is to gain the head of the Forest God, because the Emperor thinks it will grant immortality. So he has the greedy instincts of the treasure hunter, a familiar character in the adventure genre. But he's also playing the different communities against each other, pitting Lord Asano and his soldiers against Eboshi and her people. Their internecine war helps to weaken their communities, which's what the Emperor wants.

And it's Jigo who craftily tells Ashitaka just enough, to entice the youth to search for the land of the Forest Spirit. Jigo's a canny judge of people's characters, and – importantly – their values, and what they want. But he's wrong, at the end: the bigger picture is that somehow humans and nature have to get along. You can't win against fools, is how he puts it, but his cynicism and materialism is out-done here by higher values.[48]

For Hayao Miyazaki, Eboshi[49] was a tough woman who had had a hard life,[50] and that helps to make her uncompromising in her efforts to build a better life for her people. The problem is, she is one of those people who will stoop to means beyond the law, and beyond what reasonable people would do. It's not a problem for Eboshi that she is going to try to kill a god (the Forest Spirit), or the animals that

48 Miyazaki explained: 'I made the character of Jiko Bou without knowing what kind of role he would play. He could be a spy of the Muromachi government (the Samurai regime which was ruling Japan at that time), a henchman of some religious group, or a Ninja, or he could actually be a very good guy. In the end, he became a character who has all of those elements.'

49 The name Eboshi comes from where Miyazaki has his mountain cabin. There was also a Tate Eboshi in legend.

50 They made Eboshi a woman also because the staff said they preferred to draw a beautiful woman to a man (TP, 61). The costume (suggesting she was a courtesan) was part of the move towards beauty. Eboshi was a modern person – and to people of old, 20th century people might seem like the devil, Miyazaki thought (TP, 57). Miyazaki defined Eboshi as 'a heart of steel that fears no one' (TP, 23).

get in her way (the boars), or the soldiers of Lord Asano, or the wolf girl, San.

Eboshi and Irontown embody the contradictions at the heart of the themes in *Princess Mononoke*: Eboshi offers shelter to prostitutes and lepers, but she is also actively developing weapons and heavy industry (such as ironworks). In a conventional (Westernized) movie, she'd be a villain with a cigar and a nasty attitude.

One of the curious omissions from the 1997 film is the non-appearance of Lord Asano. We see his samurai and his soldiers, and his emissaries, but there isn't a scene with Asano himself. Maybe there was and it was cut before animation. But it is curious that Asano's army plays an important role in the piece, during the siege of Tatarba, but the leader isn't really portrayed. (Asano wants some of the iron that Eboshi is mining).

The *kodama*, the tree spirits, are a Miyazakian spin on traditional sprites or woodland fairies. They are small, doll-like, white, with black spots for eyes and a mouth. They spin their heads and rattle like toys. The stand-out scene with the *kodama* is when they lead Ashitaka and the two wounded soldiers into the forest: Ashitaka is trying to reach Tatarba on the other side of the mountains, but the *kodama* guide him to the heart of the forest.

Hayao Miyazaki's movies are wonderful with sidekicks and odd minor characters that pop up and disappear again, and the *kodama* are no exception. And the filmmakers give them all sorts of unusual attributes, such as fading from view (recalling the Totoros in *Totoro*), or mimicking humans (as when the *kodama* copy, like children, Ashitaka carrying the soldier on his back). Another magical scene with the *kodama* occurs at the appearance of the Nightwalker, when thousands of them materialize on the tops of the trees, and start to rattle and spin when the Night-walker arrives.[51]

51 Miyazaki described the Forest Spirit as 'nature's night': 'the creature is gathering and giving out lives during the night'.

One of the most unusual elements of *Princess Mononoke* is the ape tribe, a gorilla-like version of the legendary beast of China, the *Shoujou*.[52] The portrayal of the apes is deliberately odd, with deep, slowed-down voices, and a stylized, silhouetted approach to the animation. The apes are depicted as proto-humans: they want to absorb the power of humanity by eating them.[53] These beliefs are actually historical aspects of real incarnations of humans in prehistory. The idea that eating the bodies and particularly the brains of your enemies will give you their power was a belief that lasted for many thousands of years (and into the modern period, with the religious rituals of the Aztecs). So *Princess Mononoke* is excavating ancient prehistory with head-hunting cults in the characters of the apes. (San protests, telling the apes that those beliefs are false, that the apes would become something less than human. It's ironic, because San's been complaining about humans, and getting rid of humans from the forest).

The boars represent another level of animal life, and have their own morals, ethics and gods (Nago and Okkoto).[54] Significantly, both the giant boar-gods, Nago and Okkoto, go mad, when they are shot with iron bullets by the troops of Asano and Eboshi. Moro the wolf-god is also shot, but notice how she doesn't go mad, but bears her fatal injury with dignity (she saves up her strength to bite off the head of Eboshi, but in the end decides that San needs her help more, so she launches herself at Okkoto, to save San).

The boars are the only characters in *Princess Mononoke* that don't appeal to me so much, but that's no fault of Hayao Miyazaki and his filmmaking team: it's what the boars represent.[55] Each of the animal groups depict some aspect of humanity: the wolves are fiercely independent and fine warriors, but also have a nurturing, wise aspect, the *kodama*

52 They are charas you forget a part of the mix.

53 The apes are also planting trees. Eboshi's response is to shoot at them.

54 The name Okkoto comes from a village: the place and the *kanji* characters fascinate Miyazaki (TP, 311).

55 The boars are of course another version of a favourite Miyazakian beast – pigs.

are the spirits of the trees, or humans who are in tune with the natural world, like the Spirit God himself, and the boars represent the foot soldiers of humanity, the workers or proletariat, perhaps, whose negative traits are aggression, stubbornness, ignorance and a mob mentality. All of the animal groups are proud – it's debatable whether the wolves are prouder than the boars – and that pride and unwillingness to compromise leads to problems.

So it's not because the boars are badly visualized or dramatized in *Princess Mononoke* that I find them less than appealing, it's because of the aspects of humanity that they embody. However, the boars are certainly brave – when they go to war, they *really* go to war, launching themselves in their hundreds against the human forces. But in *Princess Mononoke* the boars, although they have their reasons, are also misguided (in Miyazaki's cinema, everyone has sound reasons for going to war – but from their point-of-view. Miyazaki's point is that when a war starts, noble motives are debased. War inevitably corrupts people).

One of the curious scenes in *Princess Mononoke* is where San goes to help Lord Okkoto, the leader of the boars. Like Ashitaka, San acts here as an intermediary and a helper. San might not agree with their tactics and ethics but she wants to help the boars, and avert a catastrophe.

THE COMMUNITIES IN *PRINCESS MONONOKE*

Hayao Miyazaki's world has been described as a fantastical, vaguely European space, with Western-looking characters and architecture. *My Neighbor Totoro, The Wind Rises, Ponyo* and *Princess Mononoke*, though, were set in Japan (but a Japan of the past – *circa* the 1950s in *Totoro*, mediæval feudal Japan in *Princess Mononoke*). Miyazaki chose the 14th century for *Princess Mononoke* because, he explained, it was a time when 'people changed their value system from gods to money'. It was an era of transition, when

> life and death were sharply delineated. People lived, loved, hated, worked and died. Life was not ambiguous. Even in the midst of hatred and slaughter there were still things that made life worth living. Marvellous encounters and beautiful things could still exist.[56]

The Emishi, being the oldest community in terms of history in *Princess Mononoke*[57] (aside from San, Moro and the wolf family), are not a matriarchy, but women hold a much higher place than the more conventional views of prehistory as patriarchal. The Emishi are linked in the 1997 film and by the filmmakers to an older group of people who lived in Japan, who were possibly the ancestors of the Japanese people. In the scene in the hut with the elders, it's mentioned (by one of the eldest of the village elders) that the Emishi were wiped out 500 years ago (by the Emperor), and are the last survivors of an ancient people. In making Ashitaka the hero, Yoshihiko Amino noted that Miyazaki 'decentered the Japanese state', because the Emishi were a small tribe in the North, while the bulk of the Japanese people were the Yamato (TP, 61).

That women held key positions in the social hierarchy of the Emishi is part of a movement in some archæological circles towards pro-women social structures. You can find it in the work of anthropologist Chris Knight,[58] British poets such as Robert Graves and Peter Redgrove,[59] with their evocation of the 'White Goddess' and the 'Black Goddess', and feminist writers and artists such as Catherine Elwes, Monica

56 Hayao Miyazaki, quoted in S. Napier, 181.
57 The other races are the Jomon and the Yamato.
58 Knight has a 1991 book on the function of menstruation in forming prehistoric social structures, *Blood Mysteries* (Yale University Press, New Haven, 1991).
59 Robert Graves wrote *The White Goddess* in the 1940s, a book which influenced filmmakers such as Orson Welles (and many poets), and *The Black Goddess* in the 1960s (which critics found more difficult to absorb). Peter Redgrove took up Graves's Black Goddess deity in the 1980s, in his study of poetic ways of living, *The Black Goddess and the Sixth Sense* (Bloomsbury, London, 1987).

Sjöo, Mary Sherfey,[60] Elinor Gadon, Geoffrey Ashe[61] and Barbara Walker, who believed that women were often leaders, and that some ancient societies were matriarchies. There isn't space here to go into the vast area of Goddess studies, but I have noted some useful starting points below.[62]

The world of *Princess Mononoke* is both prehistoric and mediæval, both mythological and historical. It is a world of self-enclosed communities – Ashitaka travels from his homeland in the East of Japan through a number of tribes, including the town under attack from the samurai warriors, to Irontown, and the forest itself. The filmmakers combine a variety of periods, from prehistory to the Renaissance.

THE FOREST

The forest. What a forest! The research trips that Hayao Miyazaki and his team made to Yakushima in May, 1995 (and Shirakami-sanchi) in Japan for *Princess Mononoke* certainly paid off:[63] this is one of the great forests in cinema (Yakushima has rainforests which includes cedars 1000s of years old; 75% of the island is forested mountains. It's off the

60 According to psychologist Mary Sherfey, there is evidence that in the Near East around 12,000-8,000 B.C., women 'enjoyed full sexual freedom and [were] often totally incapable of controlling [their] sexual drive'; to the point where this was one of the reasons that it took 'perhaps five thousand years or longer for the subjugation of women to take place' (and this also possibly delayed the early development of agriculture). ("A Theory On Female Sexuality", in S. Cox, ed., *Female Psychology*, Science Research Associates, Chicago, 1976).

61 We publish a book by Geoffrey Ashe about his American course on the female deities of old, *Discovering the Goddess* (Crescent Moon, 2007).

62 G. Ashe: *The Virgin: Mary's Cult and the Re-emergence of the Goddess*, Arkana, London, 1987; E. Gadon: *The Once and Future Goddess*, Aquarian Press 1990; M. Gimbutas: *The Language of the Goddess*, Thames & Hudson, London, 1989; S. Nicholson, ed. *The Goddess Re-awakening: The Goddess Principle Today,* Theosophical Publishing House, New York, NY, 1989; E. C. Whitmont: *Return of the Goddess*, Routledge, London, 1987; M. Sjöo & B. Mor: *The Great Cosmic Mother*, Harper & Row, San Francisco 1987; E. Neumann: *The Great Mother*, Princeton University Press, NJ, 1972.

63 The background artists 'worked frantically' on the forest, Miyazaki said (TP, 45). Japan has about 70% of forests (compared to 12% in Britain).

coast of Kyushu, in South-eastern Japan, and is regarded as a mystical island).[64]

Ancestors of *Princess Mononoke*'s forest are obviously the submerged forest in *Nausicaä of the Valley of the Wind* and the giant tree in *Laputa: Castle In the Sky,* and the neighbourhood woods in *My Neighbor Totoro* (is there a Miyazaki movie which doesn't include trees and woodland? No). And in 2010's *Arrietty*, Ghibli returned to the dense vegetation and green world of *Mononoke.*

In *Mononoke Hime* the forest is a vast, lush, green world, extending for many miles in the valleys below the mountains. It is a place of renewal, purity, growth, and a deep spirituality.[65] In short, life. It is both a fairy tale woodland and a real place, drawing on botanical studies. Dragonflies fly by and butterflies flutter by in this peaceful, dreamy place. Shafts of light beam down, there are toadstools and giant trees. The feeling that 'something is there' in the forest is a key emotion in *Mononoke*, which Miyazaki has experienced in real forests.

From a design point-of-view, the forest in *Princess Mononoke* is exquisite: large, glacial boulders, enormous trees, moss-covered tree roots, insects, and thousands of tiny plants and flowers. The level of detail in the forest is beyond obsessive.[66] As the characters walk or clamber through the forest (the forest floor is always uneven, until the central glade is reached), the viewer's eye wanders over one of the most densely detailed woodlands in movies. (You will see the influence of this forest in many subsequent movies).

And it's not just the small flowers and plants, which might have come from an Early Netherlandish painting by Jan

64 Kazuo Oga, the art director of *Princess Mononoke*, and therefore one of the stars of the movie, visited the Shirakami mountains, in Northern Honshu, Japan. One of the background designers was from Akita, and another from Kyushu.

65 If you go beyond worldly desires, Miyazaki suggested in 1994, and want to go somewhere pure, you might end up with something as simple as a stone or drops of water. There's a wealth of Asian philosophy and mysticism behind such a view.

66 'Technically, *Princess Mononoke* is a remarkable achievement, especially on the level of art direction and design: the primeval forests of Japan and the first stirrings of industrial society are depicted with ravishing realism' (J. Clements, 2006, 506).

van Eyck or Petrus Christus of the Madonna sitting with the baby Jesus in the *hortus conclusus* (enclosed garden), it's also *the light*. This is one element that is tougher to capture on celluloid: the soft light that filters through canopies of leaves. This is a misty, golden light, not the harder light of Hollywood action movies set in forests, which typically fill the area in front of the camera with smoke machines, and shoot into the sun.[67]

Sometimes the forest in *Princess Mononoke* is lit by God-rays, and sometimes the light is softer and mistier. The signature colour of *Princess Mononoke* is green (complimented by blue) – for the natural world. Colour designer Michiyo Yasuda and her team saved the brightest, richest greens for the sacred glen, which complements the golden light. But there are so many varieties of green throughout the movie (550 colours were used in *Princess Mononoke*, and 549 of them were green). This really is 'the green and the gold' that British poet Robert Graves spoke of that poets use to evoke their childhoods. (And it's red, inevitably, for the human world – of traditional Japanese costumes, of war paint (for San), of blood, etc).

And you know that the completely clear water[68] in the forest glade is pure and healing, and uncorrupted by humans. (And it proves so for Ashitaka and the soldiers – they feel refreshed and lighter after drinking the water). This is a place where you can find rest and nourishment and healing.

As well as woods and mountains, *Princess Mononoke* is also a movie of rivers: these are the cold, rushing streams of rural Japan, filled with enormous, granite glacial boulders, rounded and smooth, and often covered with moss. Some of the best scenes from the point-of-view of atmosphere and

67 Since the 1970s, forests in Robin Hood or King Arthur or mediæval flicks always have tons of smoke and backlight. Are woods really that misty and smoky? Occasionally. Most of the time, no.

68 At first, the filmmakers were going to portray water as light blue, but an artist (probably Yoshifumi Kondo) said, 'water is black', which altered the way it was portrayed (TP, 46). Black because the setting's overgrown with trees, blocking out the sky and reflections of the sky in the water.

design are those set beside the river, where Ashitaka encounters San for the first time, and where Ashitaka rescues the soldiers from the water. It's also striking how the film-makers include rivers in spate after rain, capturing the brown, muddy water churned up into waves.

Design-wise, at times *Princess Mononoke* looks like a Zen Buddhist garden,[69] with its rocks and trees, and its atmosphere of spiritual serenity. The famous Zen gardens at Kyoto might be reference points.

And when the spiritual centre of the forest is reached, the art directors (Nizo Yamamoto, Naoya Tanaka, Yoji Take-shige, Satoshi Kuroda and Kazuo Oga) have created a magical space that is at once instantly familiar and unworldly: there is juicy, green grass bordering a pool filled with perfectly clear water (which contrasts with the muddy water of the river). Small clumps of grass form islands (presumably growing atop small rocks). Large rocks are placed around the pool. It is a familiar sort of pool that one might find on a granite tableland (but the rocks and water are definitely not red with iron ore – there's no iron here in this part of the forest – the iron is left to Irontown).[70]

Hayao Miyazaki and his team certainly squeeze every ounce of possibility of using the space of the forest glade, and in particular the pool. The clear lake is employed numerous times to stage scenes: Ashitaka takes water from it; San leads Yakul and Ashitaka into the water; Ashitaka lies half in it; the Forest God walks on it; Ashitaka is hurled into it by Okkoto; Ashitaka pulls San underwater to cleanse her; even Gonza walks under the water (he can't swim) to escape the Forest God. You could give Miyazaki the most boring space in the

---

69 In the historical Japanese Zen Buddhist garden, colours are carefully orchestrated, so that a single leaf can set off a vast acreage of predominantly green or ochre. In the Oriental garden, notions of *feng shui* and *yin* and *yang* control how a landscape is shaped by humans. In the system of *feng shui*, the elements of a garden or a building must be in harmony with natural forces of air, water and earth.

70 The sacred place of the movie was also meant to be a historically real place, a holy spot which some historians believe existed.

world to use in a movie, and he'd find some way of making it incredible.

It is a symbolic forest, it is 'a depiction of a forest that has existed within the hearts of Japanese from ancient times', Miyazaki said (TP, 88). The forest and the mountains represent a place in nature of purity, of origins, of nourishment, which humans are not allowed to enter.

The forest is typically the place in fairy and folk tales where characters enter in order to encounter obstacles and mystery. The forest is the site of initiation and trial. It lies on the edge of the familiar, everyday world of the fairy tale. It is where the protagonist gets lost, meets strange creatures, undergoes transformations and spells. It is, typically, one of the first places the protagonist enters on the journey outwards from the home, in *Snow White, Little Red Riding Hood* or *Hansel and Gretel,* for example.

In *The Brothers Grimm*, Jack Zipes writes of the forest in fairy tales:

> Inevitably, they find their way into the forest. It is there that they lose and find themselves. It is there that they gain a sense of what is to be done. The forest is always large, immense, great, and mysterious. No one ever gains power of the forest, but the trees possess the power to change lives and alter destinies. (43)

The forest is a zone of otherness, strangeness, enchantment and the unknown. In (Jungian) psychological terms, it is the unconscious, or confusion, a realm of instability, a *regressus ad uterum*, a place of re-creation and re-birth, where the ego/ soul/ hero/ine is tested and initiated. The enchanted or dark forest is a place of wild things, such as dragons in caves, or witches in their gloomy houses; it is also a land of death (and dragons, witches, caves and darkness are linked with death or the 'dark side' of life).

The forest also has a feminine/ uterine/ womb association, for it is the place of rebirth. The places in fairy tales linked with the dark forest (caves, marshes, deserts, wells, seas, underworlds), are also feminine and birth spaces. Entering the dark forest is essentially the 'descent and return' process of mythology (Orpheus, Jesus, Theseus, Persephone, Isis and others descended into the Underworld or Hell and returned changed and/ or reborn). The descent is towards the foundation of life, to the secret heart of nature. The initiate (whether Orpheus, Hansel, Little Red Riding Hood or Persephone) has to overcome fear and doubt, and learn courage and resourcefulness. Often a monster has to be encountered and sometimes slain (Theseus and the Minotaur, Perseus and St George against the dragon, Marduk and the monster Tiamat, Zeus and the Titans, Jack and the giant). In *Princess Mononoke*, Ashitaka undertakes this journey, with all its mythological associations.

The Grimm brothers, in their *Children's and Household Tales*, expressed some of the Germanic love of forests, which is fuelled by awe and mysticism. There are clichés that abound about the Germanic, Bavarian mystification of groves as places of ritual and magic, sites of notions of community, race and origins. However, these clichés about the dark forest do form much of the background of fairy tales, in Jacob and Wilhelm Grimm's books especially.

But what's striking about *Princess Mononoke* is that the story doesn't develop *beyond* the forest – to a mountain top, for instance, or some castle or temple where a magic jewel or Grail is kept. Rather, the forest (and the spiritual heart of it, the glade), is the final destination of the story (although the action climax does move out onto the hills – partly for dramatic and staging reasons).

In folk and fairy tales it is often the other way around: the forest will be encountered early on, but the narrative will move on to courts or castles or an ogre's cave or a witch's house. But the most magical place in *Princess Mononoke* is a glade and a pool in the forest.

NATURE VERSUS INDUSTRY

For Hayao Miyazaki, *Princess Mononoke* was intended to be a movie of pre-industrial Japan. A country which had not yet been industrially exploited, a Japan

> when it had thick forests, few people, and a purity of nature, with distant mountains and deep valleys, abundant and clear flowing streams, narrow dirt paths unpaved with gravel, and a multitude of birds, beasts, and insects. (SP, 273)

Tatarba[71] ('Irontown' in the English language dub) is another of Hayao Miyazaki's workshops or factories or institutions, recalling the Piccolo aviation company in *Porco Rosso* or the bathhouse in *Spirited Away.* Like the bathhouse, Tatarba is presided over by an older woman. Eboshi[72] is an ambiguous character: on the one hand, she provides food and work and accommodation for (female) prostitutes, and also a group of lepers (social outcasts, you might say). The community at Tatarba seems to be thriving. On the other hand, Eboshi is developing weapons in order to kill the Forest God, and is happy to cut down the trees to support her iron works. (The ambiguity is heightened by making Eboshi a beautiful, well-mannered woman – she is not your average movie villain).

Workshops of one sort or another are a recurring motif in Hayao Miyazaki's cinema – clearly evoking the animation studio (and Studio Ghibli) itself, but also the co-operative spirit. In *Spirited Away* the workers band together to help the River God, for instance, in Tatarba (Iron Town) in *Princess Mononoke*, workers mine and develop iron,[73] and in *Porco Rosso* the workers build a plane, just like the animation team

71 The iron foundry was way too big, Miyazaki admitted: he had been inspired by a photo he saw as a youth of a foundry built in China's Great Leap Forward (TP, 97).

72 Forerunners of Eboshi include Kushana in *Nausicaä of the Valley of the Wind.*

73 Some of the ironsmithy motifs were used in *The Little Norse Prince*.

puts together a film.[74] (Kamaji in *Spirited Away* can be seen as an exaggerated caricature of the filmmaker or animator – working non-stop, doing twenty things at once with his multiple limbs, and sleeping right where he works – just as Miyazaki and his co-workers have done when the deadlines approach and the work gets intense).

Tatarba is in direct opposition to the forest: it is an iron works, felling trees to feed its furnace (and Tatarba is built from wood, too, to add to the injustice). And it's iron that drives the gods mad when the bullets pierce them. There are watch towers, a huge gate, fires, smoke and the sound of industry – all emblems of aggression and humanity arming itself against, well, everything.

Tatarba is a symbol and manifestation of humanity and what humans do: it is not an agricultural community, where people live off the land and cultivate crops. It is not a place where people live more harmoniously with the earth. It is, in short, industry: Tatarba embodies Industry, and Progress, and Capitalism.

Put it another way: Tatarba (and Eboshi and her people) embody exploitation: that is their *raison d'être*: they exploit the resources of the world. If that means clearing the forests of trees, so be it. If that means killing the Forest Spirit, so be it.

So with the community of Tatarba, Hayao Miyazaki and his team of filmmakers are exploring cultural and social oppositions such as nature vs. industry, trees/ wood vs. iron/ machines, and, ultimately, nature vs. humanity. The film's eco-friendly subtext is clear: animals live harmoniously with the world, and do not seek to exploit it. But humans can't help exploiting the Earth.

Humans, in short, don't know how *to live*.

Instead, humans have to impose themselves and their

74 And Porco Rosso, walking around and smoking and watching the women at work, recalls the film director (and perhaps Miyazaki himself) overseeing his/ her film crew at work.

will upon the Earth.[75] The contrast is between the serenity and cycles of growth and decay in the forest and the industrialization of the humans. And it's the human creation of iron in bullets that drives the gods crazy. Eboshi maybe has respect for the gods, but she has no problem with killing them if needs be.[76] Yet, also, humans are simply living, so it's not a direct opposition, it's more ambiguous.

Princess Mononoke shows that many of the groups are resisting change, and want things to stay the same. The humans in Irontown want to be able to exploit the natural resources of the area, for instance. Part of the thematic project of *Princess Mononoke* is to demonstrate that change is inescapable – and usually beneficial, too (the Forest Spirit embodies change – it is continually changing from a Day Spirit to a Night Spirit).

With Tatarba's ironworks, *Princess Mononoke* explores two historical periods: the first is the mediæval period, when the film is set (the Muromachi period, 1392-1573 [SP, 272]), with the emergent industry of working metal and the creation of modern weapons such as guns (called 'flint-fire-arrows' in the movie,[77] because the word for 'gun' wasn't known in the Muromachi era, guns were imported by the Portuguese later, in 1543).[78] The Muromachi era was the time of the first developments of industrialization on a big scale.

The second historical period is the early origins of Japan itself, a prehistoric time, roughly 10,000 B.C. to 300 B.C., known as the Neolithic Jomon period (this is also the time of

75 'Can we humans really control our egos?' Miyazaki wondered in 2006. No: 'human beings are irredeemable. We are truly irredeemable. And that is why we keep devouring this planet of ours' (TP, 401).

76 As a peacekeeper, Ashitaka continues to try to reason with Eboshi – when he's in the water, and Eboshi has shot the Forest God, Ashitaka yells at her that the Spirit is not her enemy. But then, who is? It's everyone. But Ashitaka doesn't give up trying to bring the conflicting powers together.

77 In the attack in the rain on the hillside, the guns have covers on them, and the party uses red umbrellas (and Eboshi wears a red hat).

78 Miyazaki described the gun thus: 'It's called a 'Kasou' or 'Fire Spear'. In reality, it had a longer rod, and it often exploded and injured the shooter. It was often made from copper, and was used in the Ming dynasty in the 15th century. It had been brought to Japan before matchlock guns were.'

early Shintoism, and Shinto's nature mysticism lies behind much of *Princess Mononoke*). The Emishi, where Ashitaka comes from, have affinities with both the mediæval and prehistoric periods, while Princess Mononoke herself is consciously depicted as a girl who 'resembled a Jomon pottery figure', as Hayao Miyazaki put it (SP, 273).[79] She is portrayed as someone from a very ancient time (her headdress, for instance, and her wolf family, underline that connection with the deep past).

In contemporary Japan, the Ainu (24,000 of them), now living mainly in Hokkaido in the North of Japan (they used to live in Northern Honshu), are the last links to the ancient Jomon societies. The Ainu are sometimes called Caucasian, and are related to the peoples of Siberia.

So as well as a clash between nature and industry, *Mononoke Hime* also explores conflicts between different historical periods, between the mediæval era and prehistory, and between the early modern period and the mediæval period. (And working with metal of course goes back thousands of years: there is a 'Bronze Age', an 'Iron Age', a 'Stone Age').

THE FOREST SPIRIT

During the daytime, the Spirit God (Shishigami) is a stag with enormous antlers and a mask-like, quasi-human face.[80] At night, it becomes the Nightwalker, Didarabotchi, a humanoid giant in blue-white-violet, comprised of glittering points of light inside a translucent body, trailing tendrils of energy.

79 Hayao Miyazaki and his team used the research of archæologists such as Eiichi Fujimori. 'Jomon' means 'cord pattern', the patterns that are found on prehistoric pottery (SP, 148).

80 'With its double countenance, human eyes in an animal muzzle, and the ineffable and mysterious smile of Greek *kuroi*, the Forest God appears to represent the supreme balance of Yin and Yang, death and rebirth, disrupted by men's blindness', as critic Alessandro Bencivenni put it (2003).

The design of the Forest Spirit consciously evokes the stag, an animal with a host of symbolisms attached to it, like the snake or the lion. In traditional symbolism, the stag's associated with the dawn, renewal, fire, creation, and the sun. (In Japan, the dragon is the 'celestial stag'). And the stag's linked with the cycle of the seasons, because it sheds its antlers each year. The stag form is also very ancient, and distinctly shamanic (shamen wear antlers, for instance).

The Forest Spirit 'has antlers like a deer's, the face of a human, the feet of a bird, and the body of a ram. I just made it up', Miyazaki admitted (TP, 115). And it's a low-ranking god – there are gods above it.

There's a very famous prehistoric painting, dating to the upper palæolithic era, in a cave in France. It depicts a dancing shaman or sorcerer, a figure with a man's legs, a lion's body, and a stag's antlers. The Forest Spirit in *Princess Mononoke* evokes this image both in its day and night guises – the film is a beautiful expression of prehistoric shamanism, mana and animism (animism is the foundation of all religions, including Japanese Shintoism – as E.B. Tylor defined it, animism is 'the belief in spiritual beings').

One of the unforgettable images in the 1997 Japanese animation – in a movie crammed with them – is Shishigami's feet walking towards the camera and sprouting flowers, grass and plants. It was one of those images that no other film has ever done.[81] And it occurs twice (once underwater, and in the black space of Ashitaka's dream – the dream replays the scene of Ashitaka's healing, from his point-of-view). This is a god that walks on water.

It was a key decision to keep the Forest Spirit mute – it might have been tempting to have the Shishigami speak, in the usual low, echoey voice of cinematic deities. But the silent looks that the Forest Spirit gives – towards the camera, into

81 The computer animators of Treebeard the ent paid *hommage* to this scene in *The Lord of the Rings: The Two Towers* (2002). There's also a slight pause in the medium shot of the grass, before the god's feet enter the upper part of the frame, which gives the moment even more power.

the eyes of the audience as well as into the characters' eyes – become all the more powerful. It's the same tactic that was employed in Biblical movies of the 1950s and 1960s, which portrayed Christ as a silent figure, relying on the reactions of other characters to enhance the sense of the sacred.

The head of the Forest Spirit is the film's McGuffin – this is what Eboshi and Jigo (and the Emperor) are after. This tells you what kind of movie this is: it is no ordinary flick in which the McGuffin is a suitcase full of money, or a treasure map, or the secret plans for nuclear missile sites, or the blueprint of a time travelling machine, as in your average contemporary action-adventure movie. No, it's the head of a god that can grant immortality (however, there have been movie villains of course (it's always the villains) who've wanted to obtain the secrets of immortality – it's Lord Voldemort's ultimate aim in the *Harry Potter* series, for example, or Walter Donovan's goal in the third *Indiana Jones* flick).

THE NIGHTWALKER

The most miraculous sequence in *Princess Mononoke* is perhaps the Nightwalker scene, where the Forest God first appears as the Didarabotchi. It's just before dawn, and the Nightwalker is returning to the sacred centre of the forest (there is a full moon right behind it). The god is imagined as a giant creature of light. Moving very slowly and very gracefully, wading through the trees as if through a pool of green.[82] It's an image of a nature god, the embodiment of the forest and the night.

The arrival of the Nightwalker is signalled by the appearance of the *kodama* in their thousands – the little, white figures pop up in the trees. No one else witnesses this scene:

82 This is an image which recalls the appearance of the god Pan in *The Wind In the Willows* by Kenneth Grahame.

it is a secret contract between the filmmakers and the viewers, with the human and beast characters absent (Jigo and his cronies are somewhere in the distance, and spot the Nightwalker. There's a marvellous touch of strong gusts of wind blowing down from the circular gap in the trees, until it creates golden ripples in the pool). Only Ashitaka is there, but he is maybe fatally wounded or dead, lying half in the water (that's another stroke of genius in this magical movie – that San should ensure that the wounded boy is lying half in the lake. She also cuts a plant and posts it above his head, perhaps to act as a guide for the Forest God. But when the Forest God appears in his deer form, Ashitaka has now sunk below the water; he experiences a literal, uterine rebirth).

This is mind-blowing. The incredible Nightwalker sequence continues with the transformation of the giant god into the deer with the human face (which occurs at sunrise), which materializes on the island in the centre of the pool. The filmmakers have created an authentic sense of wonder and spirituality here, which's almost impossible to do (and with bits of painted plastic!). The number of *genuinely* religious or spiritual films is very, very small. You need a filmmaking team working at their very best with superlative material to be able to evoke this kind of heartfelt mysticism.

Hayao Miyazaki and his team pull it off by using every cinematic trick at their disposal – and one of the chief of these is the *absence* of sounds and only the softest of music cues. The Nightwalker sequence unfolds in near-silence: there are electronic choral effects, and very quiet sounds (such as water and wind).[83] The episode is lit with a golden, pink light (the light of dawn), which helps too, as does the slow, graceful movement of the Forest Spirit.

In *Princess Mononoke*, the bringing back to life of a character has an authentic emotion to it, which's usually lacking in similar scenes in movies (it's quite a common scene, and not

---

83 Silence is recurring aspect of Japanese animation – moments when nothing is being said, and there is no music or sound effects.

only in fantasy cinema). The filmmakers are somehow able to re-invest a resurrection scene with the spiritual feeling it deserves.

THE NARRATIVE SWITCH

Halfway through *Princess Mononoke* there is a complete switch in the narrative, but it's so deftly done you might not notice it first-time round (I didn't the first time I saw the 1997 movie). It occurs when Ashitaka has rescued San from the clutches of Eboshi and her chums in Irontown. This is one of the big set-pieces in *Princess Mononoke*, of course, involving numerous action beats, extras, and stupendous fights. With San now unconscious (Ashitaka stuns both Eboshi and San to end their fierce duel), the prince carries her out of the village, to the amazement of the onlookers (a brilliantly staged scene, worthy of Akira Kurosawa, and rightly extended beyond the requirements of the narrative). But not before one of the irate women has fired at Ashitaka and shot him in the chest (her husband was killed in the wolf attacks – the women in *Mononoke Hime* are certainly gutsy).[84] But the wound doesn't kill Ashitaka, however, and he is able to force open the enormous, wooden gate, and leave the village on the backs on the wolves.

Then comes the switch: San wakes, and Ashitaka falls off the galloping elk (Ashitaka takes a fall on his back onto boulders that would be very difficult to achieve in live-action – it would kill a stunt guy doing it for real).[85] On the ground, face-down, Ashitaka is now near-death, there's blood down his back and over Yakul – but San is now back on fighting form, and taking charge (including preventing her wolves from chewing Ashitaka's face off).

84 It's also unusual for a minor character to get to shoot the hero. And because it's a minor chara, the hero can't be vanquished (apart from all the other reasons).
85 Although Akira Kurosawa's *Ran* features some incredible horse falls.

The dramatic switch is complete, and it's *San* who's leading the action, making the decisions, and pushing the narrative forward. And I, for one, find San a very intriguing character, and an appealing one too: right from her first appearance, she is one of Hayao Miyazaki's great heroes: independent, strong, resourceful, brave, fierce. But also tender – and the compassion comes out in the following scenes, where San takes Ashitaka into the heart of the woods, where the Forest Spirit can heal him. Whenever San is in the foreground of *Princess Mononoke*, the film is even more engrossing – the prince is a fascinating hero, too, but doesn't have the same appeal as San. Partly because you don't know what feral wolf-girl San is going to do (whereas Ashitaka is one of those heroes who is always going to 'do the right thing').

Some of the most striking scenes in *Princess Mononoke* occur next, exquisitely staged: the way that San leads Yakul into the clear water of the forest glade,[86] and pulls the unconscious Ashitaka off the animal, floating him to the island at the centre (where two trees grow). And the way that she doesn't drag Ashitaka out of the water, onto the bank, as one might expect, but leaves him partially in the water. It's details such as this that help to make Hayao Miyazaki's films far beyond your average action-adventure (down to the detail of the forest spirits appearing around the plant that San cuts, as if puzzled by what she's done – cutting a plant to heal a human).

86 The harness is taken off the beast, and later it's ridden without the harness.

WOMEN AND SEX

There is more cleavage[87] in *Princess Mononoke* than in any other Hayao Miyazaki movie: the women who work in the forge in Tatarba are former prostitutes that Eboshi has rescued from brothels.[88] The kimonos they wear are left open at the neck, emphasizing their breasts (they also go about in bare feet, and headscarves).

The eroticization of the women who work in Tatarba is part of the proto-feminism of the world of *Princess Mononoke*:[89] the women in Tatarba are more assertive and confident than the men; the ruler of Tatarba is a woman; Toki at Irontown stands up to Gonza and the other men; a woman fires a rifle at a man with intent to kill him (and she shoots him in the back); the witch doctor of the Emishi is an old woman (called Hii-sama), and the elders of the Emishi defer to her; and the wolf family is ruled by women – San and Moro. In 1997, Hayao Miyazaki explained some of his thinking:

> It's not that I wanted to make it modern. It's just that depicting Tatara Ba under the rule of men would be boring. And if I made the boss of Tatara Ba a man, he would be a manager, not a revolutionary. If it's a woman, she becomes a revolutionary, even if she is doing the same thing. So I didn't make them women who have to be protected by men, or women in their families. I intentionally cut them off (from such things).

The feminism and pro-women angle of the 1997 Japanese film is depicted strongly in the first scene at Tatarba, when Ashitaka arrives in a boat with the two soldiers he's saved. While Kohroku tells everyone that Ashitaka has saved them, and should be thanked, Gonza (captain of the guard),

87 And more nudity – even Ashitaka goes nearly naked at one point (when crossing a river).
88 The talk of brothels and prostitution puts *Princess Mononoke* in a very different place from a typical children's animated movie.
89 That Irontown is run by women is historically inaccurate, Miyazaki acknowledged, but he did that for several reasons. He also argued that before the modern period, women were strong, 'had many rights, and were very active' (TP, 84).

soon arrives to take charge. The distrust of outsiders and the way the scene is staged is thus far expected in the adventure genre. But it's rapidly subverted when the wonderful character Toki appears. She's a young, formidable presence in a red kimono, who first lays into her hapless husband Kohroku for getting wounded so he won't be any use at work. And when Gonza tries to rein Toki in, she rounds on him too (and all this is in front of everybody).

Toki standing up to Gonza and dressing him down with some choice remarks is a humorous but also important subversion of the genre. Tatarba, it seems, isn't much of a patriarchal system: at the end of the scene Toki talks with Eboshi, who watches from up the slope. Ashitaka is an observer in all this, but the introduction of Eboshi here makes it clear who is in charge (only now is Eboshi revealed as the leader of her people, although she was introduced earlier, in the caravan attack scene, and was in charge of that party).

The subversion of the action-adventure genre, the switching of gender roles, and the reversal of expectations continues throughout the 1997 film: it's Toki and her women friends who do much of the important work at the ironworks in Tatarba; it's Toki and the women who lead the defence of Tatarba; it's Toki and the women who repel the emissaries of Lord Asano.[90]

And right away there's an erotic flirtation between Ashitaka and the womenfolk of Tatarba. As soon as Toki meets him by the lake, she wonders if he's handsome, and of course she thinks he's gorgeous. The flirtation is light-hearted, but Ashitaka stands out amongst the other men as a distinctly attractive prospect. They have him in their sights: he is young, handsome, brave, a warrior, seems to be unattached, and someone new. And the women waste no time in making Ashitaka know that (there's more erotic banter in *Princess Mononoke* than in any other Miyazaki movie).

90 Though the men resent the gender reversal, and grumble that Eboshi has spoilt the women.

Hayao Miyazaki's films don't show sex, but there is a clear stand-in for a sex scene that's very obvious and bawdy. On his way back from Eboshi demonstrating the lepers who are manufacturing rifles for her, Ashitaka passes the forge, where the women are singing as they operate the bellows for the furnace by pressing down in rows of four on an enormous, wooden contraption.

So when Ashitaka shows up and decides to try his hand (or rather his legs) at the women's work, the women gather round to watch. It's a sex scene in all but name – the heat, the rhythmic movement, the squeak of the wood, the firelight, the nighttime setting, the bare feet and partially naked breasts, the giggling and laughing of the women (even down to the way that Ashitaka is a little too eager at first, and the women talk about him keeping up that rapid pace).

Yet despite all of the feminism on display in *Princess Mononoke*, and the powerful character of San, it is also very much a boy's movie, with warriors, sword fights, battles, and tons of action.

AKIRA KUROSAWA AND HAYAO MIYAZAKI

Mononoke Hime is Hayao Miyazaki's Akira Kurosawa movie: in it Miyazaki and the finest team of animators in the world consciously rework and pay *hommage* to some classic scenes from Kurosawa's cinema: sword fights, arrows fired from galloping horses, samurai attacking peasants, sieges of castles, and pitched battles, involving explosions, sword fights, fire, smoke, and fluttering flags and standards. Or simply riders galloping in misty mountains. Soldiers carrying banners (a Kurosawa favourite). Rain. Forests. Wooden forts.[91] And yet more mist (the amount of smoke and mist and atmospheric effects provided by the special effects department in *Princess Mononoke* is marked, and a striking development from Miyazaki's previous movies, which had already employed clouds like no other filmmaker. Nearly every long shot in *Princess Mononoke* has cloud, mist, fog or smoke effects added to it. And from *Princess Mononoke* onwards, Miyazaki would utilize rain and wind just as much as Kurosawa, who is well-known for it).[92]

It's easy to discern in *Princess Mononoke* elements from Akira Kurosawa's cinema such as *The Seven Samurai, Throne of Blood, Yojimbo* and *The Hidden Fortress.* Like Kurosawa's cinema, *Princess Mononoke* is storytelling on a big canvas, with the filmmakers creating scenes with a boldness and energy that are difficult to sustain (no wonder Hayao Miyazaki said he was exhausted after making *Princess Mononoke*. Ironically, *Princess Mononoke* may have been easier to shoot in live-action,[93] though that would have been very tough too).

If you like *Princess Mononoke*, I'd recommend any of Akira Kurosawa's samurai and historical movies, such as *The Seven Samurai, Sanjuro, Yojimbo, The Hidden Fortress, Throne of Blood,* and the later, colossal epics: *Kagemusha* and *Ran.* Kurosawa's 1985 adaption of *King Lear, Ran*, contains two battles which rank among the greatest ever filmed, conflicts so extraordinary and so desperately tragic you can't

91 In this mediæval world, the communities are fortified – the Emishi village has look-out towers and walls, and Irontown resembles a military fort more than a factory for extracting iron ore. It has a heavy gate that takes ten men to open, and the surrounding area has been fitted with pointed wooden stakes to repel invaders.

92 The production crew recalled how Akira Kurosawa loved rain effects; when the production manager wondered if three water pump trucks would be enough for *The Seven Samurai*, the director said double it. Kurosawa seems to have made rain one of his trademarks early on in his career, in films such as *Rashomon.* And wind, too: there are many images of sand and dust blowing around. And streams and water (the sound of water runs underneath many scenes).

93 Except for the finale, with all of those visual effects.

believe they were produced.[94]

For Hayao Miyazaki, you only need to see a few shots from a really good movie to know it's really good: from just a few shots you can discern

> the creator's philosophy, talents, resolve and character. In other words, no matter where you cut the film, you know right away whether you have hit the jackpot or not. (SP, 158)

When Hayao Miyazaki reviewed *Ikiru*, one of Akira Kurosawa's masterpieces, he talked about just one single shot in a scene which impressed him, that when he saw the scene (involving the protagonist stamping a mountain of documents), he knew that *Ikiru* 'was a film that had to be viewed with utmost respect', a movie that a filmmaker makes rarely in their career (SP, 159). The sadness of the man going through the routine of his daily work, the repetitiveness and dullness of it, was captured by Kurosawa:

> the man's dutiful, sad performance of his work is the sadness that we have in our own lives. Our lives do not take on meaning because of something we have accomplished. (SP, 160)

In taking on Akira Kurosawa in *Princess Mononoke*, Hayao Miyazaki and his team were tackling the greatest Japanese filmmaker, and you can only do that if you're feeling mighty confident. You wouldn't expect a filmmaker to mount a full-blooded, Kurosawa-style epic as their first movie, for instance (nobody ever has). However, by the time of his

---

94 The first thing to say about *Ran* is the sheer scale of the filmmaking enterprise, the scope of the battles, the vastness of the vision, the orchestration of the many levels (war, political struggle, familial strife, kingship, madness, and the natural world). If there's any doubt that a man in his mid-70s can still direct as well as a younger man, the battle sequences in *Ran* eradicates it. Not only can Akira Kurosawa still orchestrate hundreds of extras, horses and weapons, not only can he stage stunts and action, he can also do it better than anyone else. There's unequalled carnage on screen, and the image of the king sitting cross-legged on the floor of the top room of his castle in a catatonic state while smoke and flames streak through the air behind him is absolutely unforgettable.

second film (*Nausicaä of the Valley of the Wind*), Miyazaki was already staging action and narrative on an enormous canvas.

But *Princess Mononoke* does full justice to Akira Kurosawa's cinema, and the 1997 movie also understands the poetry of Kurosawa's films, the nature mysticism, the psychological and emotional drama, and the very important moral and ethical elements. Although Kurosawa's associated with *chambara*, sword-play, mediæval and 16th century historical epics, Toshio Mifune, and all the rest, those other elements are actually more significant in many respects – the nature mysticism and adventure and companionship in the astonishing and magical *Dersu Uzala*, for example, or friendship against all the odds in *The Hidden Fortress,* or the themes of morality and psychology in *Ikiru* or *The Seven Samurai.*

The amount of blood and bloodshed in *Princess Mononoke* is striking (and throughout *animé*): Hayao Miyazaki's movies have never shied away from portraying violence, and they are often more violent than viewers expect, not least because they are animation, which's often thought to be family-oriented, toned-down fare (the Walt Disney Studios, for instance, is very reluctant to show blood, and presents death on screen very carefully.) However, the bloodshed and graphic violence in Japanese *manga* are part of a cultural tradition (such as in *kabuki* theatre) which goes back 100s of years.

But in *Princess Mononoke* the body count and on-screen violence is severer than usual in a Hayao Miyazaki movie (or it's more in close-up now): there are quite a few decapitations, samurai being blown to bits by gunfire, arms being chopped off, people being stabbed and battered, and grave pits with lines of corpses (not only dead humans, but slain boars too).[95]

There's a lot of blood being sloshed around in *Princess Mononoke* too: Moro the wolf, Okkoto the boar, Ashitaka, San, and many other main characters have blood on them (and some, such as the wolf and the boar, have multiple, bleeding

95 The gravepits are disturbing images, with many modern affinities such as world wars.

wounds, the blood gushing everywhere). And San is so memorably introduced with blood on her face – a highly unusual character introduction (which you will *never* see in a Disney movie).

The violence in *Princess Mononoke* is introduced early on – when Ashitaka comes across a village under attack from Lord Asano's samurai, he rips off a guy's arms and pins them to a tree with an arrow, and decapitates another samurai on horseback.[96] From then on, the audience is going to realize they are not watching your usual action-adventure animated movie (the mad boar Nago in the opening scene has already suggested that too).

Violence is part of being human, Hayao Miyazaki insisted, and exists in children too. They may not be able to express it, but inside even gentle children 'there is an accumulation of violence and hatred in a form that they cannot control – that is the condition of our current age' (TP, 89). *Mononoke* was thus partly about the issue of whether people can control the hatred and violence inside them and dissolve it (TP, 90).

The violence I would align with the cinema of Akira Kurosawa again – Kurosawa, aside from being a genius at portraying violence and conflict, was right to portray it because his movies were evoking violent historical times. In those days, a samurai fight could be a bloody affair (although Kurosawa was happy to use violence excessively when employed in a symbolic fashion, too – *viz.*, Washizu's death by a thousand arrows in *Throne of Blood*, a much-copied demise).

In a 1985 article, Hayao Miyazaki was critical of Akira Kurosawa's stylizations of battles:[97] in *Kagemusha*, Miyazaki pointed out that the troops were set out in groups, and they charged like unified cavalry. In reality, Miyazaki reckoned that the soldiers would've all charged together (SP, 133). Also, most battles tended to be depicted in big, wide-open spaces,

96 Notice that it's the samurai who are often the targets of Ashitaka's vehemence.
97 Also, Miyazaki reckoned that the short Japanese horses wouldn't have been able to support samurai in full armour charging at speed (and anyway, there weren't grassy plains like in Europe).

not in rice fields, along footpaths, or in the undergrowth: 'won't someone make period films that more carefully depict scenes with these kinds of details?' Miyazaki asked (ibid.). And he proceeded to do just that, twelve years later, in *Mononoke Hime*.

Hayao Miyazaki was critical of the historical accuracy of the period movies of Akira Kurosawa: altho' he loved *The Seven Samurai*, the world of samurai and peasants (or farmers) wasn't how Japan was[98] (but the vision of Japan in Kurosawa's movies was influential, and cast a spell on everyone). Rather, the samurai and peasants view of history reflected the postwar period of the 1940s and the 1950s, with the samurai and peasants reflecting aspects of the Japanese psyche after its defeat and rebuilding.[99]

Hayao Miyazaki wanted to move away from the 'samurai and peasants' view of history of period films like *The Seven Samurai* – hence the decision to focus on iron-makers in the mountains[100] (and those iron-workers are definitely armed). The aim was to ignore the capital for once (where most historical movies tended to be set), and explore the marginal areas, the plains, and other classes of people than the usual samurai, peasants and merchants. (Ashitaka takes a dim view of samurai – notice that the people he kills, whether meaning to or not, are samurai and professional soldiers. This departs significantly from the usual venerated treatment of samurai in *manga* and *animé*).

The battles in *Princess Mononoke* run from the epic vista to the swift, fierce hand-to-hand fight (both reveal the influence of Akira Kurosawa). The rapidity of the sword fights and sword-and-dagger duels is lightning-swift (the film-makers seems to have been studying Hong Kong martial arts

98 'In historical Japan there were no such samurai and peasants' (TP, 80).
99 The idea that the farmers don't have weapons, and rely on the samurai to protect them isn't totally inaccurate in *The Seven Samurai*. Actually, everybody was armed, as historians have attested (including into the Edo period – with simple swords, and also with rifles).
100 And to draw on the legends of mountain people having burn marks, or one eye, or lost limbs.

movies for some of the moves, along with everyone else who makes action flicks). All in all, the staging of the action in *Princess Mononoke* is a big step-up from the knock-about humour of *Porco Rosso* or the sometimes vaguer conflicts of *Laputa: Castle In the Sky.*

And the action in *Princess Mononoke* is as accomplished as the best martial arts movies – the duel between Ashitaka and the four samurai pursing him from Irontown, for instance, is a stunning example of using space and distance and speed and camera angles and point-of-view shots. If only all action movies were this good.

Princess Mononoke is Hayao Miyazaki's Akira Kurosawa epic, yes, but it's also his *Tarzan* and *Jungle Book* movie, an action-adventure picture with the kind of characters and action that you can find in the fiction of Edgar Rice Burroughs, Jules Verne, H.G. Wells, Mark Twain and Rudyard Kipling (and thousands of comicbooks going back to the early days of magazine publishing for young people in the first part of the 20th century).

Although *Princess Mononoke* might be the only Hayao Miyazaki movie *not* featuring flying sequences, there is plenty of action up in the air, with characters leaping about – and of course much of the climactic sequence takes place in the sky, as the Nightwalker searches for its head.

THE FINALE

The climax of *Princess Mononoke* is unbelievably spectacular. You know it's going to be, when the rest of the movie is so good: you know the filmmakers are going to top everything that's already appeared. And they do. The filmmakers are throwing everything they can think of into the mix: there are incredible scenes of mass battles, some intricately intercut as flashbacks with the scenes set in the present (when Ashitaka asks the haunted soldier crouched by the graves what happened, for instance). Scenes of the boars charging,[101] with San on a wolf riding between them. Explosions and fire and smoke from mines and grenades. And deeply moving scenes after the battle, as Ashitaka explores the carnage. *Princess Mononoke* is a movie that depicts the consequences of war and the costs of violence, as in the rest of Miyazaki's cinema.

It's intriguing that the filmmakers leave Ashitaka out of the big battle towards the end of the second act of the movie: Ashitaka is riding through wind and rain as the storm breaks and the battle commences (he's heading for Irontown). But only after he's reached Irontown over the river (at some peril, avoiding soldiers, samurai and arrows – no A to B trip is easy in an action-adventure movie), and spoken to the women on the battlements, does he find out what's happening.

That's typical of Hayao Miyazaki, however: he splits the hero into two – a boy and a girl – then he places the *girl* in the centre of the battles, and has the *boy* running here and there, trying to catch up, and arriving too late! (Ashitaka continues his role as peace mediator).

At this point, the 1997 movie takes all sorts of interesting twists and turns – Hayao Miyazaki-sama and his team do everything you'd expect in an action-adventure picture – such as plenty of action, for a start, but also plenty of obstacles for the heroes, plenty of snakepit situations, plenty of cliff-hangers, and quieter interludes (though, thankfully, not the wisecracks and one-liners and silly bits of humour of too many Hollywood flicks).

Hayao Miyazaki and his animation house do all of that, and *then some*. But they also *do more*: they keep the action pinned to the major themes of the movie, which's vital; it's not simply action for the sake of it, action emptied of purpose or value or consequence. And finally they add quirky, unusual turns to the narrative.

One of the most interesting scenes in the *tour-de-force*

101 These scenes look back to the *ohmu* going into battle in *Nausicaä.*

finale of *Princess Mononoke*, for example, takes place when all of the major characters arrive at the forest glade (and what a collection of characters they are – three gods, no less, plus a cursed hero, a wolf princess, wolves, cynical treasure hunters, soldiers, and a business woman who's intent on killing a god).

Dramatically, this sequence of scenes needs to do many things, including:

(1) to bring the action to a satisfying climax,

(2) to play out many of the characters' goals,

(3) to resolve many conflicts between the groups of characters,

(4) to explore the themes of the film, and

(5) to deliver entertaining cinema.

And it does all of that, but it does it all in Hayao Miyazaki's highly individual way. How many filmmakers, for example, would choose to play out some of the action *inside* the body of a god? But Miyazaki and his team do just that when they have San being absorbed into Okkoto's body (now he's nearly all demon), and being smothered by those writhing, red, squishy, worm-like thingies.

Ashitaka acts of course like the prince or hero of fairy tales, and dives into the writhing mass of scarlet tendrils, to save his wolf princess. The imagery alone is just astounding, but the dramatic moves that *Princess Mononoke* takes continually surprise the audience. Ashitaka, for instance, is unsuccessful, and is ejected far out of the mouth of the beast, to fall into the lake, sinking, unconscious (throwing your hero into water out cold is another classic gag in the action-adventure genre).[102]

In the midst of all this thrilling drama, the filmmakers are also orchestrating other elements, such as the reappearance of the Forest Spirit, and Eboshi and Jigo waiting for their chance to kill it.[103] There's so much going on, but the climax of

102 So the once-healing water becomes a threat and potentially a grave.

103 There's an *hommage* to this moment in the 2012 *Snow White and the Huntsman.*

Princess Mononoke never feels rushed or contrived or cheated or silly. It has a dramatic and visual logic, features truly extraordinary imagery and details, and possesses a momentum that works like gangbusters (the editing, for instance, is exquisitely pin-sharp).[104]

How delightful, for instance, is the way that San is finally rescued – by Moro speaking to Ashitaka in his mind, as he floats underwater unconscious (*do you want to save the girl you love?* asks the wolf-god – well, what's a hero gonna do?!). That works because the movie has already shown how Ashitaka is telepathically linked to San and the wolves (but it's still a struggle for him to extricate San from the crazed Okkoto. It's obstacle, obstacle, obstacle for heroes – especially in the third/ fourth act).

The killing-the-god scene follows on from Ashitaka rescuing San (which he hurries to do just before the Forest Spirit blesses the boar-god with death). Multiple events play out nearly simultaneously – Eboshi has already fired a bullet thru the head of the Forest Spirit as it paces across the pool (and right in front of the re-surfaced and astonished Ashitaka). The god simply steps back onto the water[105] and continues to walk. (There's another sword-vs-gun moment here, when Ashitaka throws his blade into Eboshi's rifle).

The second time occurs as the Forest Spirit is transforming into the Nightwalker. Eboshi foolishly boasts to the men first (where fearlessness becomes hubris) – only to find her weapon sprouting vegetation – a brilliant touch (nature – life – is unstoppable). Orchestrating this headlong rush of events, getting the pacing, the parallel action, and the storytelling just right, is where a good film editor really earns their fee (and Takeshi Seyama is the best there is). This is textbook filmmaking for narrative logic, for absolutely masterful interlocking of events – and it's aided by compulsively

104 It's worth recalling that Miyazaki has the editor credit on *Princess Mononoke*, along with the incredible Takeshi Seyama.

105 Notice how the sound effects of water splashing are for Ashitaka, but the god makes no sound at all.

mesmeric, sensual and eccentric images, music and sounds.

But no, it's not over yet (though the preceding act would be enough for many a movie): the biggest, wildest scenes in *Princess Mononoke* are still to come: out burst the special effects, costing hundreds of thousands of Yen per minute, as the Forest Spirit mutates into a purple, blue and black giant searching for its head with enormous, gloopy blobs spreading thru the forest, into the lake, over the mountains. Blobs, tendrils of energy, colours, decaying trees and grass, characters fleeing in every direction – the imagery floods the screen.

You'd think that the dark goo issuing from the headless Forest Spirit would be a positive life-force – but it makes thematic sense as well as dramatic sense that the energies inside the Shishigami should be so powerful that it's death for a human who touches them. Because we are dealing with massive elemental powers here – the power of nature itself.

This section of *Princess Mononoke* is completely crazy, with the action now frantic and broad (though the human-scale dramas are still being played out fiercely back down on the ground – for instance, the scene on the island, where San is determined to finish off Eboshi, and Ashitaka does all he can to dissuade her. We are in a mythic zone now: when San stabs Ashitaka in the chest (with Kaya's gift knife), it has no effect (because the cursemark has spread further). They embrace).

The climax of *Princess Mononoke* is absolutely apocalyptic – it has everything except distant atomic explosions over Tokyo like so many Japanese *animé* (actually, there are scenes of debris and hurricane winds reminiscent of nuclear bombs, when the Forest Spirit topples into the lake. Epic scenes of devastation are one of Hayao Miyazaki's specialties – and nobody can smash stuff to bits like Japanese animators). Giant hands flying over trees, a mass of immense hands on elastic arms diving into the trees from far above, a flood of dark purple lava smothering the mountains and flowing everywhere, characters dodging out-lying tendrils speeding towards them (there are numerous split second escapes), San and Ashitaka hurtling around on wolfback, Jigo, Gonza & co. hurrying off with the Forest Spirit's head in a metal box, the frantic exodus from Irontown, the village being demolished – the action is breakneck.

It's quite right that the Forest Spirit appears to die *after* it's recovered its head. Many storytellers and filmmakers might move from that point to the happy ending, with the land reborn. No. It makes sense that after the god has found its head, it should topple into the lake (exactly at sunrise).[106] That adds a suitably jumbo-sized piece of action to close this so-spectacular part of *Princess Mononoke*, but the dramatic function is clear: the Forest Spirit's collapse seems to destroy plenty of the landscape around it, but most of the destruction is directed at Irontown (witness the shot of the remains of Irontown flying off into the mountains – as if it's the timber returning to its origins, in the trees).[107]

Only *after* Irontown has been (partially) demolished does the rejuvenation of the earth begin. The *ecological* theme (or message) of *Princess Mononoke* seems clear at this point: humans can begin again, they can have a second chance, but they'd better build something *in tune* with nature, rather than set against it. As Ashitaka states, the Forest Spirit isn't dead, it isn't all over, as San worries, because the Forest Spirit is all around, is life itself. (That piece of dialogue is what I would call 'on the nail', very blunt; but it's only stated once; in a Hollywood flick, it would be rammed home with a sledgehammer).

And when the rebirth occurs, rightly held for some moments in the extreme long shot of the mountains and the lake, and Joe Hisaishi's piano music plays (Hisaishi is also credited as pianist), it is a deeply moving and very positive

106 Jigo is banking on the Nightwalker dying at daybreak.
107 The shot is a call-back to *Totoro*.

ending. It is the right ending, and it is a happy ending, and it comes out of everything that has gone on before. It has the satisfying logic of a fairy tale, as well as the beauty and poetry of a romance from the Middle Ages.

THE ENDING

The ending of *Princess Mononoke* is not about resolving every element in the movie and rounding it all off with a happy ending, as Hayao Miyazaki insisted in his 1995 memo:

> *Princess Mononoke* does not purport to solve the problems of the entire world. The battle between rampaging forest gods and humanity cannot end well; there can be no happy ending. Yet, even amid the hatred and slaughter, there are things worthy of life. It is possible for wonderful encounters to occur and for beautiful things to exist. (SP, 274)

The *dénouement* of *Princess Mononoke* quite rightly doesn't go on and on as it so often does in American or European movies of this kind: rather, the 1997 film makes all of the pertinent points with a series of brief visits to each of the major characters: the most important scene is the two-hander between Ashitaka[108] and Mononoke, where he says he will help build a new Tatarba, and San tells him she will return to the forest because she can't forgive humans for what they've done.[109] But Ashitaka promises to visit San in the forest, and she smiles and agrees. A kiss isn't necessary here, after all they've been through.

'I have no way of replying to children who... ask why Ashitaka can control his hatred when they are unable to control theirs. That is the very reason I wanted to make this

108 We can see that the cursemark is diminished, and presumably halted.
109 'The problem presented to me was whether San's hatred of humanity could be softened by Ashitaka's love' (TP, 83).

film' (TP, 84). 'The main reason I made this film is because I felt children in Japan harbor doubts as to why they need to live' (TP, 79).

The imagery of shoots, plants and flowers growing rapidly is spiritual – authentically, properly spiritual. It really is one of the most impressive and convincing scenes of rebirth in cinema. The waves of green, and deeper greens, and then deeper greens still, are highly poetic. And when the film cuts to San and Ashitaka hugging each other on the ground in the long grass, it is the greenest, juiciest grass in movies.[110]

Princess Mononoke then cuts to the other main players: (1) Eboshi, sitting in the ruins of Tatarba, surrounded by her people, vowing to build a new and better town, and wanting to thank Ashitaka; (2) Jigo and an aide on the rock, with Jigo providing a little comic relief after all the climactic scenes, and finally (3) to the sacred centre of the film, the pool and glade.

The way Eboshi is sitting in a quiet, tired manner, and her attitude, suggests that she is humbled by what's happened. She realizes that San and the wolves helped to save them. It's not certain here if Eboshi is going to change her ways (she's still going to build a new town, which will presumably have to have some kind of industrial labour at the heart of it), but maybe she's realized that San and her wolf gods and the other animal gods had some good reasons for doing what they did.

Hayao Miyazaki knew that there were aspects of *Mononoke Hime* which weren't wrapped up neatly, that the movie contains holes, that he departed consciously from narrative formulas (TP, 80, 106). Elements were withheld which one might expect to be there (particularly in relation to Ashitaka's characterization, and his suffering).

There isn't a happy ending for the conflict between

110 And if there's one thing that Studio Ghibli can do, it is beautiful trees, flowers, plants, fields and grass. They have made reproducing the beauty of nature central to their work.

humanity and the gods, Hayao Miyazaki wrote in his proposal for the 1997 film: it is always an uneasy, ambiguous relationship: gods will never do exactly what humans want them to, and vice versa.

But the final image of *Princess Mononoke* is quite rightly the spiritual core of the piece, the lake and glade: the camera tilts down to reveal that it's still devastated but on the way to being renewed: there are new shoots growing out of the soil, and the fallen trees are sprouting new branches. But the clincher, of course, is the re-appearance of the little *kodama* – a single one, seen in long shot near the clear water, which materializes and rattles its head.[111]

And that, folks, is the last image of one of the most truly mind-bogglingly beautiful movies ever made.

111 The renewal of a land has been done in movies before, but rarely as convincing on a dramatic as well as a thematic level as in *Princess Mononoke*. The obvious counterpart in animation is *Bambi*, following the forest fire.

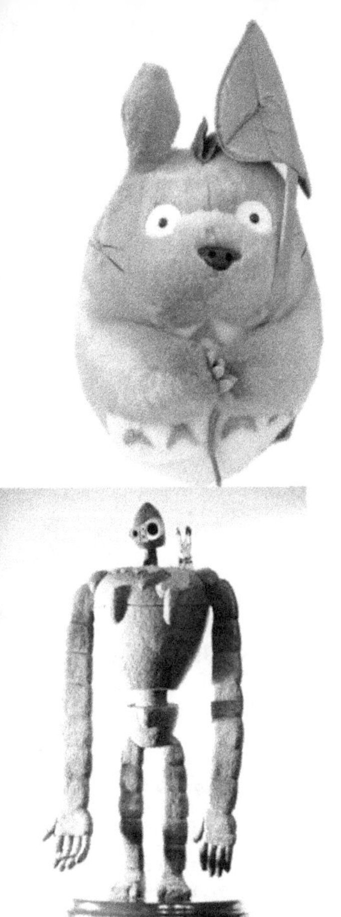

Some merchandize based on Studio Ghibli's films

RESOURCES

WEBSITES

One of the best independent sources on the internet for Hayao Miyazaki information is: nausicaa.net.

For Miyazaki-related information this is the place to start. It is a well-designed and easy to use website.

Also the Studio Ghibli websites:

onlineghibli.com, ghibli.jp and Ghibliworld.com.

The Disney sites have information on Miyazaki (such as disney.go.com). Buena Vista (Disney's distribution network) distributes Ghibli's movies in many Western territories.

Toei Animation for *Little Norse Prince* and others:

corp.toei-anim.co.jp.

Toei is one of the largest animation companies in Japan.

The Lupin III network: lupin-3rd.net. This includes info on the whole Lupin III franchise, as well as *The Castle of Cagliostro.*

And for composer Joe Hisaishi: joehisaishi.com. Hisaishi has composed the scores for most of Miyazaki's movies.

I would also recommend: Anime News Network

animenewsnetwork.com

It is excellent, and the first stop for any online research on *animé*. Anime News Network has the fullest credits on the web for animation, and each entry is linked, so you can follow your favourite actors, directors, producers and artists, across numerous shows.

Also: Gilles Poitras's site: koyagi.com.

Fred L. Schodt's site: jai2.com.

Otaku News: otakunews.com.

Midnight Eye (for Japanese cinema): midnighteyec.com.

There are fan sites, of course.

BOOKS

Among books in English, the collection of Miyazaki-san's writing, *Starting Point, 1979-1996,* is a must-have. It contains numerous articles and interviews with Miyazaki. This is an indispensable book that should've been published twenty years ago! If you are a Miyazaki fan, you will find much to enjoy in *Starting Point.* It includes his thoughts on his own movies, as well as the ones he reveres. It also gives you an insight into Miyazaki's background, his politics, his philosophies and the influences that helped to form his animation. The follow-up, *Turning-Point*, brought the selection of pieces up-to-date (to 2008).

Helen McCarthy's book *Hayao Miyazaki: Master of Japanese Animation* (1999, revised 2002) is essential reading. It was the first major study of Miyazaki, by one of the experts in *animé* studies. All of McCarthy's books on *manga* and *animé* are first-rate, and worth tracking down. Like Fred Schodt, Gilles Poitras and others, McCarthy knows *manga* and *animé* inside-out.

Dan Cavallaro's *The Animé Art of Hayao Miyazaki* is superb. Cavallaro offers many intriguing ways of approaching Miyazaki. For the illustrations alone this is worth reading. Colin Odell and Michelle Le Blanc's study of Studio Ghibli is useful, taking in Isao Takahata's work as well as that of his key collaborator, Miyazaki.

Andrew Osmond's exploration of *Spirited Away* is about the only study of this movie in book form in English. Osmond's text explores the ways in which the project developed.

The above books are some of the main studies of Hayao Miyazaki: compared to, say, Walt Disney and Alfred Hitchcock, who have stacks of books written about them, there is very, very little on Miyazaki in English.

Books by Frederik Schodt, Helen McCarthy, Trish Ledoux, Patrick Drazen, Fred Patten, Jonathan Clements, Simon Richmond, Antonia Levi, Susan Napier, Jason Thompson and Gilles Poitras are standard works. But apart from those key authors, there is surprisingly little available on *animé* in English.

And most film critics tend to focus on characters, stories, and the biographies of the filmmakers. So many books on *animé* simply tell us the stories. Very few critics grapple with the industrial, social and cultural aspects of *animé* (and even less with theory and philosophy). Which's why critics such as

Fred Schodt and Helen McCarthy are so important, because they address issues such as the modes of production, the audience and the market, and social-cultural contexts.

The single most useful book on *animé* is *The Animé Encyclopedia* (2001/ 2006/ 2015) by Jonathan Clements and Helen McCarthy. If you buy one book on Japanese animation, get this one. *The Animé Encyclopedia* provides entries on pretty much every important *animé* show, OAV and movie to come out of the Japanese animation industry, as well as numerous minor shows and oddities. This is the equivalent of a Leonard Maltin/ *Time Out/ Virgin/ Oxford/ Variety* guide to cinema. Clements and McCarthy are *animé* experts as well as fans (I would also recommend any of Clements' other books, including his entertaining accounts of working in the *animé* business in translation and dubbing, *Schoolgirl Milky Crisis*).

All of Helen McCarthy's books have become standard works: *Anime! A Beginner's Guide To Japanese Animation*, *The Animé Movie Guide*, *The Erotic Animé Movie Guide*, *500 Manga Heroes & Villains* and *500 Essential Anime Movies* (some of these were co-authored with Jonathan Clements). They contain facts, credits and background to *animé* and *manga* which will greatly enhance your studies (and enjoyment) of Japanese comics and cartoons.

Fred Schodt is one of the most valuable commentators on Japanese *animé* and *manga* in the West. His pioneering study of *manga*, *Manga! Manga! The World of Japanese Magazines*, is a marvellous book. Before it, there was virtually nothing. Because of the huge crossover between *manga* and *animé*, many of the chapters on *manga* in Schodt's studies also apply to *animé*. Schodt also offers one of the fullest and most detailed accounts of the history of *manga* and visual art in Japan. (*Manga! Manga!* also includes samples from some famous *manga*, including *Barefoot Gen* and *The Rose of Versailles,* and the illustrations – from the history of Japanese art as well as from *manga* – are stunning).

Fred Schodt's follow-up, *Dreamland Japan: Writings On Modern Manga*, is equally riveting. It includes a huge number of illuminating studies of individual artists and their works (with illustrations), as well as another history of *manga*. *Dreamland Japan* is also probably the finest, most intelligent and best-informed analysis of the *manga* market in both Japan and overseas. As well as Osamu Tezuka, Frederik Schodt also discusses Hayao Miyazaki, the relation of *manga* to *animé*, artistic styles, Japanese publishers, and the big *manga* magazines. It enhances Schodt's books that he has also interviewed many of the chief artists of *manga*, including the 'god of manga' himself, Osamu Tezuka.

Trish Ledoux and Doug Ranney edited an early guide to *animé*, *The Complete Anime Guide*, that is now a standard work. It is packed with fascinating snippets, as well as hard information, credits, etc. The companion volume, *Anime Interviews*, culled from *Animerica* magazine, is wonderful, featuring many of the key practitioners in animation (such as Masamune Shirow, Shoji Kawamori, Mamoru Oshii, Leiji Matsumoto, Rumiko Takahashi and Hayao Miyazaki).

Gilles Poitras has produced a number of works on *animé*, including *The Animé Companion* and *Animé Essentials*. Poitras offers vital links between Japanese animation and Japanese culture and society. There are objects, gestures, words and customs in *animé* that often surprise or bemuse Western viewers: Poitras' books help to explain them all. You will find yourself recognizing all sorts of elements in *animé* that Poitras includes in his books (which contain many illustrations).

Antonia Levi's *Samurai From Outer Space* is stuffed with information on Japanese society as well as Japanese animation. Clearly written and with an appealing sense of humour, Levi's book is a lesser-known but invaluable work. *Samurai From Outer Space* discusses all of the celebrated *animé* shows that've made the leap across the Pacific to the Western world. Published in 1996, you wish that Levi (like many other authors whose books came out in the 1990s), was able to update them. Many great shows have been released since 1996!

Simon Richmond's *The Rough Guide To Anime* is a superb general introduction to the wild world of *animé*. Like other *Rough Guides*, it selects fifty must-see TV shows and movies, plus providing discussions of related topics like *manga*, adaptions of *animé*, and a history of animation.

Jason Yadao's *The Rough Guide To Manga* is a companion guide to the *Rough Guide To Animé*. It has the same format and is a terrific general introduction to the world of Japanese comics. Yadao's enthusiasm is infectious: you will want to hunt out many of his recommendations. Both *Rough Guides* were published in the 2000s, so they're able to include recent classics like *Fullmetal Alchemist, Cowboy Bebop, Love Hina* and the masterpieces of Satoshi Kon.

Manga: The Complete Guide (Jason Thompson and others)

is another illuminating book, packed with short reviews and longer pieces on topics like games, sci-fi, martial arts, sport, religion, crime, *mecha, shojo*, and *yaoi*.

Manga Impact! from Phaidon is an entertaining survey of Japanese animation, with a format focussing on characters and personnel. *Manga Impact!* has short text entries, but features numerous, wonderful illustrations in colour.

Zettai! Anime Classics is another of those books that looks at 100 classic movies: Brian Camp and Julie Davis spend more time, however, on each of the familiar masterpieces of Japanese animation, exploring the films, OAVs and TV shows in much more detail than the usual single paragraph review.

Susan Napier's *Anime: From Akira To Princess Mononoke* is much more theoretical, and somewhat dry. (If you are familiar with the theoretical approaches to Western animation (see the studies noted below), you will find nothing new in Western authors exploring Japanese animation from a theoretical or philosophical point-of-view).

On animation in general, I would recommend the following studies: P. Wells' *Understanding Animation*; E. Smoodin's *Animating Culture: Hollywood Cartoons From the Sound Era*; Leonard Maltin's *Of Mice and Magic: A History of American Animated Cartoons;* James Clarke's *Animated Films; From Mouse To Mermaid: The Politics of Film, Gender and Culture* (edited by E. Bell *et al*); *Animation Art* (edited by J. Beck); and *Reading the Rabbit: Explorations in Warner Bros. Animation* (edited by K. Sandler).

For information on Walt Disney, the standard works include: Leonard Maltin's *The Disney Films*; Richard Schickel's *The Disney Version: The Life, Times, Art, and Commerce of Walt Disney*; R. Grover's *The Disney Touch;* Project on Disney's *Inside the Mouse: Work and Play at Disney World*; *Disney Discourse: Producing the Magic Kingdom* (edited by E. Smoodin); and *Walt Disney: A Guide to References and Resources* (edited by E. Leebron *et al*).

For a study of cinema, there is one book that towers above *every other book* on film (even tho' the competition is fierce!): David A. Cook's *A History of Narrative Film.* If you want one book that covers everything, this is it.

David Bordwell and Kristin Thompson have written many

meticulously researched and beautifully crafted books on cinema: *Film Art: An Introduction*, *Narration In the Fiction Film*, *Film History: An Introduction*, *The Classical Hollywood Cinema: Film Style and Mode of Production to 1960* and *Storytelling In the New Hollywood*. Anything by Bordwell and/ or Thompson is excellent.

I would also recommend Bruce Kawin's *How Movies Work*, Gerald Mast's *Film Theory and Criticism: Introductory Readings*, and Mast & Kawin's *A Short History of the Movies*.

David Cook, David Bordwell, Kristin Thompson, Gerald Mast and Bruce Kawin will give you all you could need for an in-depth study of cinema. Read their books: it's the equivalent of a degree or PhD in cinema!

AVAILABILITY

All of Hayao Miyazaki's films (and those of Studio Ghibli) are available for Western viewers on video and DVD (and, more recently, Blu-ray). They usually have the original Japanese language soundtrack, plus subtitles, and an English language dub.

The distributors of the movies of Hayao Miyazaki in Japan are: Toei Company. Tokuma Shoten. Toho.

In the U.S.A.: Buena Vista Home Video. Touchstone. Walt Disney Pictures. Miramax Films.

DIFFERENT VERSIONS

For Western viewers, the films of Hayao Miyazaki (and Studio Ghibli) are available in two main versions: the Japanese original version (usually with subtitles), and the dubbed versions.

Hayao Miyazaki's movies have been given very high profile, English language dubs, by some of the best technical people in the business (sound mixes at Skywalker Sound, for instance), and starry voice casts.

However, despite the laudable efforts of the Walt Disney corporation, in terms of the quality of filmmaking, and the significance of Hayao Miyazaki as a filmmaker, the original language versions are always the ones to go for. Why? Because Miyazaki himself has overseen or approved of the voice casts and mixes (as well as the dialogue). And Miyazaki doesn't speak English.

Think of it in the opposite direction: a film by Orson Welles or Alfred Hitchcock that was dubbed into Japanese, even by the best technical staff and the best actors in the Japanese film business, could not be regarded as conforming completely to the filmmakers' vision (unless Welles or Hitch could speak or understand Japanese and were present at the ADR and sound mixing and editing sessions). I also object to dubbing on social, cultural, political and ideological grounds.

It is also the case that Hayao Miyazaki is such a dynamically visual storyteller, dialogue, though important, is only one of numerous devices that Miyazaki and his teams employ. Unlike some movies, you really don't need to have the dialogue translated, via subtitles or dubbing, to know what's going on.

QUOTES BY HAYAO MIYAZAKI

I can't do a film after having debated it. I am unable to do a film while discussing it with my team. I issue directives. I do not achieve it otherwise.

•

We live in an age when it is cheaper to buy the rights to movies than to make them.

•

I'm not going to make movies that tell children, 'You should despair and run away'.

•

Is someone different at age 18 or 60? I believe one stays the same.

•

I never read reviews. I'm not interested. But I value a lot the reactions of the spectators.

•

Don't watch animation! You're surrounded by enough virtual things already.

•

I'm not making a film; instead, it feels like the film is making me.

•

I am an animator. I feel like I'm the manager of an animation cinema factory. I am not an executive. I'm rather like a foreman, like the boss of a team of craftsmen. That is the spirit of how I work.

•

I'm really not good at depicting the bad guys, frankly. They always wind up to be people who are at the core basically good.

•

If you watch something for three minutes, you feel like you know everything about it, even what went on backstage, and then you don't feel like watching the rest.

•

When a man is shooting a handgun, it's just like he is shooting because that's his job, and he has no other choice. It's no good. When a girl is shooting a handgun, it's really something.

•

The 21st century is a complex and unforeseeable epoch. Our thinking habits and our values, which until now looked settled, are being challenged.

•

Personally I am very pessimistic. But when, for instance, one of my staff has a baby you can't help but bless them for a good future. Because I can't tell that child, 'Oh, you shouldn't have come into this life.' And yet I know the world is heading in a bad direction. So with those conflicting thoughts in mind, I think about what kind of films I should be making.

•

Modern life is so thin and shallow and fake. I look forward to when developers go bankrupt, Japan gets poorer and wild grasses take over.

CRITICS ON *PRINCESS MONONOKE*

Extracts from reviews of *Princess Mononoke.*

A big movie for the ages, full to the brim with sympathy, imagination and sheer visual delight.

Andrew O'Hehir, *Salon.com*

•

Its breadth, profundity, and stunningly rendered vision make idealism seem renewed and breathtaking again.

Jay Carr, *Boston Globe*

•

Rarely does any film, animated or otherwise, immerse you in such a vivid landscape and engage your senses so strongly.

Marc Caro, *Chicago Tribune*

•

A more satisfying use of the medium would be difficult to imagine.

Kenneth Turan, *Los Angeles Times*

•

A visually stunning film.

Jonathan Foreman, *New York Post*

•

One of the most visually inventive films I have ever seen.

Roger Ebert, *Chicago Sun-Times*

•

The majestic pageant of images – no sylvan landscape has been this indelibly, dimensionally alive – is inextricably welded to the multifold spiritual/ecological questions about the future that Miyazaki is contemplating.

Wesley Morris, *San Francisco Examiner*

•

A dazzling movie, gorgeous to look at, involving on both emotional and intellectual levels, and often thrilling.

William Arnold, *Seattle Post-Intelligencer*

•

Complex, superbly rendered, and wildly eccentric anime – even by Miyazaki's own standards.

J. Hoberman, *Village Voice*

•

The beauty and scale of Miyazaki's vision shines through.

David Ansen, *Newsweek*

•

Exceedingly imaginative, beautifully realized animated epic adventure.

Todd McCarthy, *Variety*

•

A film for the young at heart and those who still appreciate honor, valor, love, and the earth.

Marc Savlov, *Austin Chronicle*

•

In theme and technique, it pushes the boundaries of animation and opens up new and imaginative possibilities.

Desmond Ryan, *Philadelphia Inquirer*

•

Its imagery is never less than breathtakingly beautiful, and is occasionally truly awesome

Maitland McDonagh, *TV Guide*

•

While *Mononoke* is often gorgeous to look at and has a far more sophisticated story than most Japanese animated features, it still feels overlong and dramatically unengaging.

Andy Klein, *Dallas Observer*

•

It's Miyazaki's use of sound – and silence – that takes your breath away

David Edelstein, *Slate*

•

As spectacular as it is dense and as dense as it is colorful and as colorful as it is meaningless and as meaningless as it is long.

Stephen Hunter, *Washington Post*

•

A landmark feat of Japanese animation from the acknowledged master of the genre, it's very easy to understand the film's phenomenal popularity... this intricate, epic fable is amazing to behold. No wonder the filmmaker, Hayao Miyazaki, is acknowledged as an inspiration among his American counterparts who have reinvented animated storytelling in the post-"Little Mermaid" era.

Janet Maslin, *New York Times*

FANS ON *PRINCESS MONONOKE*

Extracts from online reviews of *Princess Mononoke.*

AT THE INTERNET MOVIE DATABASE

Fantastic film! It makes me speechless.

•

Can an animated film get any better? The only other Japanese animated films I can think of that I love just as much as this are GRAVE OF THE FIREFLIES, AKIRA, SPIRITED AWAY, and GHOST IN THE SHELL. PRINCESS MONONOKE is perfection. The film is simply flawless in its storytelling, its animation, its characters, and its emotion.

•

The complexity of this movie is something never seen in the United States in an animated movie and even exceeds that of most live action movies as well. It combines love and hate, war and romance, nobility and deception in ways rarely seen in movies today.

•

Princess Mononoke is one of the most original and unique movies I've seen, even if it is a cartoon.

•

I have seen many many animated features, but none compare to the talent that is shown in this animé. After seeing this for the first time, I could see why so many animators (especially Disney animators) consider Mr. Miyazaki a GOD!

•

Princess Mononoke is my personal favorite Hayao Miyazaki flick, because I feel it has the best plot of them all. I would even go as far as to call it epic. It is beautifully animated and has a plot with a serious message, with brilliant, well drawn-out characters, each with their own unique personality.

•

Princess Mononoke is a grand, beautifully animated, heartfelt epic. It's a historical fantasy adventure, it's a melodrama, it's a race against time. Its pace is wonderful, taking us climactically through the all-embracing, outspread scope of the story. It has heart, it has violence, it has visual beauty, it has internal conflict.

AT METACRITIC.COM

This is one of the single most amazing animated movies ever created, if not the greatest movie ever created.

•

I thought this was an amazing movie. I've literally watched it tens of times and still love it.

•

Excellent film. It stunned me with its drool-worthy visuals, the characters are amazingly life-like and the plot is a fantasy masterpiece.

•

Brilliant. I love this movie. Everything from the story, to all the animations and characters were superb.

•

Of all of Hayao Miyazaki's amazing works, I'd have to say this is one of my favorites. The music, artwork, story – everything is amazing. And the whole overall feel of the film is amazing.

•

An impressive firework display with Hayao Miyazaki's loaded arsenal of visionary images going off at full blast.

•

In the end, the movie is about love, hatred, death, friendship, rivalry, happiness, anger, glee, sorrow, and being a human being. However, overall, it's about being alive. I never thought an animated film, let alone an animé, could be so purely great. If this isn't Oscar material, I have no clue in hell nor space what is.

FILMOGRAPHY

PRINCESS MONONOKE

***Mononoke Hime/ Princess Mononoke* (1997).**

Nibariki/ TNDG/ Toho. 133m.

Japanese release: July 12, 1997.
U.S.A. release: October 7, 1999.

Written and Directed by Hayao Miyazaki

CAST

Yôji Matsuda – Ashitaka
Yuriko Ishida – San
Yûko Tanaka – Eboshi-gozen
Kaoru Kobayashi – Jiko-bô
Masahiko Nishimura – Kouroku
Tsunehiko Kamijô – Gonza
Sumi Shimamoto – Toki
Tetsu Watanabe – Yama-inu
Mitsuru Satô – Tatari-gami
Akira Nagoya – Usi-kai
Akihiro Miwa – Moro-no-kimi
Mitsuko Mori – Hii-sama
Hisaya Morishige – Okkoto-nusi

ENGLISH VOICE CAST

Gillian Anderson – Moro
Billy Crudup – Ashitaka
Claire Danes – San
Jada Pinkett Smith – Toki
Keith David – Okkoto/ Additional Voices
John DeMita – Kohroku
John Di Maggio – Gonza/ Additional Voices
Minnie Driver – Lady Eboshi
Tara Strong – Kaya
Billy Bob Thornton – Jigo
K.T. Vogt – Complaining Wife
Jennifer Cihi – Tatara's Women Song
Leslie Ishii – Tatara's Women Song
Mary Elizabeth McGlynn – Tatara's Women Song
Debi Derryberry – Additional Voices
Lewis Arquette – Additional Voices
Corey Burton – Additional Voices
Pamela Adlon – Additional Voices
Alex Fernandez – Additional Voices
Jack Fletcher – Additional Voices
Julia Fletcher – Additional Voices
Pat Fraley – Additional Voices
Takako Fuji – Woman in Iron Town
John Hostetter – Additional Voices
Yoshimasa Kondô – Additional Voices
John Rafter Lee – Additional Voices
Sherry Lynn – Iron Town Woman/ Emishi Villiage Girl
Tress MacNeille – Iron Town Woman/ Additional Voices
Matt McKenzie – Additional Voices
Michael McShane – Additional Voices
Matt K. Miller – Additional Voices
Marnie Mosiman – Additional Voices
Adam Paul – Additional Voices
David Rasner – Additional Voices
Kimihiro Reizei – Jibashiri
Dwight Schultz – Additional Voices
Jessica Lynn – Additional Voices

CREW

Produced by Yutaka Narita – executive producer, Seiji Okuda – associate producer, Toshio Suzuki – producer, Yasuyoshi Tokuma – chief executive producer, Seiichiro Ujiie – executive producer, Takahiro Yonezawa – assistant producer

Original Music by Joe Hisaishi

Cinematography by Atsushi Okui
Film Editing by Hayao Miyazaki and Takeshi Seyama
Art Direction by Satoshi Kuroda, Kazuo Oga, Yôji Takeshige, Naoya Tanaka, Nizou Yamamoto
Koji Aritomi – assistant director
Masakatsu Ishizone – assistant director
Michiyo Yasuda – color designer
Hiroyuki Ito – assistant director
Tsutomu Asakura – sound mix assistant
Masahiro Fukuhara – sound recording assistant
Nobutaka Hirooka – dialogue recordist
Kazuhiko Ikai – sound effects production support
Tatsuya Ikeba – dialogue recordist
Shuji Inoue – sound recording mixer
Takahisa Ishino – sound effects assistant
Muchihiro Ito – sound effects
Mitsuharu Kanei – dialogue recordist
Takao Kato – sound effects compilation support
Rie Nishijima – dialogue recordist
Tsukuru Takagi – sound mix assistant
Shigeru Tokida – sound effects production support
Makoto Uchida – sound mix assistant
Kazuhiro Wakabayashi – sound
Motoi Watanabe – sound effects production support
Tsunahiro Yamamura – sound effects compilation support
Yuki Yasoshima – dialogue recordist
Yoshikazu Fukutome – special art effects
Tomoji Hashizume – special effects animator
Masafumi Inoue – computer graphics
Mitsunori Katâma – computer graphics
Yoshiyuki Momose – computer graphics
Masahiro Murakami – special effects animator
Toyohiko Sakakibara – special effects animator
Yoshinori Sugano – computer graphics
Kaoru Tanifuji – special effects animator
Kumiko Taniguchi – special effects animator
Michael Arias – software development
Tamaki Kojo – animation camera operator
Atsushi Okui – animation camera supervisor
Wataru Takahashi – animation camera operator
Junji Yubata – animation camera operator
Akihiko Adachi – inbetween/ clean-up artist
Akiko Aihara – ink and paint artist: Trace Studio M
Sigeko Akanuma – ink and paint artist: IM Studio
Masashi Ando – supervising animator
Kaori Anmi – ink and paint artist: IM Studio
Naomi Anzai – ink and paint artist: Trace Studio M
Sadayuki Arai – background artist

Yoriko Asai – ink and paint artist: IM Studio
Naomi Atsuta – ink and paint artist
Tsutomu Awata – key animator
Seiko Azuma – inbetween/ clean-up artist
Reiko Daigo – ink and paint artist: Trace Studio M
David Encinas – inbetween/ clean-up artist
Masaaki Endo – key animator
Kiyomi Fujihashi – ink and paint artist: Toei Animation
Kaori Fujii – inbetween/ clean-up artist
Masayo Fujikura – inbetween/ clean-up artist: Telecom Animation Film
Maya Fujimori – inbetween/ clean-up artist
Sachiko Funasaki – ink and paint artist: IM Studio
Hiromi Furuya – inbetween/ clean-up artist
Sumiko Furuya – ink and paint artist: Toei Animation
Makiko Futaki – key animator
Keiko Goto – ink and paint artist: Studio Killy
Chiharu Haraguchi – inbetween/ clean-up artist
Chie Harai – ink and paint artist: Studio Killy
Kimiko Hatano – ink and paint artist: Studio Killy
Keiichiro Hattori – digital ink and paint artist
Yoshie Hayashi – inbetween/ clean-up artist
Kazuhiro Hirabayashi – ink and paint artist: Studio Killy
Sayaka Hirahara – background artist
Kazuko Hirai – inbetween/ clean-up artist: Telecom Animation Film
Mari Hitokurai – ink and paint artist: Telecom Animation Film
Yoshiko Igarashi – ink and paint artist: Toei Animation
Natsuko Iimori – inbetween/ clean-up artist: Telecom Animation Film
Takeshi Imamura – key animator
Ryouko Ina – background artist
Mihoko Irie – ink and paint artist: Toei Animation
Michiyo Iseda – ink and paint artist: IM Studio
Megumi Ishido – digital ink and paint artist: Takahashi Production/ T2 Studio
Shizuka Ishiguro – ink and paint artist: Studio Killy
Hiroaki Ishii – digital ink and paint artist
Eriko Ishikawa – ink and paint artist: Telecom Animation
Kaori Ishikawa – ink and paint artist: Studio Killy
Shin Itagaki – inbetween/ clean-up artist: Telecom Animation Film
Toshiko Iwakiri – ink and paint artist: Studio Killy
Emiko Iwayanagi – inbetween/ clean-up artist
Megumi Kagawa – key animator
Yukiko Kakita – digital ink and paint artist: Takahashi Production/ T2 Studio

Yoshinori Kanada – key animator
Junko Kanauchi – ink and paint artist: Trace Studio M
Naomi Kasugai – background artist
Yuriko Katayama – ink and paint artist
Manabu Kawada – inbetween/ clean-up artist
Toshio Kawaguchi – key animator
Hana Kikuchi – inbetween/ clean-up artist
Yumiko Kimura – ink and paint artist: IM Studio
Yumiko Kitajima – inbetween/ clean-up artist
Kazuo Kobayashi – ink and paint artist: IM Studio
Sachiko Kobayashi – inbetween/ clean-up artist
Atsushi Kodama – ink and paint artist: Studio Killy
Komasa – inbetween/ clean-up artist
Katsuya Kondo – key animator
Rie Kondou – inbetween/ clean-up artist
Yoshifumi Kondo – supervising animator
Ken'ichi Konishi – key animator
Kitaro Kosaka – supervising animator
Yuriko Kudo – ink and paint artist: Studio Killy
Misuzu Kurata – inbetween/ clean-up artist
Kazuko Kurosawa – ink and paint artist: Toei Animation
Ikuo Kuwana – key animator
Kinuyo Maehara – ink and paint artist: IM Studio
Kiyoko Makita – inbetween/ clean-up artist
Reiko Mano – inbetween/ clean-up artist
Mariko Matsuo – key animator
Megumi Matsuo – ink and paint artist: Trace Studio M
Masaru Matsuse – key animator
Atsuko Matsushita – inbetween/ clean-up artist
Michio Mihara – key animator
Hiroko Minowa – key animator
Junko Miyakawa – ink and paint artist: Telecom Animation Film
Chiemi Miyamoto – ink and paint artist: Studio Killy
Chiyomi Morisawa – ink and paint artist: Studio Killy
Shinobu Mori – inbetween/ clean-up artist: Telecom Animation Film
Kaoru Morita – ink and paint artist: IM Studio
Noriko Moritomo – key animator
Emiko Motohashi – ink and paint artist: Trace Studio M
Yuki Murata – digital ink and paint artist: Takahashi Production/ T2 Studio
Hisashi Nabetani – ink and paint artist: IM Studio
Kyouko Naganawa – background artist
Junko Nagaoka – ink and paint artist: Telecom Animation Film
Sayuri Nagashima – ink and paint artist: Telecom Animation Film

Yoko Nagashima – inbetween/ clean-up artist
Kaoru Nakagama – ink and paint artist: Studio Killy
Rie Nakagome – animation checker
Keiko Nakaji – inbetween/ clean-up artist: Telecom Animation Film
Katsutoshi Nakamura – animation checker
Daisuke Nakayama – inbetween/ clean-up artist
Rie Niidome – inbetween/ clean-up artist
Sumie Nishido – inbetween/ clean-up artist
Hiromi Nishikawa – inbetween/ clean-up artist
Toyomi Nishimura – ink and paint artist: IM Studio
Yoshimi Nishiwaki – ink and paint artist: Telecom Animation Film
Takehiro Noda – key animator
Minori Noguchi – inbetween/ clean-up artist
Yukie Nomura – ink and paint artist
Fumiko Oda – ink and paint artist
Noriko Odaka – inbetween/ clean-up artist: Telecom Animation Film
Mayumi Ohmura – inbetween/ clean-up artist
Kumiko Ohta – inbetween/ clean-up artist
Kimiyo Okunishi – ink and paint artist: Toei Animation
Akiko Ono – ink and paint artist
Kazuyoshi Onoda – animation checker
Masako Osada – background artist
Masako Osumi – ink and paint artist: Studio Killy
Kiyomi Ota – background artist
Makiko Ota – ink and paint artist: Telecom Animation Film
Atsuko Ôtani – key animator
Shinji Otsuka – key animator
Kazumi Ouchi – ink and paint artist: IM Studio
Mito Ozaki – ink and paint artist: IM Studio
Hisae Saito – background artist
Masaya Saitou – animation checker
Masako Sakano – inbetween/ clean-up artist
Sonoe Sakano – ink and paint artist: Toei Animation
Yukie Sako – inbetween/ clean-up artist
Hiroaki Sasaki – background artist
Keiko Sasaki – ink and paint artist: Studio Killy
Shinsaku Sasaki – key animator
Keiko Sato – ink and paint artist: IM Studio
Makiko Sato – digital ink and paint artist
Kuri Sawa – inbetween/ clean-up artist
Eriko Shibata – inbetween/ clean-up artist
Kazuko Shibata – inbetween/ clean-up artist
Akira Shigino – digital ink and paint artist
Ritsuko Shiina – inbetween/ clean-up artist

Miyoko Shikibu – inbetween/ clean-up artist: Telecom Animation Film

Hiroshi Shimizu – key animator

Mariko Shimizu – ink and paint artist: Studio Killy

Rie Shimizu – inbetween/ clean-up artist

Yumiko Shimoe – digital ink and paint artist: Takahashi Production/ T2 Studio

Masako Shinohara – key animator

Sachiko Sugino – key animator

Wakako Sugiyama – ink and paint artist: Trace Studio M

Eiichi Suzuki – ink and paint artist

Makiko Suzuki – inbetween/ clean-up artist

Mariko Suzuki – inbetween/ clean-up artist

Fumiko Taira – ink and paint artist: Studio Killy

Sayuri Takagi – ink and paint artist: Studio Killy

Kanako Takahashi – digital ink and paint artist: Takahashi Production/ T2 Studio

Naomi Takahashi – ink and paint artist: Studio Killy

Atsushi Tamura – inbetween/ clean-up artist

Seiki Tamura – background artist

Masae Tanabe – inbetween/ clean-up artist

Atsuko Tanaka – key animator: Telecom Animation Film

Junichi Taniguchi – background artist

Kumiko Tanihira – inbetween/ clean-up artist

Hitomi Tateno – animation checker

Tomomi Tenma – ink and paint artist: IM Studio

Akiko Teshima – inbetween/ clean-up artist

Hiroko Tetsuka – inbetween/ clean-up artist

Tae Tochihara – ink and paint artist: IM Studio

Yoko Toju – inbetween/ clean-up artist: Telecom Animation Film

Yoyoi Toki – inbetween/ clean-up artist

Masae Tomino – inbetween/ clean-up artist: Telecom Animation Film

Keiko Tomizawa – inbetween animator

Tomoko Totsuka – inbetween/ clean-up artist

Hiromi Tsuchiya – ink and paint artist: Studio Killy

Shinobu Tsunegi – inbetween/ clean-up artist

Kazuko Tsunoda – ink and paint artist: Studio Killy

Koujirou Tsuraoka – inbetween/ clean-up artist

Akihiko Uda – inbetween/ clean-up artist: Telecom Animation Film

Mineko Ueda – inbetween/ clean-up artist: Telecom Animation Film

Kazue Urayama – ink and paint artist: Studio Killy

Keiko Watanabe – inbetween/ clean-up artist: Telecom Animation Film

Natsuko Watanabe – inbetween/ clean-up artist

Nobuko Watanabe – ink and paint artist: Studio Killy
Alexandra Weihrauch – inbetween/ clean-up artist
Hisako Yaji – inbetween/ clean-up artist
Kaori Yajima – ink and paint artist: Studio Killy
Kazuko Yamada – ink and paint artist
Ken'ichi Yamada – key animator
Tamami Yamada – inbetween/ clean-up artist
Eiji Yamamori – key animator
Mayumi Yamamoto – inbetween/ clean-up artist
Tomoko Yamamoto – ink and paint artist: Telecom Animation Film
Yukari Yamaura – inbetween/ clean-up artist
Morihiko Yano – inbetween/ clean-up artist
Hiroko Yasutome – inbetween/ clean-up artist: Telecom Animation Film
Mayu Yazawa – inbetween/ clean-up artist: Telecom Animation Film
Hiromasa Yonebayashi – inbetween/ clean-up artist
Ken'ichi Yoshida – key animator
Miyoko Yoshida – ink and paint artist: Studio Killy
Noboru Yoshida – background artist
Hideaki Yoshio – key animator
Keiko Yozawa – inbetween/ clean-up artist: Telecom Animation Film
Tatsumi Yukiwaki – ink and paint artist: trace machine: Studio Killy
Masayo Iseki – color key
Naomi Mori – color key
Kanako Moriya – color key
Kenji Furukawa – music recordist
Joe Hisaishi – music arranger and piano solos
Kazumi Inaki – music production
Hiroya Ishihara – music recordist
Hiroshi Kumagai – conductor
Yoshikazu Mera – singer: countertenor
Makoto Morimoto – music mixer
Masayoshi Okawa – music mixer
Toru Takigawa – music production
Yukio Yamashita – music production
Joe Hisaishi – orchestrator
Jack Fletcher – casting: English voices
Neil Gaiman – script adaptor: English version
Val Kuklowsky – adr editor
Eric Lewis – assistant adr engineer: English dialogue
Dan Edelstein – foley editor: US version
Warren Shaw – sound effects editor
Ernie Sheesley – dialogue recordist
Dominick Tavella – sound re-recording mixer

James Twomey – sound re-recording mixer
Garry Ulmer – dialogue recording mixer
Stephen Alpert – overseas promotion
Keiji Hamada – overseas promotion
Kenji Imura – production assistant
Haruyo Moriyoshi – overseas promotion
Minako Nagasawa – public relations
Tamami Yamamoto – public relations
Koji Otsuka – production assistant
Tara Strong – additional voices
Kin'ichirô Suzuki – production assistant

HAYAO MIYAZAKI: FILMOGRAPHY

A filmography of the chief theatrical movies directed by Hayao Miyazaki.

THE CASTLE OF CAGLIOSTRO

The Castle of Cagliostro (*Lupin III: Cagliostro no Shiro,* 1979).

Monkey Punch/ Tokyo Movie Shinsha. 100m.

Japanese release: December 15, 1979. U.S.A. release: Sept, 1980/ April, 1991.

CREW

Written and Directed by Hayao Miyazaki
Co-writer: Haruya Yamazaki
Screenplay: Yasuo Otsuka
Original Story: Hayao Miyazaki
Original Concept: Maurice Leblanc
Original Creator: Monkey Punch
Executive Producer: Yutaka Fujioka
Producer: Tetsuo Katayama
Distributor: Ghibli Museum Library and Toho
Production: Studio Telecom and Tokyo Movie Shinsha
Music: Yuji Ohno
Character Design: Hayao Miyazaki and Yasuo Otsuka
Art Director: Shichiro Kobayashi
Animation Director: Yasuo Otsuka
Director of Photography: Hirokata Takahashi
Color Design: Hiroko Kondo
Film Editing: Masatoshi Tsurubuchi

CAST

Yasuo Yamada – Lupin
Eiko Masuyama – Fujiko Mine
Kiboshi Kobayashi – Daisuke Jogen

Makio Inoue – Goemon
Goro Naya – Inspector Zenigata
Sumi Shimamoto – Clarisse
Taro Ishid – Count Cagliostro

NAUSICAÄ OF THE VALLEY OF THE WIND

Nausicaä of the Valley of the Wind (*Kaze no Tani no Nausicaä*, 1984).

Nibariki/ Tokuma Shoten/ Hakuhodo. 116m.

Japanese release: March 11, 1984. U.S.A. release: June, 1985.

CREW

Written and Directed by Hayao Miyazaki
Co-writer: Kazunori Ito
Production: Tokuma Shoten and Topcraft
Executive Producers: Yasuyoshi Tokuma, Toru Hara (Topcraft) and Michio Kondo
Producer: Isao Takahata
Distributor: Toei Kabushiki Kaisha
Music: Joe Hisaishi
Supervising Animator: Kazuo Komatsubara
Art Director: Mitsauki Nakamura
Character Design: Hayao Miyazaki and Kazuo Komatsubara
Colour Designers: Michiyo Yasuda and Fukuo Suzuki
Sound: Shigeharu Shiba and Kazutoshi Satou
Editing: Naoki Kaneko, Tomoko Kida and Shôji Sakaii
Backgrounds: Mutsuo Koseki

CAST

Sumi Shimamoto – Nausicaä
Gorou Naya – Yupa
Yoshiko Sakakibara – Kushana
Hisako Kyoda – Obaba
Mahito Tsujimura – Jihil
Youji Matsuda – Asbel
Iemasa Kayumi – Kurotawa
Ichirou Nagai – Mito
Kohei Miyauchi – Goru
Mina Tominaga – Rastel
Akiko Tsuboi – Rastel's mother

LAPUTA: CASTLE IN THE SKY

Laputa: Castle In the Sky (*Tenku no Shiro Laputa,* 1986). Nibariki/ Tokuma Shoten. 124m.

Japanese release: August 2, 1986. U.S.A. release: July, 1987/ April 1, 1989.

CREW

Written and Directed by Hayao Miyazaki
Production: Studio Ghibli and Tokuma Shoten
Distributor: Toei Kabushiki Kaisha
Producer: Isao Takahata
Executive Producer: Yasuysoshi Tokuma
Music: Joe Hisaishi
Art Directors: Toshio Nazaki and Nizo Yamamoto
Character Designers: Hayao Miyazaki and Tsukasa Tannai
Animation Director: Tsukasa Tannai
Animation Supervisor: Tsukasa Niwauchi
Head Key Animator: Yoshinori Kanada
Sound Director: Shigeharu Shiba
Colour Designer: Michiyo Yasuda
DP: Hirokata Takahashi
Editing: Yoshihiro Kasahara, Takeshi Seyama and Miyazaki
Sound Effects and Editing: Kazutoshi Satou
Visual Effects: Gô Abe

CAST

Mayumi Tanaka – Pazu
Keiko Yokozawa – Sheeta
Nou Terada – Dola
Kotoe Hatsui – Uncle Pom
Fujio Tokita – General
Ichiro Nagai – Mentor
Hiroshi Ito – Okami
Machiko Washio – Shalulu
Takumi Kamiyama – Lui

MY NEIGHBOR TOTORO

My Neighbor Totoro (*Tonari no Totoro,* 1988).
Nibariki/ Tokuma Shoten. 86m.
Japanese release: April 16, 1988. U.S.A. release: May 7, 1993.

CREW

Written and Directed by Hayao Miyazaki
Production: Tokuma Shoten, Nibariki and Studio Ghibli
Producers: Yasuyoshi Tokuma and Toru Hara
Music: Joe Hisaishi
Art Director: Kazuo Oga
Character Design & Supervising Animator: Yoshiharu Sato
Colour Designer: Nobuko Mizuta
Sound: Shigeharu Shiba and Kazutoshi Satou
Editing: Takeshi Seyama
DP: Hisao Shirai

CAST

Noriko Hidaka – Satsuki
Chika Sakamoto – Mei
Shigesato Itoi – Mr Kusakabe
Sumi Shimamoto – Mrs Kusakabe
Yûko Maruyama – Kanta
Hitoshi Takagi – Totoro

KIKI'S DELIVERY SERVICE

Kiki's Delivery Service (*Majo no Takkyubin,* 1989). Nibariki/ Tokuma Shoten. 102m.

Japanese release: July 29, 1989. U.S.A. release: May 23, 1998 (video).

CREW

Written and Directed by Hayao Miyazaki
Co-writer: Nobuyuki Isshiki
Original Creator: Eiko Kadono
Producers: Yasuyoshi Tokuma, Toru Hara, Mikihiko Ysuzuki, Morihisa Takagi and Hayao Miyazaki
Production: Studio Ghibli
Production Committee: NTV, Tokuma Shoten, Yamato Transport
Music: Joe Hisaishi
Animation Directors: Shinji Otsuka, Katsuya Kondo and Yoshifumi Kondo
Character Design: Katsuya Kondo
Colour Designers: Michiyo Yasuda and Yuriko Katayama
Production Designer: Hinoshi Ono
Production Manager: Eiko Tanaka
DP: Shigeo Sugimura
Editing: Takeshi Seyama
Sound: Naoko Asari, Kazutoshi Satou and Shuji Inoue

CAST

Minami Takayama – Kiki and Ursula
Rei Sakuma – Jiji
Mieko Nobuzawa – Kiki's mom
Kouichi Miura – Mr Okino, Kiki's dad
Keiko Toda – Mrs Osono
Kappei Yamaguchi – Tombo
Jaruko Kato – Madame
Hiroko Seki – Bertha
Keiko Kagimoto – Birthday Girl

PORCO ROSSO

Porco Rosso (*Kurenai no Buta,* 1992).
Nibariki/ TNNG. 93m.
Japanese release: July 20, 1992. U.S.A. release: October 9, 2003.

CREW

Written and Directed by Hayao Miyazaki
Production: Tokuma Shoten, Japan Airlines, Nippon Television Network and Studio Ghibli
Producer: Toshio Suzuki
Executive Producers: Yasuyoshi Tokuma, Sokai Tokuma, Matsuo Toshimitsu and Yoshio Sasaki
Distributor: Buena Vista Home Entertainment and Toho
Supervising Animators: Megumi Kagawa and Toshio Kawaguchi
Art Director: Yoshitsu Hisamura
Production Designer: Katsu Hisamura
Character Design: Toshio Kawaguchi
Colour Designer: Michiyo Yasuda
DP: Atsushi Okui
Sound: Naoko Asari and Makoto Sumiya
Music: Joe Hisaishi
Editing: Takeshi Seyama, Katsu Hisamura and Hayao Miyazaki

CAST

Shuichiro Moriyama – Porco
Akemi Okamura – Fio
Tokiko Kato – Gina
Tsunehiko Kamijô – Aiuto Gang Boss
Akio Otsuka – Curtis
Sanshi Katsura – Piccolo

SPIRITED AWAY

Spirited Away (*Sen to Chihiro no Kamikakushi,* 2001). Toho. 125m.

Japanese release: July 20, 2001. U.S.A. release: September 20, 2002.

CREW

Written and Directed by Hayao Miyazaki
Executive Producers: Yasuyoshi Tokuma, John Lasseter
Producers: Toshio Suzuki, Donald W. Ernst
Associate Producer: Lori Korngiebel
Music: Joe Hisaishi
DP: Atsushi Okui
Editing: Takeshi Seyama
Production Design: Norobu Yoshida
Art Direction: Yôji Takeshige
Animation Director: Masashi Ando
Colour Designer: Michiyo Yasuda
Sound Production: Kazumi Inaki, Tamaki Kojo
Sound Effects: Michihiro Ito, Toru Noguchi
Casting Coordinators: Keiko Yagi and Naomi Yasu

CAST

Rumi Hîragi – Chihiro/ Sen
Miyu Irino – Haku
Mari Natsuki – Yubaba/ Zeniba
Takashi Naitô – Chihiro's father
Yasuko Sawaguchi – Chihiro's mother
Tatsuya Gashûin – Aogaeru, Assistant Manager
Ryûnosuke Kamiki – Bô
Yumi Tamai – Rin
Yô Ôizumi – Bandai-gaeru
Koba Hayashi – River God
Tsunehiko Kamijô – Chichiyaku
Takehiko Ono – Aniyaku, foreman
Bunta Sugawara – Kamajî

HOWL'S MOVING CASTLE

Howl's Moving Castle (*Howl no Ugoku Shiro,* 2004). Toho. 119m.

Japanese release: November 20, 2004. U.S.A. release: June 6, 2005.

CREW

Written and Directed by Hayao Miyazaki
Original Novel: Diana Wynne-Jones
Production: Howl's Moving Castle Production Committee and Studio Ghibli
Production Committee: Buena Vista Home Entertainment, D-Rights, Dentsu Inc., NTV, Toho, Tokuma Shoten
Distributor: Toho
Producers: Toshio Suzuki, Hayao Miyazaki and Yasuyoshi Tokuma
Animation Director: Katsuya Kondo
Supervising Animators: Akihiro Yamashita, Takeshi Inaumura and Kitao Kosaka
Character Design: Akihiko Yamashita
Digital Animation: Mitsunori Katama
Music: Joe Hisaishi
Sound: Kazuhiro Hayashi, Kazuhiro Wakabayashi, Nobue Yoshinaga and Shuji Inoue
Sound Effects: Toru Noguchi
Art Directors: Yoji Takeshige and Noburu Yoshida
DP: Atsushi Okui
Editing: Takeshi Seyama
Production Managers: Ryoichi Fukuyama, Nozomu Takahashi and Hiroyuki Watanabe
Colour Design: Michiyo Yasuda
Casting: Ayumi Sati, Motohiro Hatanaka, Naomi Yasu

CAST

Chieko Baisho – Sophie
Takuya Kimura – Howl
Akihiro Mirva – Witch
Tatsuya Gashûin – Calcifer
Ryunosuka Kamiki – Markl
Akio Otsuka – King of Ingary
Haruko Kato – Madam Suliman
Daijiro Harada – Heen
Yo Oizumi – Prince

PONYO ON THE CLIFF BY THE SEA

Ponyo On the Cliff By the Sea (*Gake no ue no Ponyo,* 2008).

Toho. 101m.

Japanese release: July 19, 2008. U.S.A. release: June 6, 2009.

CREW

Written and directed by Hayao Miyazaki

Executive producers: Koji Hoshino, Seiji Okuda, Miyazaki, Naoya Fujimaki and Ryoichi Fukuyama

Producer: Toshio Suzuki

Distributor: Toho

Production: Studio Ghibli

Production: 'Ponyo on the Cliff' Production Committee

Production Committee: Buena Vista Home Entertainment, D-Rights, Dentsu Inc., Hakuhodo DY Media Partners, NTV and Toho

Music: Joe Hisaishi

DP: Atsushi Okui

Art Director: Noboru Yoshida

Animation Supervisor and Character Design: Katsuya Kondo

Key Animators: Hiromasa Yonebayashi and Atsuko Tanaka

Editing: Takeshi Seyama and Miyazaki

Sound Director: Eriko Kimura

CAST

Yuria Nara – Ponyo
Hiroki Doi – Sosuke
Tomoko Yamaguchi – Lisa
Kazushige Nagashima – Koichi
George Tokoro – Fujimoto
Yuki Amami – Ponyo's mother, a.k.a. grandmother
Kazuko Yoshiyuki - Toki
Emi Hiraoka - Kumiko
Tomoko Naraoka - Yoshie
Akiko Takeguchi - Noriko

THE WIND RISES

The Wind Rises (*Kaze Tachinu,* 2013).
Toho. 126m.
Japanese release: July 20, 2013. U.S.A. release: February 21, 2014.

CREW

Written and Directed by Hayao Miyazaki
Executive producer: Koji Hoshino
Producer: Toshio Suzuki
Associate Producers: Ryoichi Fukuyama, Seiji Okuda and Naoya Fujimaki
Production: Buena Vista Home Entertainment, Dentsu Inc., Hakuhodo DY Media Partners, KDDI, Mitsubishi Corporation, NTV, Studio Ghibli, Toho
Distributor: Toho
Music and Music Director: Joe Hisaishi
Character Design, Key Animator and Animation Director: Kitaro Kousaka
Art Director: Yoji Takeshige
Character Designer: Katsuya Kondo
Director of Photography: Atsushi Okui
Editing: Takeshi Seyama
Audio Director: Koji Kasamatsu
Color Design: Michiyo Yasuda
ADR Director: Eriko Kimura
Special Effects: Keiko Itokawa
Casting: Takashi Hayashi and Takurou Okada

CAST

Hideaki Anno – Jiro Horikoshi
Miori Takimoto – Nahoko Satomi
Hidetoshi Nishijima – Kiro Honjo
Jun Kunimura – Hattori
Keiko Takeshita – Jiro's Mother
Mansai Nomura – Giovanni Battista Caproni
Masahiko Nishimura – Kurokawa
Mirai Shida – Kayo Horikoshi
Morio Kazama – Mr Satomi
Shinobu Otake – Kurokawa's Wife
Stephen Alpert – Hans Castorp

OTHER CREDITS

Hayao Miyazaki has many credits in animation – including as storyboard artist; animator; in-between animator; concept; script; song lyrics; and planning. (For a full list, see the Anime News Network).

The following credits are for direction and script.

DIRECTOR

Lupin III (1971 and 1980)
Future Boy Conan (Conan, the Boy in Future, 1978; inc. movie)
Sherlock Holmes (Great Detective Holmes, 1981; inc. movie)
On Your Mark (1995)
Film Guru Guru (2001)
Whale Hunt (2001)
Koro's Big Day Out (2002)
Imaginary Flying Machines (2002)
Mei and the Kitten Bus (2002)
The Day I Bought a Star (The Day I Harvested a Planet, 2006)
House Hunting (Looking For a Home, 2006)
Mon Mon the Water Spider (2006)
Mr Dough and the Egg Princess (2010)
Treasure Hunting (2011)

SCRIPTS

Panda! Go, Panda! (1972)
Panda! Go, Panda!: Rainy Day Circus (1973)
Whisper of the Heart (1995)
Secret World of Arrietty (The Borrower Arrietty, 2010)
A Sumo Wrestler's Tail (2010)
From Up On Poppy Hill (2011)

BIBLIOGRAPHY

HAYAO MIYAZAKI

"Interview With Hayao Miyazaki ", *A-Club*, 19, June, 1987
The Art of Kiki's Delivery Service, Tokuma, Tokyo, 1989
"Hayao Miyazaki Interview", *Comic Box*, Oct, 1989
"Money Can't Buy Creativity", *Pacific Friend*, 18, 9, Jan, 1991
Nani ga eigaka, with Akira Kurosawa, Tokuma Shoten, 1993
"Now, After *Nausicäa* Has Finished", *YOM* special, June, 1994
Hayao Miyazaki's Daydream Note, Japan, 1997
Points of Departure, 1979-1996, Tokuma Shoten, Tokyo, 1997
"A Modest Proposal", *Manga Max*, 15, February, 2000
"The Purpose of the Film", *Spirited Away,* 2001
Tenku no Shiro Rapyuta, Tokuma Shoten, Japan, 2004
Tonari no Totoro, Tokuma Shoten, Japan, 2004
Shuna no Tabi, Tokuma Shoten, Japan, 2008
Starting Point, 1979-1996, tr. B. Cary & F. Schodt, Viz Media/ Shogakukan, San Francisco, CA, 2009
Interview, in H. Ota, *Chinese Asahi Asia Antenna*, Aug, 2013
Interview, in A. Thomspon, *Thompson On Hollywood*, Feb, 2014
Interview, in R. Collin, *Daily Telegraph*, May 9, 2014
Turning Point, 1997-2008, tr. B. Cary & F. Schodt, Viz Media/ Shogakukan, San Francisco, CA, 2014

HAYAO MIYAZAKI: *MANGA* WORKS

Puss In Boots, 1969
People of the Desert, 1969-1970
Animal Treasure Island, 1972
Nausicaä of the Valley of Wind, 1982-1994 (English version: *Nausicaä of the Valley of the Wind*, tr. D. Lewis & T. Smith, VIZ Media, San Francisco, CA, 2004)
To My Sister, 1982
The Journey of Shuna, 1983
The Age of the Flying Boat, 1990
Daydream Data Notes, 1992
The Return of Hans, 1994

Dining In the Air, 1994
Tigers Covered With Mud, 1998-1999
A Trip To Tynemouth, 2006
The Wind Rises, 2009

OTHERS

G. Adams, ed. *The Cambridge Guide To Children's Books In English*, Cambridge University Press, Cambridge, 2003

S. Adilman. "*Spirited Away* Gets Extra Word", Animation Cafe, 2002

M. Ando. Interview, *Spirited Away*, 2001

S. Ando. "Regaining continuity with the past: *Spirited Away* and *Alice's Adventures in Wonderland*", *Bookbird: A Journal of International Children's Literature*, 46, 1, 2008

The Art of Spirited Away, VIZ Media, 2002

B. Babington *Biblical Epic and Sacred Narrative In the Hollywood*, Manchester University Press, Manchester, 1993

R. Bator, ed. *Signposts To Criticism of Children's Literature*, American Library Association, Chicago, 1983

J. Beck, ed. *Animation Art*, Flame Tree Publishing, London, 2004

E. Bell *et al*, eds. *From Mouse To Mermaid: The Politics of Film, Gender and Culture*, Indiana University Press, Bloomington, IN, 1995

A. Benciveni. *Miyazaki: Il Dio Dell Animé*, La Mani, Genoa, 2003

I. Bergman. *Bergman On Bergman, Interviews with Ingmar Bergman*, eds. S. Björkman, *et al*, tr. P. B. Austin, Touchstone, New York, NY, 1986

—. *The Magic Lantern: An Autobiography*, London, 1988

S. Bigelow. "Technologies of perception: Miyazaki in theory and practice", *Animation: An Interdisciplinary Journal*, 4, 1, 2009

J. Bittner. *Approaches To the Fiction of Ursula K. Le Guin*, UMI Research Press, Ann Arbor, MI, 1984

D. Bordwell & K. Thompson. *Film Art: An Introduction*, McGraw-Hill Publishing Company, New York, NY, 1979

—. *Narration In the Fiction Film*, Routledge, London, 1988

—. *The Way Hollywood Tells It*, University of California Press, Berkeley, CA, 2006

J. Bower, ed. *The Cinema of Japan and Korea*, Wallflower Press, London, 2004

J. Boyd & T. Nishimura. "Shinto perspectives in Miyazaki's anime film *Spirited Away*", *Journal of Religion and Film*, 8, 2, 2004

M. Broderick. "Spirited Away by Miyazaki's fantasy", *Inter-*

sections: Gender, History & Culture in the Asian Context, 9, 2003
P. Brophy, ed. *Kaboom! Explosive Animation From America and Japan*, Museum of Contemporary Art, Sydney, 1994
—. *100 Anime*, British Film Institute, London, 2005
—. ed. *Tezuka*, National Gallery of Victoria, 2006
J. Brosnan. *Future Tense: The Cinema of Science Fiction*, St Martin's Press, New York, NY, 1978
—. *Primal Screen: A History of Science Fiction Film*, Orbit, London, 1991
S. Bukatman. *Terminal Identity: The Virtual Subject In Post-modern Science Fiction*, Duke University Press, Durham, NC, 1993
E. Byrne & M. McQuillan, eds. *Deconstructing Disney*, Pluto Press, London, 1999
B. Camp & J. Davis. *Anime Classics*, Stone Bridge Press, CA, 2007
H. Carpenter. *J.R.R. Tolkien: A Biography*, Allen & Unwin, London, 1977
—. & M. Prichard. *The Oxford Companion To Children's Literature*, Oxford University Press, Oxford, 1984/ 1999
L. Carroll. *Alice's Adventures In Wonderland*, Puffin, London, 1962
D. Cavallaro. *The Animé Art of Hayao Miyazaki,* McFarland, Jefferson, NC, 2006
C. Chatrian & G. Paganelli, *Manga Impact!*, Phaidon, London, 2010
D. Chute. "Organic Machine: The World of Hayao Miyazaki", *Film Comment*, 34, 6, 1998
J. Clarke. *Animated Films*, Virgin, London, 2007
J. Clements & H. McCarthy. *The Animé Encyclopedia*, Stone Bridge Press, Berkeley, CA, 2001/ 2006/ 2015
—. *Schoolgirl Milky Crisis,* Titan Books, London, 2009
Comic Box, *Nausicaä* special, vol. 98, Oct, 1995
D.A. Cook. *A History of Narrative Film*, W.W. Norton, New York, NY, 1981, 1990, 1996
J.C. Cooper: *Fairy Tales: Allegories of the Inner Life*, Aquarian Press, 1983
R. Denison. "Disembodied stars and the cultural meanings of *Princess Mononoke*'s soundscape", *Scope: An Online Journal of Film Studies*, 3, 2005
—. "Star-spangled Ghibli: Star Voices in the American versions of Hayao Miyazaki's films", *Animation: An International Journal*, 3, 2, 2008
—. 'Global markets for Japanese film: Miyazaki Hayao's *Spirited Away* (2001)", in A. Phillips, 2007
J. Donald, ed. *Fantasy and the Cinema*, British Film Institute, London, 1989

P. Drazen. *Animé Explosion*, Stone Bridge Press, Berkeley, CA, 2003
—. "Sex and the single pig: Desire and flight in *Porco Rosso*", *Mechademia: Annual Forum For Anime, Manga, and the Fan Arts*, 2, 2007
K. Eisner. "Kiki Delivers the Goods", *Variety*, July 17, 1998
M. Eisner with T. Schwartz. *Work In Progress*, Penguin, London, 1999
Mircea Eliade. *Patterns In Comparative Religion*, Sheed & Ward, 1958
—. *Shamanism: Archaic Techniques of Ecstasy*, Princeton University Press, Princeton, NJ, 1972
—. *A History of Religious Ideas*, I, Collins, London, 1979
—. *Ordeal by Labyrinth*, University of Chicago Press, Chicago, IL, 1984
—. *Symbolism, the Sacred and the Arts*, Crossroad, New York, NY, 1985
M. Eliot. *Walt Disney: Hollywood's Dark Prince: A Biography*, Andre Deutsch, London, 1994
K. Elwood. "A comparative analysis of requests in *Majo no Takkyubin* and *Kiki's Delivery Service*", *The Cultural Review*, 22, 2003
D. Fingeroth. *The Rough Guide To Graphic Novels*, Rough Guides, 2008
M.-L. von Franz: *An Introduction To the Interpretation of Fairy Tales*, Spring Publications, New York, 1970
F. Freiberg. "Tombstone For Fireflies", *Sense of Cinema*, 14, 2001
—. "Miyazaki's heroines", *Sense of Cinema*, 40, 2006
S. Fritz. "Miyazaki Came To America To Talk", Animation Cafe, 1999
L. Goldberg *et al*, eds. *Science Fiction Filmmaking In the 1980s*, McFarland, Jefferson, 1995
J. Goodwin, ed. *Perspectives On Akira Kurosawa*, G.K. Hall, Boston, MA, 1994
D. Gordon. 'Studio Ghibli: Animated magic', *Hackwriters*, 2006
J. Goulding. "Crossroads of experience: Miyazaki Hayao's global/ local nexus", *Asian Cinema*, 17, 2, 2006
P. Gravett. *Manga*, L. King, London, 2004
—. ed. *1001 Comics You Must Read Before You Die,* Cassell, London, 2011
R. Grover. *The Disney Touch*, Business One Irwin, Homewood, Illinois, 1991
P. Hardy, ed. *The Aurum Encyclopedia of Science Fiction*, Aurum, London, 1991
V. Haviland, ed. *Children and Literature: Views and Reviews*, Scott, Foresman, Glenview, IL, 1973
T. Hagiwara. "Globalism and localism in Hayao Miyazaki's

anime", *International Journal of the Humanities*, 3, 9, 2005
P. Hunt: *An Introduction To Children's Literature*, Oxford University Press, 1994
—. ed. *Children's Literature: The Development of Criticism*, Routledge, 1990
J. Hunter. *Eros In Hell: Sex, Blood and Madness In Japanese Cinema*, Creation Books, London, 1998
S. Inaga. "Miyazaki Hayao's epic comic series: *Nausicaa of the Valley of the Wind*", *Japan Review*, 11, 1999
R. Johnson. "Kawaii and kirei: Navigating the identities of women in *Laputa: Castle in the Sky* by Hayao Miyazaki and *Ghost in the Shell* by Mamoru Oshii", *Rhizomes: Cultural Studies in Emerging Knowledge*, 14, 2007
S.S. Jones. *The Fairy Tale: The Magic Mirror of Imagination*, Twayne, New York, NY, 1995
B.F. Kawin. *How Movies Work*, Macmillan, New York, NY, 1987
R. Keith. *Japanamerica*, Palgrave Macmillan, London, 2007
M. Kimmich. "Animating the fantastic: Hayao Miyazaki's adaptation of Diana Wynne-Jones's *Howl's Moving Castle*", in L. Strayner & J. Keller, eds., *Fantasy Fiction Into Films*, McFarland, Jefferson, NC, 2007
Sharon Kinsella. *Adult Manga*, University of Hawaii Press, Honolulu, 2002
U.C. Knoepflmacher. *Ventures Into Childhood: Victorian Fairy Tales and Femininity*, University of Chicago Press, Chicago, IL, 1998
C.H. Kraemer. "Between the worlds: Liminality and sacrifice in *Princess Mononoke*", *Journal of Religion and Film*, 8, 1, 2004
J. Kristeva. *Black Sun: Depression and Melancholy*, tr. L.S. Roudiez, Columbia University Press, New York, 1989
—. "A Question of Subjectivity: an interview" [with Susan Sellers], *Women's Review*, 12, 1986, in Philip Rice & Patricia Waugh, eds. *Modern Literary Theory: A Reader*, Arnold, London, 1992
A. Kuhn, ed. *Alien Zone: Cultural Theory and Contemporary Science Fiction*, Verso, London, 1990
—. ed. *Alien Zone 2*, Verso, London, 1999
A. Kurosawa. *Something Like an Autobiography*, Vintage, New York, N.Y., 1983
M. Lane. "*Princess Mononoke*", *Triumph of the Past,* 2003
—. "White moments and Miyazaki's *Kiki*", *Triumph of the Past,* 2004
C. Lanier. "Spirited Away To the Working World", mag.awn.com, 2002
T. Ledoux & D. Ranney. *The Complete Animé Guide*, Tiger Mountain Press, Washington, DC, 1997
—. ed. *Anime Interviews*, Cadence Books, San Francisco, CA,

1997
T. Lehmann. *Manga: Masters of the Art*, HarperCollins, London, 2005
U. Le Guin. *The Earthsea Trilogy*, Penguin, 1979
—. *Tehanu*, Penguin, 1992
—. *The Other Wind*, Orion, London, 2001
—. *Tales From Earthsea*, Orion, London, 2001
A. Levi. *Samurai From Outer Space: Understanding Japanese Animation*, Open Court, Chicago, IL, 1996
D. Loy & L. Goodhew, L. (2004). "The Dharma of nonviolence - Hayao Miyazaki's *Nausicaa of the Valley of the Winds* and *Princess Mononoke*", in *The Dharma of Dragons and Daemons: Buddhist Themes in Modern Fantasy,* Wisdom Publications, Somerville, MA, 2004
M. Lüthi: *Once Upon a Time: On the Nature of Fairy Tales*, Indiana University Press, Bloomington, 1976
—. *The Fairy Tale as Art Form and Portrait of Man*, tr. John Erickson, University of Indiana Press, Bloomington, 1985
P. Macias. *The Japanese Cult Film Companion*, Cadence Books, San Francisco, CA, 2001
—. & T. Machiyama. *Cruising the Anime City*, Stonebridge Press, CA, 2004
M. MacWilliams, ed. *Japanese Visual Culture: Explorations In the World of Manga and Anime,* M.E. Sharpe, Armonk, NY, 2008
L. Maltin. *Of Mice and Magic: A History of American Animated Cartoons*, New American Library, New York, NY, 1987
—. *The Disney Films*, 3rd ed., Hyperion, New York, NY, 1995
C. Manlove. *Modern Fantasy*, Cambridge University Press, Cambridge, 1975
—. *From Alice To Harry Potter: Children's Fantasy In England: Children's Fantasy In England*, Cybereditions Corporation, 2003
A. Masano & J. Wiedermann, eds. *Manga Design*, Taschen, 2004
G. Mast *et al*, eds. *Film Theory and Criticism: Introductory Readings*, Oxford University Press, New York, NY, 1992a
—. & B Kawin, *A Short History of the Movies*, Macmillan, New York, NY, 1992b
K. Matthew. "Logic and narrative in *Spirited Away*", *Screen Education*, 43, 2006
K. Mayumi *et al.* "The ecological and consumption themes of the films of Hayao Miyazaki", *Ecological Economics*, 54, 1, 2005
H. McCarthy. *Anime! A Beginner's Guide To Japanese Animation*, Titan, 1993
—. *The Animé Movie Guide*, Titan Books, London, 1996
—. & J. Clements. *The Erotic Animé Movie Guide*, Titan Books,

London, 1998
—. "The House That Hayao Built", *Manga Max*, Apl 5, 1999
—. *Hayao Miyazaki: Master of Japanese Animation*, Stone Bridge Press, Berkeley, CA, 2002
—. *500 Manga Heroes & Villains*, Barron's, Hauppauge, New York, 2006
—. *500 Essential Anime Movies*, Collins Design, New York, NY, 2008
S. McCloud. *Understanding Comics*, Harper, London, 1994
—. *Reinventing Comics*, Harper, London, 2000
—. *Making Comics*, Harper, London, 2006
K. McDonald. "Animation seminal and influential: Hayao Miyazaki's *My Neighbor Totoro*", in *Reading a Japanese Film: Cinema in Context*, University of Hawaii Press, Honolulu, 2005
K. Moist & M. Barthalow. "When pigs fly: Anime, auteurism, and Miyazaki's *Porco Rosso*", *Animation: An Interdisciplinary Journal*, 2, 1, 2007
T. Momma. "Miyazaki Hayao and Japanese animation", *Journal of Japanese Trade and Industry*, 2002
J. Morgan. "Flying with Miyazaki: Flight as a metaphor for power in *Spirited Away*", *Animatrix Magazine*, 12, 2003
A. Morton. *The Complete Directory To Science Fiction, Fantasy and Horror Television Series*, Other Worlds, 1997
S. Napier. "*Mononoke hime*: A Japanese phenomenon goes global", *Persimmon: Asian Literature, Arts, and Culture*, 1, 2000
—. *Anime: From Akira To Princess Mononoke*, Palgrave, New York, 2001
—. "Matter out of place: Carnival, containment, and cultural recovery in Miyazaki's *Spirited Away*", *The Journal of Asian Studies*, 32, 2, 2006
—. "Interviewing Hayao Miyazaki", *Huffington Post*, Jan, 2014
S. Neale & M. Smith, eds. *Contemporary Hollywood Cinema*, Routledge, London, 1998
E. Niskanen. "Untouched nature: Mediated animals in Japanese anime", *Wider Screen*, 2007
P. Nodelman: *Words About Pictures: The Narrative Art of Children's Picture Books*, University of Georgia Press, Athens, GA, 1988
C. Odell & M. Le Blanc. *Studio Ghibli: The Films of Hayao Miyazaki and Isao Takahata*, Kamera Books, London, 2009
R. Okuhara. "Walking along with nature: A psychological interpretation of *My Neighbor Totoro*", *The Looking Glass: An On-Line Children's Literature Journal*, 10, 2, 2006
I. & P. Opie: *The Classic Fairy Tales*, Paladin, 1980
T. Oshiguchi. "The Whimsy and Wonder of Hayao Miyazaki', *Animerica*, 1, 5 & 6, July, 1993

A. Osmond. "*Nausicaä* and the Fantasy of Hayao Miyazaki", *SF Journal Foundation*, 73, Spring, 1998
—. "Hayao Miyazaki", *Cinescape*, 72, 1999
—. "Will the Real Joe Hisaishi Please Stand Up?", *Animation World Magazine*, 5.01, April, 2000
—. "The Animerica Interview: Hayao Miyazaki", *Animerica*, 10, 12, Dec, 2002
— *Spirited Away*, British Film Institute, London, 2003a
—. "Gods and Monsters", *Sight & Sound*, Sept, 2003b
—. "Castles in the Sky", *Sight and Sound*, 15, 10, 2005
C. Ota. "Liminal gazes and allegorical quests: Anime of Hayao Miyazaki", in *The Relay of Gazes: Representations of Culture in the Japanese Televisual and Cinematic Experience,* Rowman & Littlefield, Lanham, MD, 2007
E. Otsuka *et al. Emu no Sedai: Bokura To Miyazaki-kun*, Ota Shuppan, Tokyo, 1989
F. Patten. *Watching Anime, Reading Manga*, Stone Bridge Press, CA, 2004
D. Peary & G. Peary, eds. *The American Animated Cartoon*, Dutton, New York, NY, 1980
A. Phillips & J. Stringer, eds. *Japanese Cinema: Texts and Contexts,* Routledge, London, 2007
C. Platt. *Dreammakers: Science Fiction and Fantasy Writers At Work*, Xanadu, 1987
G. Poitras. *The Animé Companion*, Stone Bridge Press, Berkeley, CA, 1999
—. *Animé Essentials*, Stone Bridge Press, Berkeley, CA, 2001
M. Prunes. "Having it both ways: Making children's films an adult matter in Miyazaki's *My Neighbor Totoro*", *Asian Cinema*, 14,1, 2003
M. Punch. *Lupin III*, vol. 13, Tokyopop, Los Angeles, CA, 2004
K. Quigley. *Comics Underground Japan*, Blast Books, New Yorkı, NY, 1996
E. Rabkin & G. Slusser, eds. *Shadows of the Magic Lamp: Fantasy and Science Fiction In Film*, Southern Illinois University Press, Carbondale, IL, 1985
T. Reider. "*Spirited Away", Film Criticism*, 29, 3, Mch, 2005
D. Richie. *The Films of Akira Kurosawa*, University of California Press, Berkeley, CA, 1965
S. Richmond. *The Rough Guide To Anime*, Rough Guides, 2009
C. Rowthorn. *Japan*, Lonely Planet, 2007
B. Ruh. *Stray Dog of Anime*, Macmillan, 2004
K. Sandler. *Reading the Rabbit: Explorations In Warner Bros. Animation*, Rutgers University Press, Brunswick, NJ, 1998
R. Schickel. *The Disney Version: The Life, Times, Art, and Commerce of Walt Disney*, Pavilion, London, 1986
M. Schilling. "The Red Pig Flies To the Rescue", *Japan Times*, July 28, 1992

—. "Miyazaki Hayao and Studio Ghibli", *Japan Quarterly*, 44, 1, 1997
—. *Contemporary Japanese Film*, Weatherhill, New York, NY, 1999
—. "Majesty of 2-D", *Japan Times*, Nov 24, 2004
F. Schodt. *Inside the Robot Kingdom: Japan, Mechatronics and the Coming Robotopia*, Kodansha, Tokyo, 1988
—. *Manga! Manga! The World of Japanese Magazines*, Kodansha International, London, 1997
—. *Dreamland Japan: Writings On Modern Manga*, Stone Bridge Press, Berkeley, CA, 2002
—. *The Astro Boy Essays*, Stone Bridge Press, CA, 2007
J. Seward, ed. *Japanese Eroticism: A Language Guide To Current Comics*, Yugen Press, Houston, TX, 1993
T. Shippey. *J.R.R. Tolkien: Author of the Century*, Harper-Collins, London, 2000
C. Shiratori, ed. *Secret Comics Japan*, Cadence Books, San Francisco, CA, 2000
G. Slusser. *The Farthest Shore of Ursula K. Le Guin*, Borgo Press, San Bernardino, CA, 1976
E. Smoodin. *Animating Culture: Hollywood Cartoons From the Sound Era*, Roundhouse, 1993
—. ed. *Disney Discourse: Producing the Magic Kingdom*, Routledge, London, 1994
V. Sobchack. *Screening Space: The American Science Fiction Film*, Ungar, New York, NY, 1987/ 1993
Spirited Away Roman Album, Tokuma Shoten, Tokyo, 2001
A. Stibbe. "Zen and the art of environmental education in the Japanese animated film *Tonari no Totoro*", *Journal For the Study of Religion, Nature and Culture*, 1, 4 2007
M. Stokrocki & M. Delahunt. "Empowering elementary students' ecological thinking through discussing the animé *Nausicaa* and constructing super bugs", *Journal for Learning Through the Arts*, 4, 1, 2008
Rosemary Sutcliffe. *The Mark of the Horse Lord*, 1965
A. Suzuki. "A nightmare of capitalist Japan: *Spirited Away*", *Jump Cut*, 51, 2009
T. Suzuki. *Work As Entertainment*, Iwanami Shoten
—. *The Ghibli Philosophy*, Iwanami Shoten
I. Takahata. "Interview", *Grave of the Fireflies*, DVD, 2004
—. "The Fireworks of Eros", in H. Miyazaki, 2009
M. Tatar. *The Hard Facts of the Grimms' Fairy Tales*, Princeton University Press, Princeton, NJ, 1987
—. *Off With Their Heads: Fairy Tales and the Culture of Childhood*, Princeton University Press, Princeton, NJ, 1992
S. Thill. "The wizard of awe: Hayao Miyazaki's *Spirited Away*", *Bright Lights Film Journal*, 38, 2002
J. Thomas: *Inside the Wolf's Belly: Aspects of the Fairy Tale*,

Sheffield Academic Press, 1989
J.B. Thomas. "Shukyo asobi and Miyazaki Hayao's anime", *Nova Religio: The Journal of Alternative and Emergent Religions*, 10, 3, 2007
J. Thompson. *Manga: The Complete Guide*, Del Rey, New York, NY, 2007
K. Thompson & D. Bordwell. *Film History: An Introduction*, McGraw-Hill, New York, NY, 1994
—. *Storytelling In the New Hollywood*, Harvard University Press, Cambridge, MA, 1999
J.R.R. Tolkien. *The Letters of J.R.R. Tolkien*, ed. H. Carpenter & C. Tolkien, Allen & Unwin, London, 1981/ 1999
—. *The Monster and the Critics and Other Essays*, ed. C. Tolkien, Allen & Unwin, London, 1983
J. Tucker. "Anime and historical inversion in Miyazaki Hayao's *Spirited Away*", *Japan Studies Review*, 7, 2003
V. Watson, ed. *The Cambridge Guide To Children's Books in English*, Cambridge University Press, Cambridge, 2001
P. Wells. *Understanding Animation*, Routledge, London, 1998
M. West, ed. *The Japanification of Children's Popular Culture: From Godzilla to Miyazaki*, Scarecrow Press, Lanham, 2009
J. Whalley & T.R. Chester: *A History of Children's Book Illumination*, John Murray, 1988
C. Winstanley, ed. *SFX Collection: Animé Special*, Future Publishing, London
I. Wojcik-Andrews, ed. *The Lion and the Unicorn, Children's Films* issue, 20, 1, June, 1996
C. Wood. "The European fantasy space and identity construction in *Porco Rosso*", *Post Script: Essays in Film and the Humanities*, 28, 2, 2009
L. Wright & J. Clode. "The animated worlds of Hayao Miyazaki: Filmic representations of Shinto", *Metro: Australia's Film & Media Magazine*, 143, 2005
—. "Forest spirits, giant insects and world trees: The nature vision of Hayao Miyazaki", *Journal of Religion and Popular Culture*, 2005
—. "Wonderment and awe - the way of the kami", *Refractory: A Journal of Entertainment Media*, 5, 2004
J. Yadao. *The Rough Guide To Manga*, Rough Guides, 2008
M. Yokota. "A psychological meaning of creatures in Hayao Miyazaki's feature animations", *Japanese Journal of Animation Studies*, 1, 1A, 1999
S. Yoshioka. "Heart of Japaneseness: History and Nostalgia in Hayao Miyazaki's *Spirited Away*", in M. MacWilliams, 2008
J. Zipes. *Breaking the Spell: Radical Theories of Folk and Fairy Tales*, Heinemann, London, 1978
—. *Fairy Tales and the Art of Subversion: The Classical Genre for Children and the Process of Civilization*, Heinemann,

London, 1983
—. *Don't Bet On the Prince: Contemporary Feminist Fairy Tales In North America and England,* Methuen, New York, NY, 1986
—. *The Brothers Grimm: From Enchanted Forests To the Modern World*, Routledge, New York, NY, 1989
—. ed. *The Oxford Companion To Fairy Tales*, Oxford University Press, 2002a
—. *Breaking the Spell: Radical Theories of Folk and Fairy Tales*, University of Kentucky Press, Lexington, 2002b
—. *Sticks and Stones: The Troublesome Success of Children's Literature from Slovenly Peter To Harry Potter*, Routledge, London, 2002c
—. *The Enchanted Screen: The Unknown History of Fairy-tale Films*, Routledge, New York, NY, 2011
—. *The Irresistible Fairy Tale*, Princeton University Press, Princeton, NJ, 2012

Jeremy Robinson has written many critical studies, including *Hayao Miyazaki*, *Walerian Borowczyk*, *Arthur Rimbaud*, and *The Sacred Cinema of Andrei Tarkovsky*, plus literary monographs on: William Shakespeare; Samuel Beckett; Thomas Hardy; André Gide; Robert Graves; and John Cowper Powys.

It's amazing for me to see my work treated with such passion and respect. There is nothing resembling it in the U.S. in relation to my work.
Andrea Dworkin (on *Andrea Dworkin*)

This model monograph – it is an exemplary job, and I'm very proud that he has accorded me a couple of mentions… The subject matter of his book is beautifully organised and dead on beam.
Lawrence Durrell (on *The Light Eternal: A Study of J.M.W. Turner*)

Jeremy Robinson's poetry is certainly jammed with ideas, and I find it very interesting for that reason. It's certainly a strong imprint of his personality.
Colin Wilson

Sex-Magic-Poetry-Cornwall is a very rich essay... It is a very good piece… vastly stimulating and insightful.
Peter Redgrove

John Hughes (1950-2009) is one of the best-loved figures in 1980s America filmmaking, and considered by many to be among the finest and most celebrate comedy writers of his generation. His memorable motion pictures are insightful, humanistic, culturally aware, and paint a vibrant picture of the Unite States in a decade of rapid social and political change.

Bibliography, notes, illustrations 372pp.

ISBN 9781861713896 Pbk ISBN 9781861713988 Hbk

Also available: *Ferris Bueller's Day Off: Pocket Movie Guide*

andy goldsworthy
touching nature

WILLIAM MALPAS

Contemporary British sculptor Andy Goldsworthy makes land and environmental art, a sensitive, intuitive response to nature, light, time, growth, change, the seasons and the earth. Goldsworthy's sculpture is becoming ever more popular, appearing in TV documentaries, public works, and Holocaust memorials. Goldsworthy has exhibited around the world, and has become one of the foremost contemporary sculptors in Great Britain.

The book has been updated and revised for this new edition.

ISBN 9781861714122 Pbk ISBN 9781861714138 Hbk

Fully illustrated www.crmoon.com

In the Dim Void

Samuel Beckett's Late Trilogy: *Company, Ill Seen, Ill Said* and *Worstward Ho*

This book discusses the luminous beauty and dense, rigorous poetry of Samuel Beckett's late works, *Company, Ill Seen, Ill Said* and *Worstward Ho*. Gregory Johns looks back over Beckett's long writing career, charting the development from the *Molloy-Malone Dies-Unnamable* trilogy through the 'fizzles' of the 1960s to the elegiac lyricism of the *Company* series. Johns compares the trilogy with late plays such as *Ghosts, Footfalls* and *Rockaby.*

Bibliography, notes. Illustrated. 120pp

ISBN 9781861712974 Pbk and ISBN 9781861712608 Hbk
9781861713407 E-book

ARTS, PAINTING, SCULPTURE

web: www.crmoon.com • e-mail: cresmopub@yahoo.co.uk

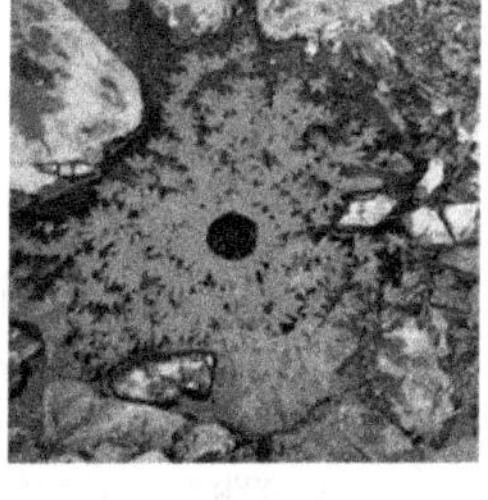

The Art of Andy Goldsworthy
Andy Goldsworthy: Touching Nature
Andy Goldsworthy in Close-Up
Andy Goldsworthy: Pocket Guide
Andy Goldsworthy In America
Land Art: A Complete Guide
The Art of Richard Long
Richard Long: Pocket Guide
Land Art In Great Britain
Land Art in Close-Up
Land Art In the U.S.A.
Land Art: Pocket Guide
Installation Art in Close-Up

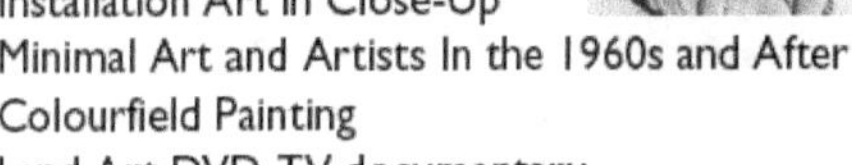

Minimal Art and Artists In the 1960s and After
Colourfield Painting
Land Art DVD, TV documentary
Andy Goldsworthy DVD, TV documentary
The Erotic Object: Sexuality in Sculpture From Prehistory to the Present Day
Sex in Art: Pornography and Pleasure in Painting and Sculpture
Postwar Art
Sacred Gardens: The Garden in Myth, Religion and Art
Glorification: Religious Abstraction in Renaissance and 20th Century Art
Early Netherlandish Painting

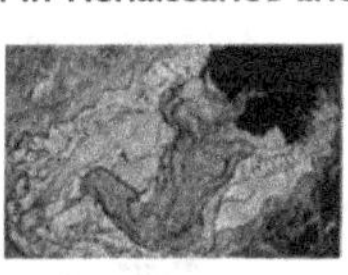

Jasper Johns
Brice MardenLeonardo da Vinci
Piero della Francesca
Giovanni Bellini
Fra Angelico: Art and Religion in the Renaissance
Mark Rothko: The Art of Transcendence
Frank Stella: American Abstract Artist
Alison Wilding: The Embrace of Sculpture
Vincent van Gogh: Visionary Landscapes

Eric Gill: Nuptials of God
Constantin Brancusi: Sculpting the Essence of Things
Max Beckmann
Gustave Moreau
Caravaggio
Egon Schiele: Sex and Death In Purple Stockings
Delizioso Fotografico Fervore: Works In Process 1
Sacro Cuore: Works In Process 2
The Light Eternal: J.M.W. Turner
The Madonna Glorified: Karen Arthurs

LITERATURE

J.R.R. Tolkien: The Books, The Films, The Whole Cultural Phenomenon
J.R.R. Tolkien: Pocket Guide
Beauties, Beasts and Enchantment: Classic French Fairy Tales
Tolkien's Heroic Quest
Brothers Grimm: German Popular Stories
Sexing Hardy: Thomas Hardy and Feminism
Thomas Hardy's *Tess of the d'Urbervilles*
Thomas Hardy's *Jude the Obscure*
Thomas Hardy: The Tragic Novels
Love and Tragedy: Thomas Hardy
The Poetry of Landscape in Hardy
Wessex Revisited: Thomas Hardy and John Cowper Powys
Wolfgang Iser: Essays and Interviews
Petrarch, Dante and the Troubadours
Maurice Sendak and the Art of Children's Book Illustration
Andrea Dworkin
Cixous, Irigaray, Kristeva: The *Jouissance* of French Feminism
Julia Kristeva: Art, Love, Melancholy, Philosophy, Semiotics and Psychoanalysis
Hélene Cixous I Love You: The *Jouissance* of Writing
Luce Irigaray: Lips, Kissing, and the Politics of Sexual Difference
Peter Redgrove: Here Comes the Flood
Peter Redgrove: Sex-Magic-Poetry-Cornwall
Lawrence Durrell: Between Love and Death, East and West
Love, Culture & Poetry: Lawrence Durrell
Cavafy: Anatomy of a Soul
German Romantic Poetry: Goethe, Novalis, Heine, Hölderlin
Novalis: *Hymns To the Night*
Feminism and Shakespeare
Shakespeare: *The Sonnets*
Shakespeare: Love, Poetry & Magic
The Passion of D.H. Lawrence
D.H. Lawrence: Symbolic Landscapes
D.H. Lawrence: Infinite Sensual Violence
The Ecstasies of John Cowper Powys
Sensualism and Mythology: The Wessex Novels of John Cowper Powys
Amorous Life: John Cowper Powys (H.W. Fawkner)
Postmodern Powys: New Essays on John Cowper Powys (Joe Boulter)
Rethinking Powys: Critical Essays on John Cowper Powys
Paul Bowles & Bernardo Bertolucci
Rainer Maria Rilke
Joseph Conrad: *Heart of Darkness*
In the Dim Void: Samuel Beckett
Samuel Beckett Goes into the Silence
André Gide: Fiction and Fervour
Jackie Collins and the Blockbuster Novel
Blinded By Her Light: The Love-Poetry of Robert Graves

POETRY

Ursula Le Guin: *Walking In Cornwall*
Peter Redgrove: Here Comes The Flood
Peter Redgrove: Sex-Magic-Poetry-Cornwall
Dante: Selections From the *Vita Nuova*
Petrarch, Dante and the Troubadours
William Shakespeare: *The Sonnets*
William Shakespeare: Complete Poems
Blinded By Her Light: The Love-Poetry of Robert Graves
Emily Dickinson: Selected Poems
Emily Brontë: Poems

Thomas Hardy: Selected Poems
Percy Bysshe Shelley: Poems
John Keats: Selected Poems
John Keats: Poems of 1820
D.H. Lawrence: Selected Poems
Edmund Spenser: Poems
Edmund Spenser: *Amoretti*

John Donne: Poems
Henry Vaughan: Poems
Sir Thomas Wyatt: Poems
Robert Herrick: Selected Poems
Rilke: Space, Essence and Angels in the Poetry of Rainer Maria Rilke
Rainer Maria Rilke: Selected Poems
Friedrich Hölderlin: Selected Poems

Arseny Tarkovsky: Selected Poems
Paul Verlaine: Selected Poems
Novalis: *Hymns To the Night*
Arthur Rimbaud: Selected Poems
Arthur Rimbaud: *A Season in Hell*
Arthur Rimbaud and the Magic of Poetry
D.J. Enright: By-Blows
Jeremy Reed: *Brigitte's Blue Heart*
Jeremy Reed: *Claudia Schiffer's Red Shoes*
Gorgeous Little Orpheus
Radiance: New Poems

Crescent Moon Book of Nature Poetry
Crescent Moon Book of Love Poetry
Crescent Moon Book of Mystical Poetry
Crescent Moon Book of Elizabethan Love Poetry
Crescent Moon Book of Metaphysical Poetry
Crescent Moon Book of Romantic Poetry
Pagan America: New American Poetry

MEDIA, CINEMA, FEMINISM and CULTURAL STUDIES

J.R.R. Tolkien: The Books, The Films, The Whole Cultural Phenomenon
J.R.R. Tolkien: Pocket Guide
The *Lord of the Rings* Movies: Pocket Guide
The Ghost Dance: The Origins of Religion
The Cinema of Hayao Miyazaki
Hayao Miyazaki: *Princess Mononoke*: Pocket Movie Guide
Hayao Miyazaki: *Spirited Away*: Pocket Movie Guide
The Peyote Cult
HomeGround: The Kate Bush Anthology

Tim Burton : Hallowe'en For Hollywood
Ken Russell
Cixous, Irigaray, Kristeva: The *Jouissance* of French Feminism

Julia Kristeva: Art, Love, Melancholy, Philosophy, Semiotics and Psychoanalysis
Luce Irigaray: Lips, Kissing, and the Politics of Sexual Difference
Hélene Cixous I Love You: The *Jouissance* of Writing
Andrea Dworkin
'Cosmo Woman': The World of Women's Magazines
Women in Pop Music

Discovering the Goddess (Geoffrey Ashe)
The Poetry of Cinema
The Sacred Cinema of Andrei Tarkovsky
Andrei Tarkovsky: Pocket Guide
Andrei Tarkovsky: *Mirror*: Pocket Movie Guide

Walerian Borowczyk: Cinema of Erotic Dreams
Jean-Luc Godard: The Passion of Cinema
Jean-Luc Godard: Pocket Guide
John Hughes and Eighties Cinema
Ferris Buller's Day Off: Pocket Movie Guide
The Cinema of Richard Linklater
Liv Tyler: Star In Ascendance

Blade Runner and the Films of Philip K. Dick
Paul Bowles and Bernardo Bertolucci
Media Hell: Radio, TV and the Press
Detonation Britain: Nuclear War in the UK
Feminism and Shakespeare
Wild Zones: Pornography, Art and Feminism

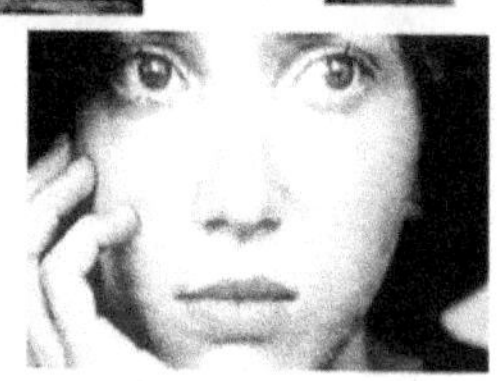

Sex in Art: Pornography and Pleasure in Painting and Sculpture
Sexing Hardy: Thomas Hardy and Feminism

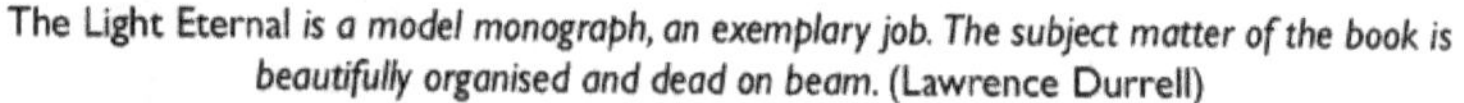
The Light Eternal *is a model monograph, an exemplary job. The subject matter of the book is beautifully organised and dead on beam.* (Lawrence Durrell)
It is amazing for me to see my work treated with such passion and respect. (Andrea Dworkin)
Sex-Magic-Poetry-Cornwall *is a very rich essay... It is like a brightly-lighted box.* (Peter Redgrove)

CRESCENT MOON PUBLISHING P.O. Box 1312, Maidstone, Kent, ME14 5XU, Great Britain
0044-1622-729593 cresmopub@yahoo.co.uk www.crmoon.com

www.ingramcontent.com/pod-product-compliance
Lightning Source LLC
LaVergne TN
LVHW010608100826
845148LV00014B/2894